TEACHING STUDY SKILLS
A GUIDE FOR TEACHERS

Thomas G. Devine
University of Lowell

Allyn and Bacon, Inc.
Boston • Sydney • London • Toronto

Library of Congress Cataloging in Publication Data

Devine, Thomas G
  Teaching study skills.

  Bibliography: p.
  Includes index.
  1. Study, Method of—Handbooks, manuals, etc.
I. Title.
LB1049.D48   371.3'028'12   80-39784
ISBN 0-205-07269-0

Printed in the United States of America

10 9 8 7 6 5 4 3   86 85 84 83 82

To Claire and Tom,
who have shaped the book more than they know

CONTENTS

3

READING FOR STUDY   41

4

STUDY SKILLS IN MATHEMATICS, SCIENCE, AND LITERATURE   65

5

STUDY SKILLS AND THINKING PROCESSES   93

6

STUDY SKILLS AND VOCABULARY DEVELOPMENT   121

7

NOTETAKING, HOMEWORK, AND STUDY GUIDES   155

8

USING RESEARCH SKILLS: THE LIBRARY AND
THE RESEARCH PAPER   181

9

STUDY SKILLS IN COMPREHENSION 219

10

REPORTING 239

11

REMEMBERING, RELATING, AND TEST-TAKING   279

12

MOTIVATION, SELF-CONCEPT, AND
THE STUDY SKILLS PROGRAM   307

PREFACE

This book describes specific ways teachers may assist their students master skills needed to succeed in school. It is based upon the beliefs that thinking can be improved, human intellect sharpened, and academic ability increased. These beliefs rest upon a number of observations and realizations gained through my decades of teaching, research, and reflection. For example:

☐ Although they permeate the professional literature and daily conversation, we do not really understand such notions as *thinking*, *academic ability*, or *intelligence*.

☐ Agreement exists that these "things" (whatever they are) are influenced by heredity and environment.

☐ Despite decades of investigation, we are still not sure of the relative effect of these influences.

☐ We can be fairly sure that schooling plays a part in whatever influence environment has.

☐ It appears that a student's motivation and self-concept play a role in whatever influence schooling has.

☐ Evidence indicates that training (teaching) may improve certain mental operations.

☐ Knowing what we know (and realizing what we still do not know), we would be foolish not to make the best use we can of schools and teachers.

The book, based as it is on such observations, realizations, and beliefs, must be a paean of sorts to teaching and teachers. Those of us who have chosen to teach have powers (sometimes more incredible than we recognize) to affect our students—as we discover what does and what does not motivate them; as we help them develop positive images of themselves as successful, learning, growing human beings; as we teach them how to better use those skills and mental processes which seem to be involved in *thinking, academic ability,* and *intelligence.*

This book is a description of successful teaching strategies, a kind of how-to-do-it book. But it is intended to be more than a simple manual or guidebook. It is the expression of a point of view about teaching and learning, about how "intelligence" works, and about the ways our feelings work with our intellects. This point of view is documented in the various chapters by references to research and scholarship and, particularly, by examples of successful teaching practices that run through its pages.

It is surely appropriate in this context to say some words about the teachers who have influenced this point of view. A full declaration of acknowledgement and thanks is, unfortunately, beyond the scope of a brief preface. Certain teachers, friends, and colleagues, however, should be recognized for their obvious impact on my thinking and/or their assistance in the development of the book:

☐ Dr. Thomas E. Culliton, Jr., whose interest in study skills led to many productive discussions (and who gave me the idea for writing the book in the first place);

☐ Mary Agnella Gunn, my own advisor and supporter through the years;

☐ Drs. Donald D. Durrell, Olive S. Niles, Roy O. Billett, and John Gilmore, all professors of mine, at one time or another, who influenced my way of looking at teaching;

☐ My sister, Dr. Judith A. Devine, and colleague, Dr. J. Richard Chambers, who generously shared their professional libraries with me; and

☐ Drs. Adeline Oakley and Kenneth A. Lexier, who read sections and made suggestions.

When students have asked, during recent months, the nature of my current writing project, they have been told, "It's my autobiography." This is not entirely a flippancy. This book, after all influences and assistances are acknowledged, *is* autobiographical. It is one viewer's picture of reality. Indeed, it was shaped by my own teachers, by all the teachers I have known, by countless students, friends, family, by all the books and articles I have read and thought about, by all my experiences in life. Nevertheless, the final product (and any errors, inconsistencies, or biases) remains mine. I believe teachers can teach their students to think and study more effectively. This particular "autobiography" was written to support that belief.

Thomas G. Devine

INTRODUCTION

OVERVIEW OF CHAPTERS

In what ways may a book such as this aid teachers who want to teach basic study skills? The case for study skills is made in Chapter 1. (Teachers who wish to further explore the arguments for and against study skills may begin their reading with some of the books and articles cited at the end of each chapter.) The next chapters focus on specific areas of study skills, examine research findings and successful classroom practices in each, and suggest strategies for teaching.

Much classroom instruction is largely oral-aural, yet students are rarely taught *how to listen!* Chapter 2 provides guidelines for the immediate improvement of classroom listening, describes important research findings in listening upon which teaching needs to be based, and concludes with descriptions of successful lessons at elementary school, high school, and college levels.

Reading specialists in recent years have developed a variety of effective approaches to textbook reading. Many of these work as well for college students as for fourth graders. Chapter 3 highlights specific techniques and suggests ways for improving textbook use in general.

The three content areas of mathematics, science, and literature present several unique problems. Some techniques for teaching study skills in these fields, however, are applicable in social studies, health education, language study, and other content areas. Chapter 4 presents a variety of teaching ideas for teachers of all areas.

Most of the study skills examined (certainly the most important ones) are actually *thinking* skills. Chapter 5 looks at the relationships between study and thinking and thinking and intelligence. It concludes with a discussion of critical thinking and ways in which it may be promoted through lessons in critical listening and critical reading.

Words, word attack skills, word meanings, and vocabulary growth are topics of concern to all study skills teachers at every grade level. Chapter 6 looks at the research in the field and at specific teaching strategies.

Chapter 7 reviews research findings about notetaking, homework, and study guides. Suggestions are made for improving students' notetaking skills, guidelines are given for maximizing the benefits of home assignments, and sample study guides for different levels are described.

Students regularly come to college unable to use the card catalog or locate basic information in their school or community libraries. Chapter 8 lists needed library research skills and offers ideas for teaching them. It concludes with specific suggestions for teaching students how to write a library research paper.

Skills associated with comprehension, synthesizing, reflecting, organizing, and "getting meaning" are difficult to pin down and teach because the topics themselves are slippery and not generally understood. Chapter 9 suggests a model for better understanding and teaching those processes involved in comprehension, and it presents specific ideas for helping students recognize and use organizational patterns.

Reporting helps students organize, focus, and assimilate their learning. Chapter 10 reviews approaches to teaching written reports and skills in expository writing, spelling, and proofreading. Model formats, teaching suggestions, and a sample lesson are given. Ways of reporting orally and visually (through charts, graphs, pictures, and models) are also examined.

Successful students (successful test-takers!) remember because they relate new material to old, the unknown to the known, and, in the process, see patterns of relevance for them. Chapter 11 examines research findings in the study of memory and important insights teachers may derive from the research. It includes ideas for improving memory as well as tips for testees.

Mastery of study skills is contingent upon a student's image of himself or herself as a successful learner and, of course, upon motivation to learn. Chapter 12 reviews the research in these two crucial areas and presents suggestions for improving both in the context of the study skills program.

FRAMEWORK

Five points about these chapters and their arrangement should be noted by teachers who use this book:

The plan of organization is arbitrary. Earlier books and articles about study skills spoke of three major areas of competency: receptive, reflective, and expressive. It seemed to their authors that certain skills are associated with the reception of material (such as using an index or reading for main ideas), others with reflection (such as making inferences or drawing conclusions), and others with expression (such as supporting a topic sentence with examples or writing a research paper). Chapter 1 notes six areas of competencies:

1. Gathering new information and ideas (in listening and reading)
2. Recording them (through notetaking, outlining, or summarizing)
3. Making sense of them (by synthesizing and relating)
4. Organizing them (through patterning, outlining, recording)
5. Remembering (by relating and using specific devices)
6. Using the new material (in reporting, writing, and test-taking).

Clearly, the two ways of organizing skills are related (the first two on the above list with receptive, the second with reflective, the last with expressive). Just as clearly, however, there is much overlap of skills to areas. Relating new with old ideas, or organizing new information and ideas into patterns, for example, may be reflective and expressive all at once! In the following chapters, reference is sometimes made to the first schema, sometimes to the second; skills are often neatly slotted into categories labeled *recording skills* or *reporting skills*, yet referred to elsewhere as *receptive* or *expressive*. It should be recognized here that these classifications (and, indeed, most classification made by the human mind) are arbitrary conveniences for thinking and reporting. Chapter titles serve as focal points around which related material is gathered, not as signposts signaling a well-developed or widely-accepted system of organizing study skills.

Teaching ideas cut across grade levels. Can a single book presume to address teachers at all grade levels, from upper elementary school through college? Yes! This book can and does. Those teachers (unfortunately, few) who have taught at several grade levels testify that *approaches to teaching* remain remarkably the same whether one is teaching middle-school students or college sophomores. No matter which grade level, the general techniques are more alike than different when teaching students how to listen to a lecture, read a textbook assignment, take notes, use the library, organize, synthesize, relate, remember, write, report, and succeed in school. Such teachers recognize, as they must, that course content and materials must differ, as must the language they use in talking to students and the examples and anecdotes they use to illustrate their teaching objectives. However, the general strategies and approaches are essentially the same. (Perhaps too much attention in education has been paid to artificial grade distinctions. As one teacher points out, "We tend to treat high school and college students as if they are more adult than indeed they are, and elementary school students as if they are more child-like than *they* really are.") The suggested approaches to study skills teaching in this book may act as a corrective, reminding teachers at all grade levels that they have more in common than the traditional system of schooling allows them to see. The basic thinking processes involved in receptive, reflective, and expressive area skills remain much the same for fourth-graders and fourteenth-graders. The problem associated with motivation and building positive self-concepts remain similar for elementary school children and for their teachers and parents!

The Idea Boxes are repositories of "triggers." Each chapter ends with several teaching ideas. Some are clearly aimed at elementary school students, and some are geared for students in high school and college. All have been used successfully in the classroom. They are not coded as to grade level or subject matter because they are intended as "triggers" to stimulate individual teachers to create strategies for specific students or specific classes. An idea which at first glance appears to be designed for an elementary school language arts class may suggest another idea for a high school science class. The creative teacher, like the cutpurse Autolycus in *The Winter's Tale*, takes what he or she finds, changes it a bit here and a bit there, polishes it up, and reshapes it to fit the needs of the teaching moment.

The lists of skills are "starters." Most of the following chapters conclude with a list of study skills. Chapter 2, for example, ends with twenty basic study skills in listening; Chapter 3 details skills needed to read textbook assignments; and so on. These lists are not intended to be exhaustive, comprehensive, or final. References are made in the chapters to books and articles which often contain other lists. Many teachers and curriculum specialists have developed still other lists. Those provided in this book are intended to give teachers a frame of reference so that they may more effectively develop their own lessons and programs.

Research and theory are appropriately referenced. Research findings which support the guidelines, recommendations, and suggestions in each chapter are cited by the author's last name and date within the text. Complete names and titles, with appropriate bibliographic data, are given in a reference section at the end of each chapter. An attempt has been made consistently throughout the book to include not only the results of recent research and reports of recent theoretical discussions, but also important books and articles from the past which have helped shape current thinking about the topics. For example, Chapter 5 notes recent research

About the Author

Thomas G. Devine received his M.A. in English and Ph.D. in Education from Boston University. Dr. Devine has been Professor of Education at the University of Lowell. He has also served as president of state and local councils of both the International Reading Association and the National Council of Teachers of English, a national director of N.C.T.E., and a member of its standing committee on research. In addition, Professor Devine has been a consultant to several state education departments and many individual school systems and was General Chair for N.C.T.E.'s 1981 National Convention.

Professor Devine's other publications include several junior high school textbooks, a college text in the teaching of reading, and more than many articles in professional journals.

and discussion on information processing theories as well as "classic" studies done several decades ago. The references on listening extend from the first formal study done more than fifty years ago to the most recent doctoral studies. The reference sections, as well as the lists of skills, are not intended to be comprehensive or final. They can provide interested teachers with a starting point for further reading and study in each area.

1

TEACHING STUDY
SKILLS

Can thinking be improved? Can school learning be made more effective?
Is the ability to think and learn predetermined by forces outside the control of teachers and schools? Do heredity and home environment set
limits on a student's success in school? Is IQ an index of a student's capacity to acquire higher cognitive skills? What part does motivation and
self-concept play in school achievement? Can students be taught to be
better listeners and readers? Can they be taught to effectively handle
mathematics problems, science textbooks, and readings in literature?
Can they be taught to take notes, use the library, increase their vocabularies, organize, synthesize, relate, remember, write and report, and take
tests? In short, can students be taught to study?

These are some of the questions around which this book is organized.
Some have provoked acrimonious, even bitter, disputes through the
years. Others have been answered satisfactorily by research. The purpose
of the following chapters is to examine certain important questions about
school learning and study and to point the way to answers. As will be
seen, the picture is generally encouraging. Evidence from research and
successful practice in the classroom indicates that (1) thinking and learning may be improved; (2) intelligence and preschool background, while
setting certain vague limits on school achievement, do not hamper teaching as much as has been sometimes believed; (3) student motivation and
self-concept may be improved; and (4) *study skills can be taught.*

This chapter looks at some of the basic issues involved in the development of a successful study skills program. Underlying the chapter
and the book is the strong conviction that teachers must make a major,
personal commitment to doing what can be done—teaching their students how to better study, learn, and think.

WHY STUDY SKILLS?

Some students move easily through school, achieving academic success, good grades, honors, prizes, and eventual admission to college. Others stumble year after year, requiring special help, remediation, individual tutoring, and developing along the way negative images of themselves as students and people. The majority, in the great middle bump of the bell-shaped curve of the school population, hover between success and failure, experiencing their share of each.

The conventional wisdom has explained the extremes glibly enough. The nonsucceeders are the unfortunate victims of their genes and environments; they are the way they are because of the families they come from, their neighborhoods and communities, and their social and economic class backgrounds. The succeeders in school are accounted for in comparable terms—they are lucky in their genes and culture. School success and failure, then, are explained in terms of "IQ" and "background." All the explanations derived from the conventional wisdom have merit: academic success and failure may be predicted using measurements of such factors as scores on tests of intelligence and academic aptitude and ratings on scales of socioeconomic background. However, enough exceptions exist to the general rule ("IQ and background predict school achievement") to raise questions about the conventional wisdom. It is becoming increasingly apparent that at least three other factors influence school achievement:

1. The student's desire to learn
2. The student's self-image of himself or herself as a successful learner
3. The student's ability to manage certain key competencies necessary for school learning.

Heredity and environment and the interaction between them certainly affect ultimate school learning (Anastasi 1958). Serious psychological, neurological, and physiological impairments put constraints on the amount of learning that may take place. Motivation, learner self-esteem, and competencies in using study skills also influence learning, but, unlike other factors, they are more or less controllable in school situations. Motivation and self-esteem have been freshly examined by researchers in recent years (Kolesnik 1978), but few specific strategies have been tested thoroughly enough to allow recommendations for the classroom. On the other hand, the development of instructional strategies for teaching students how to study have been collected over the decades and tested in classrooms, educational clinics, and study centers (see, for example, Herber 1965; Robinson 1978). Research and combined experience currently allow for minimal equivocation about direct instruction in study skills—they can be taught, to all students, at all levels. Despite possible handicaps of inherited intelligence and aptitude, family and neighborhood backgrounds, and/or social and economic status, students can be taught to more effectively read, listen, write, compute, think, and study. In short, students can be taught to learn.

One important dimension to the study skills approach to learning is that it is manageable in a school setting. Teachers have little control over those hypothetical concepts of IQ and academic background; they have little or no control over family, neighborhood, and social class influences; but they *can*, in the daily operations of the classroom, teach specific study skills in an organized, systematic way and give students practice in using the skills in school subjects. In the process of teaching students to learn, teachers *may* also affect changes in the crucial matters of motivation and self-esteem. Students who regularly experience successes in learning do develop more positive images of themselves and do begin to care about and strongly desire further successes. Teaching study skills to all may be the single most valuable contribution of teachers and schools.

What Are Study Skills?

Academic ability, as presently understood, is a composite of discrete skills or competencies, all of which are teachable and testable. The first research in this area seems to have come from the reading specialists who isolated the particular reading skills needed by a student to effectively read a given passage. In the past, reading textbooks and research articles asked teachers not to teach reading as a holistic or global activity, but to focus on specific skills such as recognizing main idea sentences, noting examples and details, noting the author's plan of organization, or predicting outcomes. As basal reading series were developed, these lists of skills or competencies were extended to include: noting typographical clues to organization, noting head notes, using graphs and tables, and using the index and table of contents. Reading teachers and others added to the growing list such items as outlining, notetaking, summarizing, and underlining. Even before the current debate between reading specialists who see reading as a bottom-to-top process (in which students first learn specific skills in order to understand total passages) and those conceiving reading as a top-to-bottom process (in which readers first examine the total passage for meaning) (Shafer 1978), some reading specialists (Robinson 1946) were suggesting the SQ3R method. This method teaches students to skim a text, ask their own questions of it, and then read it, recite back their answers to their own questions, and later practice recalling the answers. All of these skills—from finding main idea sentences to using the SQ3R method—are study skills.

Teachers in other areas have added skills peculiar to or especially important to their own subjects. History teachers, for example, are concerned about teaching students to recognize and place events and ideas in chronological order and to evaluate evidence. Mathematics teachers teach students to interpret materials used for showing functional relationships and to interpret verbal problems. Science teachers teach students to formulate hypotheses and to organize pertinent evidence. More frequently than not, teachers interested in teaching study skills have found many study skills common to all subject-matter areas.

One example of commonality may be seen in the skill of recognizing and using the generalization-plus-evidence plan of organization. Here students are taught that authors of most paragraphs found in textbooks and articles develop a "main idea" by supporting it with "evidence." The reading teacher may approach this by teaching the specific reading skills of recognizing main idea sentences and recognizing supporting details and examples. The social studies or science teacher may get at the same underlying processes by teaching students to note an author's generalizations and inferences and then checking the evidence offered to support them. An English teacher may focus on writing topic sentences and developing topic sentences with examples. All these skills are clearly hitting at the same mental processes—using terminology appropriate and traditional in their fields. In a school-wide study skills program, the same processes would be taught in an organized and systematic way, perhaps using similar terminology but always stressing the general usefulness of the skills involved to successful academic achievement.

What are study skills? They are those competencies associated with acquiring, recording, organizing, synthesizing, remembering, and using information and ideas found in school. Many should be valuable in non-academic settings, but all seem more or less indispensable for school success. All are teachable at all levels to all students.

Study Skills and Academic Ability

Any school-wide program in study skills is posited upon the belief that, while academic ability, academic aptitude, talent for learning, and similar terms are still not satisfactorily defined, teachers can isolate the components of academic ability and translate them into teachable skills. It is not known, for sure, that academic talent is inherited or somehow distributed in different amounts to different students (Anastasi 1958). It is known that students can be taught to find and use a main idea sentence or to organize material they have learned (Kuethe 1971). It seems also reasonable to note that as long as some teachers accept the notion that academic ability or talent is unevenly distributed (because of biological inheritance or environmental factors), then those teachers can rationalize, at worst, their failure to teach at all, and, at best, their failure to teach with assurance, optimism, or enthusiasm. This may be illustrated by comparing much teaching of reading and writing in schools.

Through the years, most reading teachers have recognized that, within certain parameters set by physiological, neurological, and intellectual constraints, reading skills are teachable. Thus, developmental and remedial programs and clinics have purposed to teach reading skills to all clients above an established (but low) point of so-called normal intelligence if they were relatively free of severe neurological or physiological impairments. (Some clinicians and teachers regularly attempt to teach reading to clients with low IQ's and a variety of ocular, auditory, and neurological problems.) On the other hand, some teachers of composition operate from the assumption that writing competence is the result of a specific academic ability called "writing talent," and therefore set up a self-fulfilling prophecy that leads to ineffective teaching and learning. The teacher who accepts expository writing ability, not as a set of learned competencies, but as an aptitude inherited or predetermined by environmental factors, tends to bifurcate classes into the "gifted" and "nongifted," those who have talent and those who do not. The teacher who treats writing achievement as the result of high motivation, positive self-image, and the master of specific writing ("study") skills is free to teach students how to write.

Most skills necessary for academic success are teachable and most, upon examination, seem to be components of the abstraction "academic ability." To accept writing achievement—or achievement in mathematics, science, social science, or school in general—as somehow set in preschool life of the student permits the great educational "cop out."

(Does this study skills point of view deny all inherited talents? If writers of expository prose are made and not born, what about mathematicians, painters, and musicians? The answer to these questions must be, simply, that *no one knows.* It may be that there is a special verbal dimension to intelligence, an inborn mathematical, pictorial, or musical ability. The conventional wisdom has made much of such talents; the honest reaction must be: no one *knows.* For example, evidence in the form of test scores on a test of verbal intelligence is suspect because the high scorer may simply be a test-taker who has somehow learned many verbal skills, in or out of school. The student who demonstrates unusual ability in mathematics, art, or music may also be a student who has been somehow powerfully motivated to learn the skills needed to successfully compute, draw, or play an instrument. The evidence on this question is not in; in fact, it has not even begun to come in.)

The distinction between study skills development and academic ability is important because a teacher's beliefs about the relative primacy of one over the other shapes the teacher's daily behaviors in the classroom. To admit that, despite the conventional wisdom and the educational myths of the ages, it is not known scientifically that academic achievement is predetermined allows teachers to expect success. To expect "inborn" ability to be the sole explanation for achievement in school delimits all instructional possibilities.

Study Skills and General Intelligence

Any program for the improvement of study skills is also predicated upon the belief that, while intelligence may be influenced by inherited factors, intelligence is capable of improvement. The nature-nurture controversy has never been settled. Some psychologists still believe that intelligence is predetermined by heredity (for example, Jensen 1969); others maintain that it is the result of prior learning experiences and that, while genetic factors may fix the upper limits of growth, most abilities are built through a complex process of transfer among countless learning situations (for example, Ferguson 1956; Lewontin 1970; Block and Dworkin 1976). Many argue that there is no reason to believe IQ is an index of capacity to acquire higher cognitive skills (Layzer 1976). Some contemporary psychologists suggest that intelligence, at least as it is presently understood, may be trained and improved by "cognitive therapy" (Whimbey 1975). The teacher who sets out to design a program to teach study skills may be well guided by Snow (1971), who noted:

1. For educational purposes, it appears reasonable to assume that a significant portion of observed variation in abilities is due to environmental influences.
2. Efforts to alter educational environments to promote ability development are thus not likely to be wasted.

This point of view was neatly summed up by Carol Hovious (1939, p. 6) many years ago. "Suppose," she said, "we have two steel knives, both dull. One is of poor quality, the other is finely tempered metal. Both can be made sharper, but the fine steel will take a better edge." The teacher, said Hovious, "is doing something analogous to sharpening these knives; he is putting on the student's mind the sharpest edge it will take, given the kind of mind it is (and avoiding the question of whether or not we know how to measure the quality of a mind!)" (Hovious, 1939, p. 6).

A Look at Present Practices for Teaching Study Skills

Many teachers do teach students how to study (often in developmental reading classes, in special lessons and units, and in various remedial situations); many others teach study skills as part of courses in content areas. Unfortunately, much of this instruction is unorganized, unsystematic, and unfocused; sometimes it is casual and perfunctory. All too generally, teachers give reading assignments, ask questions, talk about lesson topics, distribute and collect exercises, suggest enrichment activities, allow for classroom discussion, and test. They generally do not explain and demonstrate to students how to read an assignment, how to deal with new vocabulary, how to listen to teacher presentation, how to take notes, outline, review, participate in discussions, or how to take a test.

The following lesson was videotaped recently in a suburban school:

> Mr. B., in his eighth-grade social studies class, noted that homework would be to read the next twenty-five pages in the American history textbook. Students were to prepare themselves for a quiz the next day on the causes of the American Revolution. Mr. B. then presented a well-organized lecture on the causes of the conflict, using the chalkboard to list his points, and, throughout, enlivening his talk with interesting anecdotes. At various points in an otherwise teacher-dominated lesson, he asked for and received student comment and a few questions.

Most observers of the videotape would agree that this was a relatively effective history lesson for eighth graders. The material was well-presented, and the students were receptive, orderly, and interested. Most students probably learned something about the causes of the American Revolution. Observers who accept the conventional wisdom about academic ability and/or prevailing myths about intelligence will explain away the varying test results (which ranged from low scores to high) by noting that "bright" students obviously learned more than "slow" ones. Observers of the lesson who accept the point of view that students can be taught to learn may alternatively note that some students had somehow learned to listen and read better than others and consequently scored higher on the tests; hence, some students were not necessarily "brighter" than others but more adept at handling necessary study skills.

How could the same lesson have been taught so that learning would be maximized for *all* students? Research and decades of teacher experience point to a variety of approaches to teaching students to study more effectively. An examination of the professional literature and successful practices suggest the following strategies:

☐ Have the students open their textbooks to the pages assigned and skim through them quickly to discover what the writer is writing about

Then ask the students to jot down in their notebooks three questions that they personally want answered.

☐ Note that there are certain key ideas or concepts in these pages that all eighth-grade students may not understand. Explain the concept *in advance* of reading.

☐ Next call attention to difficult words that might trouble readers, and then provide students with practice in using the SSCD method (try to *S*ound out the new word to see if it is already in your listening vocabulary; next look for *S*tructure clues to see if there are familiar roots and affixes to help unlock the word's meaning; then seek *C*ontext clues to discover if the author gives away the word's meaning by the way he or she uses the word; and finally, of course, check the *D*ictionary). Distribute a list of words found in the assignment with synonyms or definitions or write these on the chalkboard. This is still *before* students actually read the assignment.

☐ Provide students with questions in addition to their own, so that they may have them in mind (or in their notebooks) *before* they read.

☐ Provide an *advance organizer* which sums up the content in a few lines, or a *study guide* to lead students systematically from point to point.

☐ Show students, in advance, the author's plan of organization. (Does the author use a chronological pattern? Cause and effect? Simple enumeration? Does the author offer evidence to support generalizations?)

☐ Once the class is prepared in advance for the reading assignment, tell the students what *you* are going to talk about! Explain the "hard" words that you will be using (many from the assigned reading), clear up concept problems before beginning to talk, and share *your* plan of organization.

☐ After students have read the assignment, have them write in their notebooks three pieces of evidence found in the book to support three of the author's inferences, relate five main points in the reading to events in their own lives, or break up into groups to write multiple-choice test items.

This, of course, is only a beginning. A teacher who structures a lesson so that students will *learn to learn* may, in this and similar lessons, teach (1) outlining, (2) notetaking, (3) summarizing, (4) memory devices, (5)

critical reading-listening skills, (6) report writing skills, (7) library techniques, and other study skills appropriate to the grade level. The important feature of this approach is that the emphasis is redistributed from
straight content assimilation to content-plus-study skills.

Summary

Why study skills? The question is answered here in a series of operating
assumptions (or best lines for action):

1. Many factors influence school learning (heredity, family, social-
   economic class status, etc.).
2. Of these, a student's motivation, self-image, and understanding
   and use of efficient study skills seem of most direct importance in
   the classroom.
3. Teachers have little or no control over heredity, preschool, and
   out-of-school influences.
4. Teachers can affect motivation, self-image, and instruction in
   study skills.
5. Of these, the teaching of study skills seems most immediately
   manageable in the classroom (and, in turn, can affect motivation
   and the student's view of himself or herself as a learner).

Underlying these operating assumptions, of course, are others about
the nature of intelligence and special abilities and the place of schooling
in our society. However, this book is not intended to be a treatise on educational psychology or educational philosophy; it is a handbook for
teachers who want to teach students how to study more effectively.

The following pages will treat those skills and competencies students
need to:

1. Gather new information and ideas (in reading, listening)
2. Record what they have gathered (through notetaking, outlining,
   summarizing)
3. Make sense of it all (by synthesizing, relating it to previous learning)
4. Organize it (through outlining, patterning, writing, recording)
5. Remember it (by memory devices, recall techniques)
6. Use the new information and ideas (in reporting, writing, test-taking).

Why teach study skills? Kuethe (1971), a researcher in the teaching-
learning process, answers the question this way:

A student who develops efficient study methods has in a true sense learned how to learn. He has not changed his innate capacity for learning but rather discovered how to get the maximum mileage out of what ability he has. The student thus becomes more efficient at mastering academic content because he has learned to concentrate, to organize the material he has learned, to employ mnemonic aids, and to follow study with review and self-testing. Such a person has learned to learn in an effective manner that which he intends to learn.

The teacher who accepts the operating assumptions suggested here and then teaches students the skills needed to gather, record, organize, understand, remember, and use the information and ideas presented in the classroom will—to use Hovious's analogy—be "putting on the student's mind the sharpest edge it will take."

Idea Box
Study Habits Inventory

Many successful teachers of study skills start the school year, course, or semester by having students complete a Study Habits Inventory such as the one suggested below. They use the information in planning lessons and programs and as the basis for individual conferences. They say it is a first step in getting a study skills program off the ground.

	Hardly Ever	Sometimes	Frequently	Most Always
1. Do you follow a daily schedule?	___	___	___	___
2. Do you have a regular place to work and study?	___	___	___	___
3. Do you keep track of home assignments in a book or log?	___	___	___	___
4. Do you keep a long-term schedule or calendar of tests, projects, reports, etc.?	___	___	___	___
5. Do you plan weekly reviews?	___	___	___	___
6. Do you take class notes?	___	___	___	___
7. Do you keep a notebook?	___	___	___	___
8. Do you have a notetaking system?	___	___	___	___
9. Do you study with friends?	___	___	___	___
10. Do you listen well in class?	___	___	___	___
11. Do you look up new words?	___	___	___	___
12. Do you keep track of new words you learn?	___	___	___	___
13. Do you use the glossary?	___	___	___	___
14. Do you underline in textbooks?	___	___	___	___
15. Do you outline reading assignments?	___	___	___	___
16. Do you skim assignments before reading them?	___	___	___	___
17. Do you read tables, charts, and graphs?	___	___	___	___
18. Do you have a private short-hand system for taking notes?	___	___	___	___
19. Do you use the index of a book?	___	___	___	___

	Hardly Ever	Sometimes	Frequently	Most Always
20. Do you use the card catalogue in the library?	___	___	___	___
21. Do you use the periodical index?	___	___	___	___
22. Do you organize papers before you write?	___	___	___	___
23. Do you do a first draft?	___	___	___	___
24. Do you proofread for spelling and punctuation errors?	___	___	___	___
25. Do you study effectively?	___	___	___	___
26. Do you learn in school?	___	___	___	___
27. Do you get eight hours of sleep each night?	___	___	___	___
28. Do you get regular exercise?	___	___	___	___
29. Do you make good use of your mind?	___	___	___	___
30. Do you try to improve your study habits?	___	___	___	___

In order to get to know their students better, many teachers have them complete a brief questionnaire such as the following.

1. What do I really like to do best? Least?
2. What do I do especially well? Poorly?
3. What do I get praised for doing?
4. What are my favorite school activities? Courses?
5. What do I dislike most about school?
6. What do I really want to do when I finish school?
7. What are my strongest skills and abilities?
8. What do I want from school? From this class or course?

To better understand how students spend their time, some teachers have students keep a log for a week. Each day (including weekends) is blocked off in thirty-minute periods, and students are asked to fill in what they do.

Some teachers begin the study skills program by (1) having students respond (on a 3 × 5 index card) to the question, "Why *study* study skills?"; (2) allowing them time to share responses in small groups; and, then (3) listing on the chalkboard all the suggested answers to the question. Some teachers have the list neatly lettered for a giant wall chart to hang in the classroom as a regular reminder of students' reasons for participating in the program.

The Idea Box for Chapter 12 contains a suggested Master List of Basic Study Skills. Some teachers start the program by having students "out-guess" the compilers! They suggest that students—individually or in small groups—prepare a list of all the skills *they* believe are important for success in school. Teachers have the student's list edited and duplicated for the class, and then distribute duplicated copies of the master list so that students may compare and contrast the two. This also serves as a preview and overview of the depth and variety of the program.

Many teachers find it useful to assess their own attempts to improve student study skills by completing an inventory such as the following:

	Hardly Ever	Sometimes	Frequently	Most Always
I *teach* my students to:				
1. Recognize a speaker's or writer's purpose	___	___	___	___
2. Identify their own purpose in listening or reading	___	___	___	___
3. Predict the plan of organization	___	___	___	___
4. Outline	___	___	___	___
5. Note signal words	___	___	___	___
6. Recognize main points	___	___	___	___
7. Note supporting details and examples	___	___	___	___
8. Follow sequence of ideas	___	___	___	___
9. Summarize	___	___	___	___
10. Take notes	___	___	___	___
11. Draw conclusions	___	___	___	___
12. Make inferences	___	___	___	___
13. Predict outcomes	___	___	___	___
14. Predict test questions	___	___	___	___
15. Take tests	___	___	___	___
16. Note emotive language	___	___	___	___
17. Distinguish fact from opinion	___	___	___	___
18. Note emotional appeals	___	___	___	___

	Hardly Ever	Sometimes	Frequently	Most Always
19. Recognize bias	____	____	____	____
20. Follow directions	____	____	____	____
21. Use the card catalog	____	____	____	____
22. Use the periodical index	____	____	____	____
23. Use the SQ3R method	____	____	____	____
24. Use study guides	____	____	____	____
25. Use the dictionary or glossary	____	____	____	____
26. Note unfamiliar concepts	____	____	____	____
27. Note unfamiliar words	____	____	____	____
28. Use sound, structure, or context clues to get the meaning of new words	____	____	____	____
29. Use maps, charts, graphs, etc.	____	____	____	____
30. Use headings and other typographical aids	____	____	____	____
31. Use the table of contents and index	____	____	____	____
32. Relate material to their own lives	____	____	____	____
33. Distinguish relevant from irrelevant material	____	____	____	____
34. Organize material according to a plan	____	____	____	____
35. Keep personal notebooks	____	____	____	____

References

Anastasi, Anne. *Differential Psychology: Individual and Group Differences in Behavior*, 3rd ed. New York: Macmillan, 1958.

Block, N. J. and Gerald Dworkin, eds. *The IQ Controversy: Critical Readings.* New York: Pantheon Books, 1976.

Ferguson, George A. "On Transfer and Abilities in Man." *Canadian Journal of Psychology* 10 (1956): 121–131.

Herber, Harold L., ed. *Developing Study Skills in Secondary Schools.* Newark, Del.: International Reading Association, 1965.

Hovious, Carol. *Suggestions for Teachers of Reading.* Boston: D. C. Heath Co., 1939.

Jensen, Arthur R. "How Much Can We Boost IQ and Scholastic Achievement?" *Harvard Educational Review* 39 (Winter 1969): 1–123.

Kolesnik, Walter B. *Motivation: Understanding and Influencing Human Behavior.* Boston: Allyn and Bacon, 1978.

Kuethe, James L. "Processes of Education: Psychological Viewpoint." In *Encyclopedia of Education*, vol. 7, p. 230. New York: The Macmillan Company and the Free Press, 1971.

Layzer, David. "Science or Superstition? A Physical Scientist Looks at the IQ Controversy." In *The IQ Controversy.* Edited by N. J. Block and Gerald Dworkin. New York: Pantheon Books, 1976, pp. 194–291.

Lewontin, Richard. "Race and Intelligence." *Bulletin of the Atomic Scientists* 26 (March 1970): 2–8.

Robinson, Francis P. *Effective Study.* New York: Harper and Brothers, 1946.

Robinson, H. Alan. *Teaching Reading and Studying Strategies: The Content Areas*, 2nd ed. Boston: Allyn and Bacon, Inc., 1978.

Shafer, Robert F. "Will Psycholinguistics Change Reading in Secondary Schools?" *Journal of Reading* 21 (January 1978): 305–316.

Snow, Richard E. "Mental Abilities." In *Encyclopedia of Education*, vol. 6, p. 306. New York: The Macmillan Company and the Free Press, 1971.

Whimbey, Arthur. *Intelligence Can Be Taught.* New York: E. P. Dutton, 1975.

2

LISTENING IN THE CLASSROOM

Despite decades of advice to the contrary, teachers at all levels still lecture. Most recognize the values of silent reading, guided study, individualized learning, group interaction, media, and other approaches to learning, but, in the actual classroom, teachers talk. After all, talk is the most direct and, perhaps, the easiest way of getting across new information and ideas. It is also one of the most effective ways of communicating certain aspects of the affective dimension of the lesson, such as important values, attitudes, and feelings. Because teacher-talk is ubiquitous, easily-justified, and probably impossible to avoid completely, teachers need to teach students how to listen to lectures and classroom talk. Of all areas of study skills, those associated with listening are, in many ways, primary. Research evidence indicates that these listening skills may be improved significantly with instruction (Lundsteen 1979). Strategies are available; they need only to be used (Devine 1978).

This chapter presents guidelines for the immediate improvement of classroom listening, discusses important research findings in listening, and offers consideration for developing programs in study skills associated with listening.

GUIDELINES FOR IMPROVING
CLASSROOM LISTENING

Teachers can improve learning in oral-aural situations by acting upon the following guidelines.

Prepare Students for the Talk

Certainly, much oral communication takes place in the classroom spontaneously, informally, and semi-formally. When the talk is intended as part of the lesson or course (a lecture or planned presentation), the class should be prepared. Early teachers' manuals accompanying basal readers for the intermediate grades often recommended prereading activities which included: (1) setting up a purpose for reading, (2) teaching difficult words in advance of reading, and (3) explaining new concepts to children before they encountered them in the books. Elementary school teachers who followed the suggestions in the manuals found time spent in prereading activities helped children better understand the selections in the basal readers. Considerable research evidence indicates that preteaching at all levels is important for maximizing learning (see, for example, Ausubel 1960; Grotelveshar and Sjogren 1968; Barnes and Clawson 1975). Preteaching in the form of so-called "advance organizers" is regularly suggested for improving reading comprehension (see, for example, Spache and Spache 1977; Smith 1975; Burmeister 1978). Few teachers, however, exploit this knowledge in preparing students for classroom talk.

The following are some pretalk possibilities that have proved successful at every grade level from grade four to college:

☐ Tell students what the talk or lecture is to be about. State clearly the major concerns, the topics, the subtopics, and the purpose underlying the teacher's preparation.

☐ Clear up vocabulary problems before beginning. If you know (and you should know) the unfamiliar or difficult words to be used, these may be duplicated or listed on the chalkboard. Students may define and use in sentences those they already know; they may be given definitions and synonyms for the others. A few minutes' talk about the words helps increase general vocabulary and improves listening comprehension.

☐ Explain difficult concepts in advance. If you can predict the ideas and concepts most puzzling to students at that level (whether grade four or fourteen), you need to take time to explain them at the board.

☐ Give students a few questions in advance so that they may listen to answer the questions. These may be derived from your lesson plan or from the students' prelecture discussion.

☐ Set up a purpose for listening. The old basal readers' teachers' manuals "set a purpose for reading" in the belief that, while adult readers usually read for a specific purpose, children read only because they are told to. The purpose was often to find an answer to an interesting question, to solve a problem, or to relate the selection to their own lives. Purpose in classroom listening is generally ignored, yet disgruntled teachers are heard to say, "Students don't listen in class!" Purpose is important enough to suggest the second guideline.

Give Students Something to Anticipate

The most successful teacher-talkers in elementary school, high school, and college have always known that the best listening occurs when student-listeners anticipate. A popular university lecturer on one campus regularly hints in his opening remarks that he plans to "drop a bombshell" today. His hundreds of listeners more-or-less sit on the edges of their chairs waiting for his latest antiestablishment criticism or his newest attack on the military-industrial complex or the university administration. Countless teachers in earlier grades follow the same procedure, telling students that in the next few minutes they will learn "something shocking," or "a piece of information that very few know," or even some information important to school routine, the extracurricular program, or a coming examination.

Clearly, some imagination is required of teachers, but strategies do exist.

☐ After previewing the topic with students, ask them to list five questions they would like to hear answered in the following talk.

☐ Ask students to outguess the teacher-talker. ("I am going to start by telling you about X. What do you think I'm going to conclude?")

☐ Ask students to write down the ways in which they see this particular talk relating to preceding discussions or to next week's work.

☐ Even more effective (but perhaps more dangerous) is to ask students to relate the talk to what they know of life in general. ("Is this really true? Does it fit with what *you* know of the world?")

Any kind of question or problem that can serve as the organizing point for the presentation increases the opportunities for building anticipation, but even a lesson that does not lend itself to questioning or problem solving can have built into it simple devices for encouraging listeners to anticipate.

Personalize the Talk

One of the early readability formulas included, along with counts of average sentence length and polysyllabic words, counts of "personal references" (Flesch 1948). Most of the current readability formulas discard the personal factor, yet it remains enormously important in reading-writing and listening-speaking situations. (Some authorities (see Harris and Jacobson 1979) have recently recommended that future investigations into readability include study of the relationships of cognitive and affective variables, and that "the development of a formula to predict affect should receive high priority.") Every time a writer includes the listener into the discussion, the level of involvement and, consequently, the amount of learning is heightened. Teachers often have little or no control over the reading material in class, but they do have considerable control over their own speech in class. Every time the teacher uses a personal reference, involvement and learning are increased. Personal references include personal pronouns ("*I* discovered" or "*You* will find"), anecdotes, illustrations, examples, and evidence culled from the teacher's life, from the lives of individual students past and present, and from the life of the school. Listeners are less apt to let their attention wander when speakers relate the content of the talk to the listeners and their immediate world. This is a truth well known to rhetoricians and advertisers but often ignored by some teachers.

Encourage Students to Respond During the Talk

This guideline leads to the often misunderstood topic of notetaking. Students need to be frequently reminded that the human memory is a fragile and untrustworthy aspect of the mind and personality. People forget. Students need to see that immediate response of one kind or another helps them organize and remember the information and ideas they hear in the classroom. Written notetaking may be the most effective way of capturing and later making sense of the flow of ideas in class. For students not yet ready to "listen-with-pen-in-hand," other response strategies are available and need to be used.

☐ Give (on the chalkboard, on duplicated sheets, or by dictation) five or ten questions to be answered during the talk. Ask students to then jot down answers as the talk proceeds, or you stop at various points in the talk to allow students to share their answers.

☐ Have the students listen to answer questions they have generated in pretalk discussions. Stop regularly for oral responses or to share written answers.

☐ Later, duplicate a rough outline of the presentation with places left blank for one-word or complete sentence responses.

☐ Some teachers have suggested the heading "New to Me." Students are asked to simply jot down as much information as they can that was not in their memories before the talk.

☐ Others have varied the "New to Me" heading by trying "Facts Important to My Survival" or "What's Worth Knowing." The important feature of any of these approaches is that they insure some immediate response, preferably, with middle-school and secondary-school students, a physical response ("listening-with-pen-in-hand").

☐ More sophisticated students in high school and college may be introduced to more formal notetaking systems (see, for example, Castallo 1976; Palmatier 1973). In the Cornell System (Pauk 1974), students take notes of main ideas in a right-hand column during the lecture and afterwards jot down key words and phrases in a smaller (2½-inch) left-hand "Recall" column. After class, they cover the right-hand column and try to reconstruct it in memory using only the cues in the "Recall" column.

Learning in the typical classroom, characterized by much teacher-talk, may be increased by immediate student response, and especially by listening "actively" (that is, listening with a notebook open on the desk and a pen or pencil in the hand). Whether students tell or write down the main points, fill in blanks, note items that puzzle them, or use a system such as Pauk recommends is less important than that they do respond during the talk. (For more on notetaking, see Chapter 7.)

Share an Outline with Students

Much valuable teacher-talk is, and should be, "on the spur of the moment." Any kind of formal presentation implies preplanning by the teacher and, presumably, some organization. The organization may be simple enumeration in which important points are listed in sequence, or more sophisticated patterns of generalization-plus-evidence, climax, or comparison and contrast. Most successful teachers and lecturers have always sketched in their organization pattern on their lesson plan or lecture notes. Some have shared these with listeners, thus giving listeners an overview of the talk, increasing its effectiveness, and, in the process, teaching listeners more about outlining. Recent research in *discourse analysis* suggests that reading or listening with the author's or lecturer's organizational plan in mind improves comprehension (Catterson 1979). Strategies may be simple or complex:

☐ Give students a whole outline in duplicated form and encourage them to follow it as they listen.

☐ Give students the outline with a few supporting details missing and ask them to "fill in the blanks."

☐ Give students the main headings with blanks for the supporting details and ask them to supply these as they listen.

☐ Give students only the supporting details and ask them to fill in on blank lines the main points or generalizations.

☐ After practice, give students *only* the blank lines of the outline and ask them to fill in major headings and supporting details.

☐ Supply everything to the students but the transitional devices (*next, second, on the other hand, therefore, finally*) and ask them to supply these from a list at the bottom of the page or on the board.

☐ Eventually give students practice in reproducing an entire outline without printed cues. This, of course, is the eventual goal of all instruction in outlining. Instruction toward this goal needs to be supplemented by additional activities in reading and composition. (For more on outlining see Chapters 7 and 9.)

Teach (or Reteach) a Specific Listening Skill in Each Talk

Listening is best viewed—at least for teaching purposes—as a composite of separate skills, not as a global ability. To help students become more effective listeners in the classroom (and outside it), they need to be taught discrete skills, such as listening for main ideas, listening to follow directions, or listening to follow a sequence of events. The guidelines presented here are suggested for the more-or-less immediate improvement of classroom listening, but teachers need to start thinking of each separate talk or lecture as one part of an over-all program for improving study skills in listening. Therefore, in planning for the classroom talk, teachers should focus, if possible, on one or two listening skills that seem especially appropriate to the lesson and focus student attention on the skill or skills. For example, while using the outline as a device for improving lecture comprehension, development of the skill of listening for main ideas might also be highlighted. A history lesson on events leading up to the American Revolution might provide opportunities for emphasizing the skill of listening to follow a sequence of events. A list of specific study skills in listening appears at the end of this chapter.

Use Visual Aids

Students at all grade levels benefit by visual presentations while listening. Most teachers realize this, but many still neglect the usefulness of visuals in the teaching-learning process. Of course, one explanation for the neglect is that time is needed to prepare transparencies or duplicate appropriate material. Fortunately, time spent in preparing visuals may be justified if teachers remember that they may be used with many classes, reused with the same class, and shared with other teachers. Fortunately, too, many students in today's schools are capable of assisting in making such material, and they may profit hugely from the experience (see, for example, Morrow and Suid 1977). Some of the many possibilities for duplicated items and overhead projector transparencies include:

☐ Pictures (of people, places, objects, or whatever is mentioned in the presentation). It is one thing to hear a name (Lincoln, Bombay, Lenin, turbine) and quite another to look at its visual representation as it is heard.

☐ Graphs and tables. Relationships, quantities, dimensions, and other properties are often meaningless to many students in verbal form. If they can *see* them, they begin to understand the teacher's oral explanations.

☐ Diagrams and charts. Often restricted to science and mathematics textbooks, visual representations of concepts are also useful in English (in teaching syntactical relationships in grammar or paragraph patterns in expository writing) and in social studies (in explaining time sequences or governmental structures).

Teachers without time or material resources may exploit the visual dimension at the chalkboard. Student understanding of a talk is often increased by a teacher who simply spells out a new word in the board, sketches in a rough bar graph, or draws an illustrative cartoon. The purpose of all visual aids, crude or sophisticated, is to assist students in following and understanding the classroom presentation.

Allow Time for Students to Respond at End of Talk

Some presentations may end at the conclusion of the period, but a carefully planned talk should be followed by time for students to react. They should have opportunities to explore their answers to the guide questions posed by the teacher and the questions they may have formulated themselves in the prelistening sessions. They should have a chance to review the new words and concepts introduced in the talk and their written responses, whether lists of new ideas or outlines. The time spent in prelecture activities and in teaching students how to listen-with-pen-in-hand may be wasted unless there is organized follow-up. As many teachers have noted, even a brief paper-and-pencil test (of the fill-in-the-blanks or true-false type) provides for at least minimal postlecture response. Others have found a brief (one-sentence or single-paragraph) summarizing statement, orally or in writing, a useful device for allowing each student a personal concluding response.

Give Students a Study Guide

All the previous guidelines lead to this. There is much that a teacher can do to increase listening comprehension during the lesson. A planned study guide helps to utilize what is known to be effective in listening instruction and helps to pull it all together in one package (Thomas and Cummings 1978). Each guide may be different because each teacher, each class, and each lesson is different, but an effective guide probably includes the following:

☐ A preview of the talk (with a statement of its purpose and a general plan)

☐ A list of new words, ideas, and concepts to be used

☐ Questions for students to think about as they listen

☐ Space for students to write down questions *they* want answered as they listen

☐ Provision for "anticipation" (that is, some problem, question, or student concern that students can look forward to learning about as they listen)

☐ Questions or strategies for relating the student-listener *personally* to what is being said (for example, "In what way does this affect your own life? Have you ever had an experience like this?")

☐ Space for students to respond in writing (for example, completing an outline, making lists)

☐ Appropriate visuals that may be duplicated in the guide

☐ Follow-up activities (possible test questions, an actual test, discussion of key questions, related writing activities, related reading)

A study guide for listening has two values: it assists students in learning while they listen and it forces teachers to carefully prepare what they plan to say. Both are important for the development of basic study skills in listening. (For more on preparing study guides, see Chapter 7.)

RESEARCH FINDINGS IN LISTENING

The preceding guidelines for improving classroom listening are based upon observation of successful teaching. Whether they are used as presented here, used only in part, rearranged, reshaped, or otherwise modified, the experiences of many teachers indicate that they can immediately improve learning in the typical classroom.

Are guidelines such as these validated in any way by research? Or are they simply good hunches of good teachers or the result of inspired intuitions of inspired practitioners? Interestingly enough, research in listening and listening study skills extends back more than fifty years, and enough studies have been completed and replicated to permit certain generalizations to be made. The guidelines do, indeed, seem to be supported by theoretical and research findings. At least six research-based generalizations about listening and listening study skills are significant to teachers as they attempt to improve students' study skills. They are presented here in some detail because, as will be seen, they have important implications for all study skills improvement programs.

Listening Is Central to All Classroom Learning

It is not a peripheral matter for teachers to quickly read about a topic, discuss it for a few minutes, and then tuck it in the back recesses of the mind. In fact, listening seems to be the primary means by which all incoming ideas and information are taken in, both by children and adults. In one of the first studies done in this area it was found that of all time spent in daily verbal communication with friends, relatives, associates, and strangers,—people in general devote 45 percent of their time in listening, as compared with only 30 percent in speaking, 16 percent in reading, and 9 percent in writing (Rankin 1926). In school the percentages go even higher: elementary school children, for example, spend as much as 60 percent of their time listening (Wilt 1958). And, as many teachers, researchers, and linguists have frequently noted, listening is primary in all learning, in that it comes before speaking, reading, and writing in the development of all communications skills (Lundsteen 1979). Certainly, in school, whether elementary, secondary, or college, almost all instruction rests to an incredibly large degree upon the ability of students to listen well.

Listening Is Not the Same As "Paying Attention"

The belief that listening, like walking, is "naturally developed" survives; more than a few teachers still believe that some students learn to pay attention while others do not. However, in a careful analysis of listening, one researcher pinpointed a working definition that helps in structuring research and teaching in the area. Lundsteen approached a definition by asking: What is listening like? (comparative definition), What goes along with it? (definition by attribute), Where does it fit? (definition by classification and clarification), What parts does it have? (structural definition), and How does it work? (operational definition). She concluded that listening is "the process by which spoken language is converted to meaning in the mind" (Lundsteen 1979). It is not a set of naturally developed behaviors, nor is it simply "heeding" or "paying attention." A student's motivation and emotional-physical condition obviously influence listening, but listening itself is more than the forces which might affect it at any given time.

Listening Is Not the Same As Intelligence

Because the point is central to this entire book, it is important to examine it closely. Can it be that students who follow lectures and classroom talk better than others are simply more intelligent? Are poor listeners simply less intelligent? What is known about comprehension in general indicates that comprehension, as presently understood, is contingent upon such a variety of factors (for example, previous learning, experiential background, physical and emotional predispositions to learn, etc.) that the old notion of "IQ" is not as crucial as has been sometimes believed. What is known about listening and intelligence leads one to suspect simple generalizations about relationships between the two. Regularly in the research, one finds correlational studies in which intelligence tests are examined in relation to listening tests. Coefficients of correlation between the two kinds of test scores range from .22 to .78, but, as has been often pointed out, both kinds of tests involve language comprehension and the interpretation of verbal symbols; overlapping is to be expected. However, enough variation exists between scores not accounted for by common elements to lead researchers to believe that listening does, indeed, depend upon something besides intelligence (Devine 1968). Until much more is learned about intelligence, it is probably unwise for teachers to assume good listeners are "bright" and poor ones "dull."

Listening Is Probably Related to Thinking

"Thinking," defined as the use of certain higher mental processes (such as making inferences, predicting outcomes, generalizing, organizing, etc.) may or may not be related to intelligence (see Chapter 5). Enough is known about thinking, however, to conclude that the higher mental processes involved are teachable (Russell 1956, p. 287). Listening, at its most basic level, is akin to decoding in reading; it is a matter of dealing with incoming sounds in syntactical and larger units so that the listener may make sense out of them. At its higher levels, it appears that listening is much more like thinking as thinking is defined here. Listening to a speaker's main ideas, listening for a speaker's inferences, or listening to predict outcomes may simply be thinking processes used in an oral-aural context. Moffett has pointed out, "If a reader can translate print into speech—read it aloud as sentences with normal intonation patterns—and still fail to grasp the idea or related facts or infer or draw conclusions, then he has a *thinking* problem, traceable to many sources, none of them concerning words" (Moffett 1968). Wilt (1970) has noted, "The same thing may be said of listening and not comprehending. It is probably a thinking problem." Listening, then, involves a good deal of high-level mental activity. Critical listening, to give one example, seems to involve much critical thinking of a rather high level and may approach facets of syllogistic reasoning of a distinctly high order (Hackett 1966).

Study Skills in Listening Can Be Taught

Of the hundreds of studies done in this area in the past decades, most have focused upon the teachability of listening skills and almost all have found that these skills are markedly influenced by instruction (Duker 1968; Devine 1978; Lundsteen 1979).

Two early studies provide examples of the dozen done each year. Sr. Mary Hollow wanted to discover if she could teach boys and girls in the fifth grade four study skills in listening: summarizing, drawing inferences, recalling facts in sequence, and remembering facts accurately. She pretested more than six hundred students, then gave thirty twenty-minute lessons to half the group, and allowed the other students to follow their usual language arts program. Both groups were then retested at the end of the program. She found that the differences between the two groups at the end of her carefully-conducted experiment were statistically different. Fifth-graders could be taught to listen better (Hollow 1955).

Professor Charles Irwin tried a similar study at about the same time at Michigan State College with college freshmen. In four sections of Freshman English, he gave lessons in how to listen, and tested, before and after a seven-week period, these students and an equated group of freshmen. He, too, found that students who were taught study skills in listening improved in a well-designed experimental study. He concluded that "a sufficient number of processes involved in listening can be positively influenced by teaching as to result in improvement in listening" (Irwin 1952). These two well-known studies have been replicated so often that there seems little doubt that teachers can—if they try—teach study skills needed to listen more effectively in the classroom.

Listening Can Be Tested

Since listening first became a curriculum consideration, teachers have been testing these skills. There are now several standardized listening tests available (for example, the Brown-Carlsen Listening Comprehension Test and the STEP Listening Test) and several dozen good tests developed in master's and doctoral studies. Data on the validity and reliability of the tests have been published so that teachers who want to develop more formal programs in the teaching of these study skills can find available measuring instruments (see Lundsteen 1979). However, interested teachers can prepare tests in the classroom. For example, exercises used to develop the skill of listening for main ideas may be used later as tests. The teacher can simply select one of the exercises used in the series of lessons and use it at the end of the unit, course, or marking period to discover how effective the lessons have been. Students, too, may be encouraged to develop tests for classroom use to check on their own growth in key skills.

SOME CLASSROOM CONSIDERATIONS

Observation of classroom practices and examination of recent theorizing and research findings lead to three final considerations for teachers planning to teach and develop programs in listening study skills:

1. Teachers must teach students how to listen.
2. Strategies for doing this are available.
3. A framework, in the form of a Scope and Sequence of Listening Skills, may be developed for any class or school.

The Need for Teaching Listening Study Skills

Surveys of actual classroom practices indicate little time is devoted to listening instruction (Landry 1969). Yet, listening is basic to all school learning, important in life outside of school, teachable, and testable. And it is not based directly on intelligence. The reasons for the neglect have often been cited. Landry (1969) noted three: tradition (many teachers believe that listening, like walking, is "naturally developed" and, consequently, needs no special attention from schools); time (in an already over-crowded curriculum, listening must take a distinctly subordinate place to "important" subjects); and training (little emphasis, if any, is given to listening in the professional training of teachers or in textbooks used in most education courses).

Students are not born good or poor listeners. Teachers need to show them how to take maximum advantage of each listening situation. This means that they must prepare students for classroom talk by presenting an overview and explaining difficult concepts and vocabulary in advance, by giving student listeners something to anticipate, by personalizing presentations, by teaching notetaking and outlining skills to more advanced groups, by using visual aids, by encouraging responses during and after the talks, and by teaching specific listening skills. Teachers who complain that "Students don't listen!" have rarely taught them how.

Strategies for Teaching Listening

Often, direct lessons in specific skills may be incorporated into regular lectures and classroom presentations in subject matter areas. At other times, it is necessary to teach separate skills apart from the regular unit or course. Fortunately, many teaching strategies are available. Several are suggested here to indicate the wide range of possibilities.

☐ To teach elementary school students the basic skill of listening for details, simple listening games may be played in which increasingly difficult instructions are given first to one student and then another. For example, you may say, "Tom, take the chalk and carry it to the window. Harold, you take it from the window and place it on the desk. Mary, you take it, walk around the room and draw a circle on thc board." Such a game may increase in difficulty so that each student is challenged to listen carefully for each detail.

☐ To develop attentive listening, the old game of Simon Says is useful because it involves careful listening to directions. A leader gives a command ("Simon says touch your toes") and the group must do as ordered. If the leader gives a command without the "magic" words *Simon Says*, students should not obey, and those that do must sit down. Variations of the game, such as "Airplanes Fly" (in which students raise their arms and flap them only when the leader mentions something that can fly, such as a bird or rocket, and must sit down if they flap for a nonflying object, such as an automobile or boat), may be developed for different classes and age groups.

☐ To teach the skill of listening to follow directions in a more formal setting, you may give specific directions, such as, "Draw a one-inch margin down the left side of your paper, a four-inch box one inch over from the margin to the right, and a word with five letters over the box." Directions may be made increasingly complex. Various contests may be developed to discover "Who Listens Best?" Students may also be paired, back to back, to give one another similar directions. This tests the speaker's skill in giving directions and the listener's skill in following them.

☐ To provide further practice in following directions in an oral-aural context, you may tape record messages such as this:

> You are working part-time in a local service station. The manager is extremely busy and gives you these instructions in a hurry: "Go to the back room (the key is in the top left-hand drawer of the office desk) and get three five-gallon cans of that new synthetic motor oil. Put them on the edge of the back drive because Harry will pick them up. Then, run down the street to the Mobil station and tell Ted that I need that wrench he borrowed from me yesterday. Ted is the big guy with the red mustache. Give the wrench to Sam as soon as you get it and then relieve me at the pump. Don't forget to put the synthetic oil out first."

After students have listened to the tape, tell each to recount (on paper or orally) the exact direction in correct order. The tape may be played several times so that students may check and double-check their responses. Students may later volunteer to make similar tapes based upon their own job experiences for use in class.

☐ To help secondary school students gain practice in recognizing and remembering a speaker's main points, you can list on the chalkboard (or duplicate) twenty items selected in advance from a brief tape-recorded talk. Students should then listen several times until they decide, individually and then as a group, what they think the main points really are. After you and the students have a discussion (during which, of course, much subject matter is taught), the chief points should then be starred or underlined. To help students remember better, ask them to relate each main point to a personal memory or association (no matter how "crazy") and use the personal associations as memory joggers. In a later class, post or distribute the original list of twenty items, and ask students to check their decisions and the efficacy of their memory joggers.

☐ To give high school and college students practice in the critical listening skill of recognizing a speaker's bias, you may tape record short talks from radio or television and have students indicate the speaker's purpose and possible bias. Follow-up discussions may focus on the speaker's use of emotionally-charged words, slanted language, preference for opinion rather than factual statements, and emotional appeals. (See Chapter 5 for further discussion of critical listening skills.)

☐ To teach college sophomores the skill of listening to distinguish fact from opinion, one professor prepares a twenty-minute talk on a famous American poet and instructs the class before the lecture to list at least ten statements which clearly reflect *his* opinion. After the presentation, he spends the remaining time discussing distinctions between the fact and opinion statements and then encourages students to share their lists.

☐ Developing the important skill of predicting the direction or outcome of a talk may be accomplished by stopping the lecture or talk at certain points and having students either write down or tell orally what they think the speaker will say next. (This kind of exercise, which is effective at all grade levels, has the additional advantage of focusing attention on the content of the talk.)

☐ To teach high school and college students several key skills in listening and notetaking, show them REAP (Relating, Extending, Actualizing, and Profiting). Tell students to take notes only on one side of each page of a large, loose-leaf notebook, using short sentences and skipping lines to indicate where they think one idea ends and another begins. *Immediately after the lecture*, have students take the page to the left in the notebook and draw two columns, one labeled "Triggers" and one labeled REAP. The open notebook should look like this:

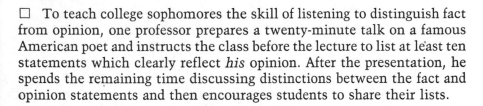

In the Triggers column, students should write any word or phrase that will "trigger" for them the idea on the opposite page of class notes. Later in reviewing, they should be able to cover the right-hand page of notes and use their personal triggers to stimulate in their minds the material covered in class.

In the REAP column, students should be encouraged to write any words or phrases which help them *relate* the material to their own lives, *extend* the content material outward from the classroom into the outside world, *actualize* the material by noting ways these ideas might actually work in the world the student knows, and indicate how the student or society as a whole might *profit* from the ideas. Clearly, the purpose of the REAP column is to make course content somehow more personal to student listeners.

Consider this example of how REAP works: A college professor might say, "One of the key concepts of Alfred Adler's theory is inferiority. As he noted very clearly in his books, Individual Psychology begins and ends with the problem of inferiority. I believe his social ideas are also very important, but we should begin with his thinking about inferiority." Under Class Notes, an individual student would perhaps write: "Adler. Basic concept in Individual Psychology is his idea about inferiority. Social ideas important. Inferiority basic." In the Trigger column, the student might write: "Adler's basic concept?" In the REAP column, a particular student might later write: "Not me. Brother? Famous people? Maybe Jimmy Carter. If true, make a list. Can I control others by knowing their inferiorities as they see them?)"

The professional literature on study skills and notetaking includes descriptions of the several excellent systems for taking lecture notes (see, for example, Palmatier 1973; Pauk 1974, pp. 126–139). Research indicates that students who use notetaking skills profit (see Chapter 7). Most have the advantage of giving practice in several listening skills. REAP, for example, encourages listeners to (1) recognize a speaker's main points, (2) note details and examples, (3) guess the speaker's plan of organization, (4) note transitional words and phrases, and (5) select main points to remember. It seems especially valuable in that it forces students who use it to relate the ideas and information they hear in class to their own lives, extend school learning out into the nonacademic world, and see ways in which the material may be used.

Other strategies (and ideas to "trigger" strategies for the individual teachers) may be found in professional literature, especially in books about language arts instruction (see, for example, Anderson and Lapp 1979; Green and Petty 1971; Savage 1977; Smith 1972). Weber's book on teaching the "adolescent slower learner" suggests many teaching ideas (Weber 1974). One of the most complete collections is still *Listening Aids through the Grades* (Russell and Russell 1959), which includes almost 200 teaching ideas, ranging from general to specific, and simple to complex.

The Need for a Framework of Instruction

Separate lessons, activities, or exercises scattered throughout the school year by individual teachers (or throughout the school curriculum by many teachers) represent a shot-gun approach to improving listening study skills. Underlying instruction ought to be some coherent framework—a listening taxonomy or a Scope and Sequence of well-defined skills from "easiest" to "hardest." Unfortunately, such a framework does not yet exist. Lundsteen (1979, pp. 53–78) has examined approaches to the development of progressions of listening skills and a tentative hierarchy of general and critical listening skills. Until a great deal more is known about cognitive development, a definitive and widely-accepted list may not be made. However, *for teaching purposes*, individual teachers and groups of teachers attempting to set up school-wide study skills programs need some kind of framework in listening study skills. The following is based upon an examination of the research literature and observations of successful classroom practices.

1. Determining one's own purpose for listening
2. Guessing the speaker's purpose for talking
3. Following spoken directions
4. Guessing the speaker's possible plan of organization
5. Noting transitional words and phrases
6. Using a study guide or outline when provided
7. Recognizing the speaker's main points
8. Noting the speaker's supporting details and examples
9. Following the sequences of ideas
10. Keeping track of the main points by notetaking or mental recapitulations as the talk proceeds
11. Distinguishing between new and old, relevant and irrelevant
12. Noting possible speaker bias
13. Noting emotional appeals
14. Distinguishing between fact and opinion statements
15. Predicting possible test questions
16. Recognizing the speaker's inferences
17. Drawing conclusions from the talk
18. Asking one's own personal questions (mentally or on paper) as the talk proceeds
19. Summarizing the speaker's main points (mentally or on paper) after the talk
20. Relating the speaker's ideas and information to one's own life.

Idea Box
Learning to Listen

To encourage students to listen to directions in class, give directions only once. When a student misses important steps, ask others in the group to recall and restate the directions. Some elementary school teachers have a "Good Listener's Club." Membership is acquired by a student successfully repeating a set of your directions. Members' names should be posted in a special place in the room.

Divide a planned teacher "lecture" into three or four short segments. Note in advance that there will be a pause after each so that students may offer their own oral summaries of the main points. Individuals may volunteer or teams may be developed to compete to discover who best understands and reproduces the material presented.

To make students more aware of sounds around them, have them close their eyes and listen carefully. After a minute, go around the group and have students tell what they heard. What were the expected sounds? The unexpected sounds? Which "made sense"? Which didn't? An out-of-class assignment may be to gather information for an Unusual Sound Collection. (Each student locates and tries to describe sounds not noticed before.) Time may be spent the next day in telling about student collections.

To make students more aware of inference-making, encourage them to make up Sound Stories. A series of four or five distinct sounds are produced outside the classroom door or on tape (for example, a dog barks, a chair is overturned, a person cries out, a shot-like sound is heard). Students try to guess the story behind the sounds (a dog detected a burglar in the house, attacked the burglar, and was shot; or the electricity failed and the darkness caused a boy to stumble over his dog and a chair before finding the porch door, which he slammed as he ran out). Volunteers may create their own Sound Stories for the class to solve.

Have students develop their own Class Listening Guide. Suggest that it include questions such as: What is the speaker's purpose? Does he or she have a "hidden" purpose? What can I learn from this talk that I didn't know before? What are the main points to remember? The guides may be duplicated for student notebooks or posted conspicuously in the room for use during lessons.

To give practice in following spoken directions, have volunteers prepare in advance detailed directions for completing an activity in class (such as drawing a musical staff with the first notes of a familiar melody on it, or drawing a simple map representing a familiar area). Give the class time to follow the directions and to then talk about their success (or lack of it) and the importance of good direction-giving and good direction-taking.

In his book, *Adventures in Communication*, James A. Smith (1972, p. 115) gives two suggestions for elementary language arts teachers that should be heeded by teachers at *all* grade levels:

1. Praise the children for good listening. When you give directions and they are carried out well, motivation for listening is enhanced when the teacher says, "Good, I am proud that you did such a good job! It shows that we listened well!"
2. Be a good listener yourself. Teachers so often only half-listen to a child as their eyes roam around the room taking in all the other children at work. Develop the habit of looking directly at a child when he talks and responding specifically to him.

To help students realize the importance of purpose in listening, tell them that teachers try to send out signals so that a class will know what it is supposed to do. Some of these might be:

1. Here are four important parts.
2. The most important thing to remember is what I'll say last.
3. Listen to this and see if you can tell me. . . .
4. There are three explanations for this situation.

After the class has had practice in noting your signals, encourage them to listen for and write down similar signals they hear in other classes, on radio and television, and in conversation. List these on the chalkboard, and note in class the reasons why speakers use them, by asking such questions as: In what way did the sentence or phrase signal the speaker's purpose? Did the speaker really follow the indicated purpose? Would your listening have been as effective if the speaker forgot to tell you what to listen for? How may signals be improved?

Some teachers in elementary and secondary school make it a regular practice to begin each period with a review of the previous day's lesson. Ask a member of the Good Listeners Club to volunteer to summarize the main points of the lesson, or ask a volunteer in a high school class to recapitulate for students who were absent the previous day.

To encourage accurate listening, some middle-school teachers read a short magazine article and ask ten questions about it. They then reread (or have a student read again) the same article so that listeners may correct their own papers. Second-Chance Listening is useful, too, with passages from school textbooks or material that relates to the content of the course.

To develop the skill of following spoken directions, have each student plan a two-minute talk on "How to Put on an Overcoat." As the directions are spoken, ask some volunteers to do *exactly* what the speaker says. The practice is valuable for both listeners and speakers.

Some teachers have discovered that listening for details is improved when they have students prepare possible test items while listening to the presentation. Each student tries to create three or four multiple-choice, true-false, or completion items. Then, after the talk, a student committee puts the better items together to form a short test. The test is projected by overhead transparencies or dictated.

For additional practice in listening to follow directions, have volunteers give oral directions to others for locating some object within the classroom. While speaking, they cannot point or move facial muscles. The directions should be given completely before the "seeker" begins the search.

Students at all grade levels should be encouraged to discuss in class the importance of listening skills in daily life and in school learning. Ask some volunteers to gather information through library research (the *Readers' Guide to Periodical Literature* will direct them to recent magazine articles) and share their findings with the class. Some may conduct "action research" at home and in school to discover exactly how much time people do spend in listening compared to reading, speaking, or writing.

Time may be spent in some classes on developing Rules for Listening Courtesy. Initial discussion may be stimulated by such questions as: What can you learn by listening? In what ways can you improve speaking-listening situations? How can you respond to a speaker (by gestures or facial expressions) to show you understand the talk? Should you ever interrupt? Why? The "rules" should be duplicated or posted in the classroom.

To maximize lecture attention, some teachers tell their students in advance that there will be at least one factual error in the talk. Students who have read the related textbook assignment previous to the class session may then note errors on cards which are passed to the front of the room after the talk.

Introduce high school and college students to the *non-sequitur* (an inappropriate or unreasonable remark which does not follow from the material in the talk). Ask them to first find examples in class presentations, and then in radio, television, or other talks.

To help students follow items in sequence, you may list, out of order, the five most important points of the talk on the chalkboard before the presentation. Instruct students to listen for the correct placement and to then write the items in order before the talk concludes.

To encourage more careful listening, try a "contest." In any class presentation, you may announce that five points will be awarded at the end of the talk for each idea or fact remembered. At the conclusion of the lecture, allow a few minutes for students to jot down all facts and ideas they can recall, and then award the points. Afterwards, the group can check to make sure all recalled material is accurate. The "contest" serves as an excellent device for reviewing the content of the lesson.

Introduce high school and college students to a variety of structured note-taking systems, such as Pauk's "Cornell System" (Pauk 1974), Castallo's "Listening Guide" (Castallo 1976), or the REAP plan (presented in this chapter). Encourage the students to try them out. Later, they may tell the merits they find in each system and/or develop an original system to share with the class.

References

Anderson, Paul S., and Diane Lapp. *Language Skills in Elementary Education.* New York: Macmillan Publishing Co., 1979.

Ausubel, David P. "The Use of Advance Organizers in the Learning and Retention of Meaningful Verbal Material." *Journal of Educational Psychology* 51 (1960): 267–272.

Barnes, Buckley R., and Elmer V. Clawson. "Do Advance Organizers Facilitate Learning? Recommendations for Further Research Based on an Analysis of 32 Studies." *Review of Educational Research* 45 (Fall 1975): 637–659.

Burmeister, Lou. *Reading Strategies for Secondary School Teachers.* Reading, Mass.: Addison-Wesley, 1978.

Castallo, Richard. "Listening Guide—A First Step Toward Notetaking and Listening Skills." *Journal of Reading* 19 (1976): 289–290.

Catterson, Jane. "Comprehension: The Argument for a Discourse Analysis Model." In *Reading Comprehension at Four Linguistic Levels.* Edited by Clifford Pennock. Newark, Del.: International Reading Association, 1979.

Devine, Thomas G. "Reading and Listening: New Research Findings." *Elementary English* 45 (March 1968): 346–348.

Devine, Thomas G. "Listening: What Do We Know After Fifty Years of Research and Theorizing?" *Journal of Reading* 21 (January 1978): 296–304.

Duker, Sam. *Listening Bibliography,* 2nd ed. Metuchen, N.J.: Scarecrow Press, 1968.

Flesch, Rudolf. "A New Readability Yardstick." *Journal of Applied Psychology* 32 (June 1948): 221–233.

Green, Harry A., and Walter P. Petty. *Developing Language Skills in the Elementary Schools,* 4th ed. Boston: Allyn and Bacon, 1971.

Grotelveshar, Arden, and Donald D. Sjogren. "Effects of Differentially Structured Introductory Materials on Learning Tasks on Learning and Transfer." *American Educational Research Journal* 5 (1968): 191–202.

Hackett, Herbert. "A Null Hypothesis: There Is Not Enough Evidence." In *Listening: Reading.* Edited by Sam Duker. Metuchen, N.J.: Scarecrow Press, 1966.

Harris, Albert J., and Milton D. Jacobson. "A Framework for Readability Research: Moving Beyond Herbert Spencer." *Journal of Reading* 22 (February 1979): 390–398.

Hollow, Sr. Mary K. "An Experimental Study of Listening at the Intermediate Grade Level." Ph.D. dissertation, Fordham University, New York, 1955.

Irwin, Charles. "An Analysis of Certain Aspects of a Listening Training Program among College Freshmen at Michigan State College." Ph.D. dissertation, Michigan State College, 1952.

Landry, Donald L. "The Neglect of Listening." *Elementary English* 46 (1969): 599–605.

Lundsteen, Sara W. *Listening: Its Impact on Reading and the Other Language Arts,* rev. ed. Urbana, Ill.: ERIC Clearinghouse on Reading and Communications Skills and the National Council of Teachers of English, 1979.

Moffett, James. *A Student-Centered Language Arts Curriculum, Grades K–13.* Boston: Houghton Mifflin, 1968.

Morrow, James, and Murray Suid. *Real-world Learning in the Schools: Media and Kids.* Rochelle Park, N.J.: Hayden Book Co., 1977.

Palmatier, Robert A. "A Note-taking System for Learning." *Journal of Reading* 17 (1973): 36–39.

Pauk, Walter. *How to Study in College,* 2nd ed. Boston: Houghton Mifflin Co., 1974.

Rankin, Paul. *The Measurement of the Ability to Understand Spoken Language.* Ph.D. dissertation, University of Michigan, 1926.

Russell, David H. *Children's Thinking.* Boston: Ginn and Co., 1956.

Russell, David H., and E. F. Russell. *Listening Aids through the Grades.* New York: Bureau of Publications, Teachers College, Columbia University, 1959.

Savage, John F. *Effective Communication: Language Arts Instruction in the Elementary School.* Chicago: Science Research Associates, Inc., 1977.

Smith, Frank. *Comprehension and Learning: A Conceptual Framework for Teachers.* New York: Holt, Rinehart and Winston, 1975.

Smith, James A. *Adventures in Communication: Language Arts Methods.* Boston: Allyn and Bacon, Inc., 1972.

Spache, George D., and Evelyn B. Spache. *Reading in the Elementary School.* Boston: Allyn and Bacon, Inc., 1977.

Thomas, Keith J., and Charles K. Cummings. "The Efficacy of Listening Guides: Some Preliminary Findings with Tenth and Eleventh Graders." *Journal of Reading* 21 (1978): 705–709.

Weber, Kenneth J. *Yes, They Can! A Practical Guide for Teaching the Adolescent Slower Learner.* Toronto, Canada: Methuen, 1974.

Wilt, Miriam. "A Study of Teacher Awareness of Listening As a Factor in Elementary Education." *Journal of Educational Research* 43 (1958): 626–636.

Wilt, Miriam. "Listening: What's New?" Paper presented at the NCTE Elementary Language Arts Section Conference, St. Louis, Missouri, 1970.

3

READING FOR STUDY

It may very well be that the reading done by students "outside the curriculum" will have more influence upon their attitudes, values, and behaviors than the study reading done in association with their classes. No one knows. Study skills type reading, however, is so much a part of schooling that a student's academic success is contingent upon his or her relative mastery of a set of rather specific and teachable skills and approaches to textbooks and other school-related materials.

This chapter builds upon many of the suggestions, generalizations, and research findings presented in the previous chapter on classroom listening. It begins by presenting specific suggestions for the immediate improvement of classroom reading, then offers ideas for teaching students how to deal with the textbook as a learning tool. Also provided is a list of basic skills in study reading and an Idea Box. The following chapter will treat special kinds of problems students encounter in study-reading in science, mathematics, and literature.

IMPROVING CLASSROOM READING

There are still teachers who naively assign chapters or sections of textbooks by saying, "Read Chapter 9 for tonight" or "Read the chapter on labor unions for discussion tomorrow." Just as in teaching students how to listen to a lecture or other classroom talk, it is important to teach students what to do *before* they read the chapter or selection, what to do *during* the reading, and what to do *after* the completion of the reading assignment. The following suggestions are derived from observations of successful practice and some of the research that has been done in this area.

Prereading Activities for Students

Before reading a textbook chapter, an article or essay, an anthology selection, or, indeed, any assigned school reading, students need to be given an overview of the assignment, explanations of new or difficult concepts and ideas, assistance in handling unfamiliar words, and a structure for organizing their responses to the material. Research findings supporting the value of preteaching have been noted in the previous chapter on classroom listening. Some ideas are given here.

Give Students an Overview

Teachers should tell students what an assignment is about before they begin to read. A brief oral presentation, an outline, an appropriate film, or a succinct statement may be enough to give students an orientation to the new material. They should have a general notion of what the author intends, why the material has been chosen for the lesson or course, what the teacher's goals are, and what they are expected to gain from the expenditure of time and energy.

Explain New and Difficult Concepts in Advance

Just as the actual reading is made less difficult when students are given help with possibly unfamiliar words, so it is made easier when concept problems are cleared up prior to reading. Items may include concepts, names, historical events, literary references, scientific terms, and any word or phrase which may not in the background of students in the class. A good rule of thumb is for the teacher to explain *any* items he or she has the least suspicion about. A popular and relatively easy-to-read middle-school anthology assumes readers will know about *napkin rings, asphalt, public swimming baths, prisoner in the dock, G.I.,* and *Doré Bible.* Clearly, young students (and many older ones) will have trouble understanding the selections that the teacher wants to teach, unless such items are explained, not simply as new vocabulary words but as words representing rather difficult concepts. A glance at any social studies or science book acts as a reminder that students often know less than the textbook writers assume.

Teach Unfamiliar Words in Advance

Despite advice to the contrary, some teachers assign passage that include many words not in their students' vocabularies. Some words are new to some students even when material has been carefully selected for a given grade level. One way to help students with unfamiliar words is to teach the SSCD approach.

SSCD approach.   Effective at upper elementary levels and beyond, the SSCD approach includes four basic techniques for attacking unfamiliar words. These four techniques follow (suggested directions for the teacher are in parentheses):

☐ Use *sound* clues. (Point out that some "new" words which may be encountered may not be new at all. They may be unfamiliar when seen in print but not when heard. This is an appropriate time to remind students that their listening vocabularies may be larger than their speaking, reading, and writing vocabularies. You may then ask *why* one is larger or smaller than another. Encourage the students to realize that they already have many words in their listening vocabularies that they have yet seen in print. Show how sounding out syllables helps one to recognize a word and arrive at its meaning. To demonstrate how sound clues may be used, have students locate unfamiliar words in the assignment and help them sound out the words.)

☐ Use *structure* clues. (Explain that another way of dealing with an unfamiliar word is to analyze its parts by examining the word for familiar prefixes, suffixes, and roots. Demonstrate with words from the assignment how previously known information of widely-used affixes and roots can unlock the meanings of many unfamiliar words. (Lists of frequently used affixes and roots, plus ideas for teaching, are given in Chapter 6.))

☐ Use *context* clues. (Point out that if use of sound and structure clues fail to unlock a word's meaning, a word may be studied in the context of its sentence or paragraph. Before they begin to read the assigned pages, encourage the student to skim and find words not in their listening vocabularies and without known roots or affixes. Then, with the entire class or groups, have the students guess at the meanings using clues in the surrounding passages to verify the guesses.)

☐ Use a *dictionary*. (Explain that sound, structure, and context clues sometimes do not help readers. Have students find words they cannot understand using these techniques and then explain that in such cases they must resort to the "D" in SSCD: the dictionary. If the textbook has a glossary, this is an appropriate time to demonstrate its use and value.)

The SSCD approach to unfamiliar words is not intended as a single lesson. Time should be spent early in the school year on a careful explanation of and practice in using the four techniques. The teacher needs to review the approach with words in assignments throughout the year aiming to have students "internalize" it. The approach is valuable because it reminds students and teachers that vocabulary is important, that it can be developed, and that it needs to be attacked from several angles—phonetic, structural, contextual, and semantic. An extended discussion of these four approaches and vocabulary development in general is found in Chapter 6.

Set Up a Purpose and Plan for Reading

Just as students need purpose and structure in classroom listening, so do they in class reading tasks. They need to have a general plan of the author's intentions and organization, to ask questions of the text, to read actively to discover how the author answers their questions, and to respond afterward to what they read.

SQ3R method.   One of the most effective approaches to study reading is the SQ3R method. Students may be taught the five steps of the method from textbook chapters, magazine articles, anthology selections, or newspaper editorials. The steps, as outlined originally by Robinson, are: (1) *survey* the headings and summarize quickly to get the general ideas that will be developed in the assignment; (2) turn the first heading into a *question*; (3) *read* the whole section through to answer that question; (4) at the end of the headed section stop to *recite* from memory the answer to the question, and jot the answer down in phrases (steps 2, 3, and 4 are repeated on each succeeding headed section); and (5) at the end of reading the assignment in this manner, then immediately *review* the lesson to organize the ideas and recite on the various points to fix them in the mind (Robinson 1970). Robinson points out that this approach is not learned simply by reading about it but that *it must be practiced under supervision.* He also notes that various modifications have been developed for different grade levels and for different subject-matter materials.

Some of these modifications are used regularly and appeal to individual students and particular classes. They constitute attractive and effective alternate study approaches, especially for students who have not had success with SQ3R. Five are given here:

1. PQRST: Preview, Question, Read, State, Test (Staton 1954)
2. The Triple S Technique: Scan, Search, Summarize (Farquhar, Krumboltz, and Wrenn 1960)
3. OARWET: Overview, Achieve, Read, Write, Evaluate, Test (Norman and Norman 1968)
4. OK5R: Overview, Key Idea, Read, Record, Recite, Review, Reflect (Pauk 1974, p. 151)
5. PQ4R: Preview, Question, Read, Reflect, Recite, Review (Thomas and Robinson 1972)

One guide sheet written directly for students explains the SQ3R method as follows:

HOW SQ3R WORKS

S Survey   Here is where you skim or survey the material. It means looking over the whole assignment *before* you actually start to read it.

1. Check the title first to get an idea of what the material is about.
2. Note the beginning and end to get a notion of how much material the author uses to get across the ideas.
3. Pay attention to headings and subheadings. They can help you get an over-all picture of the author's plan.
4. Look at charts, pictures, graphs, and other illustrative material. Check the captions under each. These can also help give you clues to the over-all plan.
5. Quickly read any headnotes, introductory paragraphs, and summary sections. They can give you a better overview.

Q Question This is the crucial stage in personalizing the assignment, making it really yours. On a separate sheet of paper, jot down the questions that you, personally, want answered. What might the author be able to tell you about the topic that you don't already know? What are *you* curious about here? Sometimes, turning the headings and subheadings into questions helps.

R Read   Now you are ready to actually read the assignment.

1. Read the introductory paragraphs rather carefully.
2. Add to your personal list of questions if you need to.
3. Skim the less important points.
4. Add difficult words to your question sheet so that you can verify the meanings later.
5. Keep asking yourself: What is the author's main purpose in writing this material?

R Review   After you have completed the reading, try to remember each section. What was the author's main purpose? What were the chief points? What was the over-all plan? Try to keep the key points in mind.

R Recite   One of the best ways of understanding anything is to tell it to someone else in your own words. At this final stage, "tell" your answers to the questions, either to yourself in writing or to another student in conversation. Making a synopsis or summary (which includes answers to your questions) is also a powerful learning method.

Research since Robinson suggests that the SQ3R method is soundly based on an information processing theory of learning (Tadlock 1978). Such a theory implies that human beings strive to make sense of their world and reduce their uncertainty about the world around them by (1) taking in information through their sensory organs, (2) processing it through their memory systems, (3) structuring and categorizing it in the most meaningful manner possible, and (4) storing the information for recall and later use. (For descriptions of such a theory, see Neisser 1967; Newell and Simon 1972.) Tadlock points out that each component of SQ3R serves to facilitate the processing of information. Recitation and Review components also encourage evaluation and selection of the most relevant information, slow down the input of information to allow the processing system time to transfer information from short-term to long-term memory, and interfere with the forgetting process, thus aiding in more complete retention (Tadlock 1978, p. 111). She suggests that high school and college students be shown *why* SQ3R works so that they will use it in their independent reading and study.

Try an "Advance Organizer"

The suggestions given here for prereading activities are based upon the experiences of successful teachers who have noted that students who receive preparatory instruction tend to learn more than students who do not receive such help. Recent research now suggests that these prereading activities that increase learning may be summarized in a printed aid explaining the text, distributed, and discussed prior to reading (see, for example, Karahalios, Tonjes, and Towner 1979). Such "advance organizers" may note the author's purpose and plan of presentation, explain major concepts, and provide synonyms for difficult words; or they may simply paraphrase the text in language students can readily understand. More elaborate printed handouts in the form of study guides have been used by teachers for many years to improve learning by encouraging students to identify specific reading tasks and offering strategies for working through assignments. Interlocking guides, which carefully guide readers from literal to interpretive and applicative levels of meaning, and non-interlocking guides, which provide less-structured directions to help readers process information and ideas, have proved successful in many classrooms (see, for example, Tutolo 1977). Traditional study guides, if distributed and discussed prior to reading, may serve as advance organizers, especially when they present an overview of the assignment. Either kind of printed handout, detailed study guide or simple advance organizer, evidently helps to establish a certain mind set conducive to learning. Both are specific devices for improving study skills in classroom learning.

Activities for Students during Reading

The value of listening-with-pen-in-hand has been noted in lecture and teacher-talk situations. Its importance in study reading is also widely recognized. Readers may indeed read for pleasure and to casually acquire information and ideas, but in reading a school assignment they need to *do something, to react, to respond while reading.* The SQ3R method provides for active response while reading. Other strategies have been used successfully by students who have been taught how to learn.

Completing teacher-prepared outlines. Provide duplicated *partial* outlines (with main headings or supporting examples) to the students and show them how to fill in the blanks with missing material. This technique works for middle-school, high school, and college students in a lecture situation, and it works well for most students in a reading situation.

Jotting down "new" information. Instruct students to read the selection and write down (in complete sentences or phrases) a specific number (perhaps five or ten) of pieces of information that they did not have before.

Asking questions of the text. To promote active rather than passive reading, tell the students to write a specific number of questions they would like to ask the author. (These may be addressed in a postreading session to the teacher acting as author.)

Noting personal responses. Ask students to list a specific number of responses that they personally have to the text (for example, What seems to be true? False? What makes a difference to me as a person? How does this relate to my life? to my future?).

Preparing a "lesson plan." Ask students to consider how *they* would teach the material in the text. They need to see a sample lesson plan with its objectives or main points, its teaching ideas or strategies, and its follow-up questions or test. Then allow them to try out their plans on other students or share them with you. (See Peer Teaching in this chapter.)

Obviously, a teacher does not use *all* these techniques everyday. Outline-completion may be used with one assignment, "lesson planning" with another, question-asking with another. Variety and change of pace are also important in respect to *how* classroom reading is done. It is assumed here that most study reading is done silently. However, assignments may sometimes be read aloud by the teacher or by volunteers who have prepared in advance for the oral reading. Prereading and during-reading activities, of course, should be included in an oral reading experience as in the silent reading of the assignment. One caution needs to be made about oral reading: indiscriminate selection of student readers, as in row-by-row or around-the-circle oral reading, is generally nonproductive in that it embarrasses and alienates those students who are unprepared or unable to read aloud. Unless a reading specialist is using oral reading for diagnosis of reading difficulties, it is better to call on volunteers or those prepared in advance.

In choosing activities for students to do during the actual reading of the assignment, whether a "pen-in-hand" response or some variety of oral reading, the goal is the same: to minimize passivity and maximize learning. As one teacher said, "When I see students sitting, quietly reading, I'm pleased, but I really don't know whether they are daydreaming about Saturday's ball game or what they'll wear to the dance! When I see the pens responding to the pages, I feel that minds *may* be reacting to ideas!"

Postreading Activities for Students

Once students have completed the assigned reading, they need to follow-up the experience in some structured, meaningful way. Again, SQ3R or one of its variants provides for postreading activities (especially, the final "R" in SQ3R). Other possibilities exist.

Testing Self

Many teachers recommend that students try to out-guess them. They have each student make up ten questions about the assignment that may go on a test. After the reading is completed, the questions may be discussed in small groups. Each group then selects the ten questions they believe most important. These may be duplicated or written on the chalkboard to be used as the basis for an examination. Some teachers have each student write one, two, or three questions on a card and later post the cards on a bulletin board. Others have had students write their questions directly on a ditto master for duplication. However the teacher gathers and shares them, the students' questions become the basis for each student's self-testing, done either at home or in the classroom.

Learning Different Kinds of Questions

Whether students create their own questions or not, they should learn something of the kinds of questions they may be asked. One simple breakdown to share with students includes: (1) factual questions, (2) questions that relate the reader to the text, (3) questions that "extend horizons," and (4) questions that are peculiar to the content area being studied. The first, because it is best-known to students, is easily dealt with by explaining that these include true-or-false types, fill-in-the-blanks types, incompleted-sentence types, and multiple-choice questions. The students should be given opportunities *to make up their own using the assigned reading.* This kind of practice is valuable in freeing students from some of the fear they have of tests and test questions, and it also gives them practice with the study material.

Questions that relate the reader to the text include such items as "What would you do if this happened to you? or "How would you behave in a similar situation?" Such questions personalize the book and, again, lessen student intimidation by testing.

Questions that "extend horizons" are intended to encourage divergent rather than convergent thinking. They force the reader to think of matters he or she would not have thought of without reading the assignment. Students need help responding to such questions in general; one way of helping them answer ones they encounter is to give them practice in creating their own. Some examples might be: "What reminds you—even remotely—of a film you once saw? Or a television program? Or something you read?" Students need to be made secure in their attempts to see new relationships, different points of view, and odd angles of experience. Traditional schooling has often been criticized because too much questioning has encouraged convergent thinking rather than divergent, creative thinking. In postreading sessions, teachers can do much to promote creative thinking and reading by the kinds of questions they ask and the questions they encourage students to ask.

Questions that relate to content areas need special attention. Each school subject has its special terminology, its individual approach, and its own intellectual bias. Teachers of study skills need to give students much practice in framing the kinds of test questions peculiar to each subject area. Science teachers need to teach students how to ask questions about hypothesis formulation, scientific observation, and technical symbols and terms. Literature teachers need to demonstrate how to ask relevant questions about plot (What is the turning point or climax?), setting (What clues does the author give to the time and place of the story?), and characterization (In what ways does the author reveal certain qualities of the character? What specific speeches reveal the quality? Which of the character's actions reveal the quality?).

Determining the Main Points

After reading, students can list what they believe are the main objectives of the author. This can be done simply in a list or, after practice, in an outline form. Students ought to be able to write a one-sentence summary or a short paragraph "digest" of the study passages. These should be shared aloud or duplicated and then discussed. Many teachers have used the newspaper writing technique by asking students to turn the assignment into a newspaper story which answers the "Five W's" (What? Where? When? Why? Who? and perhaps How?). All class reading does not lend itself to this kind of rewriting, but much does. A chapter in a history textbook may be turned into a newspaper page by the class; science and literature assignments may be rewritten as articles for a duplicated *Reader's Digest*-type class publication.

Rewriting for Others

Many teachers have found that school textbooks seem to be too frequently written over the heads of the readers for whom they are planned. (Some teachers have shown students how to apply a simple readability formula, such as the Fry or SMOG, in order to discover the reading grade level of their own books; it is usually a grade level or two too high. See Two Preventive Measures in this chapter.) A postreading activity may be for students to rewrite an assignment "so that *anyone* can understand it." This may be suggested as a group project or a series of individual activities. Either way, the goal is to produce a simplified version of the assigned reading for another ("younger") class or for later review. These rewrites may be collected in a loose-leaf book, posted, or duplicated for all.

The value of rewriting has been noted by many teachers and researchers. Henry (1974), for example, points out the way most readers deal with written tasks: "We read at our own pace, finish with an inchoate lump of meaning unformed by language, and go on to other activity." He suggests that it is not until readers try to communicate the ideas they have read to others that readers begin to conceptualize them and discover what meanings they have. Research evidence suggests that Henry and teachers who encourage rewriting are correct. Some studies indicate that the most effective learning takes place when one undertakes a task that requires meaningful processing and an overt response (Anderson 1970). Eanet and Manzo (1976) have developed the REAP approach (Read, Encode, Annotate, Ponder) which formalizes this rewriting aspect of study.

Teaching Peers

Rewriting, as well as all of the suggestions for postreading activities, leads to one of the most effective strategies of all: teaching the assigned material. It is an axiom fairly common to the world outside the schools but rarely followed in the actual classroom that the best way to learn anything is to teach it to someone else. After students have decided what the author's main points are, after they have learned to ask questions, and after they have had practice in rewriting the text, they should then teach the lesson to one another. Some teachers do have students teach their peers in class; they find it time consuming but effective. Students may be paired to teach or review materials, they may teach small groups, or they may teach the entire class.

The Problem of Assumptive Teaching

Underlying all discussions of ways to improve study skills needed in reading school assignments is this important teaching consideration: *Many reading assignments are made by teachers on the assumption that student readers possess certain learnings and understandings which, in fact, they do not have!* Some teachers regularly assign readings that are based on ideas, information, terminology, concepts, and skills which student readers have not yet acquired. Some of them develop excellent teaching activities, strategies, study guides, exercises, and lessons which are interesting and potentially effective but, when put into operation, do not work. Often, students are blamed ("They are dull, uninterested, unmotivated, stupid.") and, less often, teachers blame themselves.

The problem, which has been frequently pointed out but is still not generally recognized by teachers, is that students may not have reached the point where they can profit from a particular assignment. Teachers sometimes take for granted that students have acquired the skills and understandings needed to read the assignment when actually the students have not.

Herber (1978) calls this "assumptive teaching": the tendency of teachers at all educational levels to assume key learnings and skills have been taught by their predecessors. Middle-school teachers assume elementary teachers have taught the skills, terminology, and understandings necessary for students to successfully complete their current assignments; high-school teachers assume middle-school or junior high-school teachers have done the work; college teachers take for granted the mastery of basic skills and learnings. Thus, an eleventh-grade history teacher (whose students believe maps, charts, and graphs are fillers in the book to reduce the number of words they have to read) does not bother to teach study skills needed to read maps, charts, or graphs because "that sort of thing has been taught in junior high school." An eighth-grade teacher does not teach the use of context clues or how to use the index because "It's been covered in the grades." As Herber (1978) noted, "Clearly, the students are shortchanged."

Assumptive teaching serves as a convenient label to describe the classroom practices of those teachers who take for granted that all teachers of prior grades have successfully taught all the vocabulary, all understandings and concepts, and all the skills needed by students to manage assignments *they* make at *their* grade level. Given the realities of American public education, it is increasingly difficult to assume that (1) all previous teachers were equally successful; or (2) all students were psychologically, emotionally, physically, socially, and developmentally ready to receive instruction when it was offered; or (3) all students were present in school when important lessons were presented.

Clearly, teachers need to be aware of the pitfalls of assumptive teaching. They need to carefully select materials for their particular students, ascertain (as well as possible) the present developmental level of their students, and make sure that their students have the skills and understandings to deal with the reading assignment. In short, teachers should *assume* as little as possible.

USING THE TEXTBOOK

Despite the much advertised advent of technological aids to instruction, textbooks remain ubiquitous. Teachers of almost all school subjects rely on them. Students at all grade levels are "burdened" with them. And yet, as has often been pointed out, students often cannot use them with ease and few teachers offer guidance in their use. As Arno Jewett (1965, p.32) once noted, "Even a high school or college student looking for a name, a fact, or a principle in a textbook may skim through it like a rat in a maze hunting for a piece of cheese, but without," he added, "the special advantage of the rat's keen olfactory organ." Learning how to learn certainly involves learning how to use the textbook. How may teachers help students to better understand and use these valuable tools?

Talk with Students About Textbooks

Even older students sometimes stand in unnecessary (and unhealthy) awe of the weighty, impressive, well-designed books upon which so much course content seems to rest. One hears, "But it's in the book!" or "That's what it says in Chapter 9." or "It must be true. It says so in the textbook." Students need to know that textbooks are human creations, generally written by teachers and specialists in the field; that they become outdated as new information and new points of view are made available; that they are almost all produced commercially to make profits; and that they range in scope and quality. When a book is first distributed or discussed at the beginning of the year or semester, attention should be called to the copyright date, the name of the publisher, the number of revisions, the author's name and credentials, the estimated cost of the book, and other features that will help students realize that their text represents a view from one point in time as expressed by one author (or group of authors) for a certain market of readers. Even younger students need to have some insight into book preparation and intention (Who wrote this? Why? For whom?). Upper-level students should have some background on the history of textbooks in education and the strengths and weaknesses of such tools in general.

Go Over the Title Page Together

Many students (and teachers) do not know the exact title of the book used daily in class ("You know, the one with the blue cover"), the name of the author or authors, the publisher, or the date published. A few minutes at the beginning of the course should be spent in close examination of the title page. Much of the information about textbooks in general may be incorporated into this brief but important examination. Discussion questions may include: How can several authors write a book together? Why are several cities listed beside the publisher's name? What is a copyright? How is one obtained? What is a revision? Discussion may lead to independent research projects done as library research (see Chapter 8).

Examine the Table of Contents with the Class

Teachers should take class time to examine the organization of the book as revealed in the table of contents, calling attention to chapter and sectional divisions, subheadings, topics, and subtopics. They can point out the interrelation of topics and the table's resemblance to outlines students have prepared or examined in connection with lectures or reading assignments. When the book is introduced, discussion questions may include: What content is covered? What are the main topics? How can you tell? What is missing? What would you like to see included?

Discussion of the table of contents is also useful throughout the year in reviewing what has been studied and what needs to be studied in the future. Topics for review, for term papers and research projects, for independent study and reading, and for student-prepared tests may also be derived from a later examination of the contents page(s).

Examine the Index Together

Many students fail to take advantage of the index. Teachers need to explain what an index is, how it is developed, how it can be used, when it can be used, and how it differs from the table of contents. Then time should be allotted for the students to practice using an index through exercises (What was the exact date of Martin Luther King's death? When was the zipper invented? By whom? What pages give information on the stock market? What is an indirect object?); games (for example, individuals compete to locate certain information the fastest); evaluations (Which available textbook on American history, for example, has the most complete index?); or index-building (in which students may develop an index for their own research paper or theme).

Check the Glossary

Students are sometimes unaware of the glossary in the textbook they are using. They need to learn how to distinguish between a glossary, a dictionary, and an index. Discussion questions may include: Why did the author include these particular words? Why did he or she omit others? Where did the author get the definitions? Who defines words for dictionaries? What may you learn from a dictionary that you cannot from a glossary? If textbooks differ in scope and quality, do their glossaries differ too? Do dictionaries differ? Teachers may use glossary study as part of the general vocabulary program of the class and as a springboard into introductory lessons in lexicography. Students should at least know the glossary exists and how to use it.

Discuss the Reference and Footnote System

Students in high school and college encounter textbooks with footnotes and other references, but they often do not understand their purpose or use. Teachers have a responsibility to explain why an author is obligated to use a footnote and the ways an author may make a reference (for example, in a bottom-of-page note, end-of-chapter note, or end-of-book note). Because several systems are used in American publishing, time needs to be spent, in upper-level classes especially, on demystifying such scholarly "tricks-of-the-trade." Elementary school students should at least know how to read a reference note in their own textbooks and how to use a simple form in their own report writing. High school and college students need help in distinguishing between the several different systems used in the United States (those of the Modern Language Association, the American Psychological Association, etc.) and in reading frequently-used abbreviations, such as *ibid.* (for *ibidem* or in the same place), *loc. cit.* (for *loco citato* or in the place cited), and *op. cit.* (for *opere citato* or in the work cited).

Any scholarly apparatus that acts as an obstacle to a student's pleasure and potential for learning has to concern the teacher. The teacher may sometimes wish that textbooks for students were written with less scholarly pretension, but if the apparatus is in the textbooks, there is an obligation to explain it and show students how to use it. (For more information on reference systems, see Chapter 8.)

Call Attention to the Typographical Aids

Many of the better textbooks have been so well-designed that a variety of typographical aids assist readers in locating information quickly, seeing relationships, following the author's plan of organization, and defining new words. If the class textbook has such aids built into it, the teacher should take advantage of them by calling attention to and explaining such aids as marginal notes, outsize print, special headings, graphs, charts, pictures, and italicized passages. As numbers of college teachers testify, many undergraduates fail to take advantage of the most obvious aids. Teaching students to use textbooks certainly includes regular explanation and frequent reminders so that students will not pass over these valuable study aids.

Select Textbooks Carefully for the Appropriate Readability Level

Too many textbooks used in American schools tend to be unnecessarily difficult. Time and time again, reading specialists have found that books designated by authors and publishers for "grade 7" or "grade 10" or "grade 12" are actually written at the ninth-, twelfth-, or fourteenth-grade levels as ascertained by use of standard readability formulas. Some authors write over the heads of their readers; some publishers publish books without researching their readability; and some schools purchase books without asking for specific information on readability. Textbooks are often two, three, or five grade levels above the reading levels of students. Studies of mathematics, science, and social science books have regularly revealed mismatches. "Classics" chosen for literature anthologies are too often found to be several reading-grade levels beyond students for whom the anthologies were compiled. While most authors, publishers, and teachers have become increasingly aware of readability, many textbooks still present students with learning difficulties that are not caused by poor study habits, ineffective teacher planning, or lack of student motivation, but by printed language that is too difficult.

What can classroom teachers do to cope with the readability problem? Two preventive measures, four tested strategies, and two "desperate remedies" are presented below.

Preventive Measures

To avoid problems in the first place, teachers can find out the readability of a textbook being considered for adoption. A reading specialist is needed to apply one of the more sophisticated reading formulas, but most subject-matter teachers can use the FOG Reading Index, the SMOG Read-

ability Formula, or the Fry Graph for Estimating Readability (Fry 1968).
Most current formulas, based only on word familiarity, word length, and
sentence length, have limitations. They do, however, provide some help
in textbook selection. (For a discussion of the concept of readability, see
Harris and Jacobson 1979.) For example, one easy-to-use formula is the
Fog Reading Index (see Gunning 1952). Directions for using it follow.

1. Select a sampling of approximately one hundred words (with the
   last word completing a sentence).
2. Count the number of sentences within this sample.
3. Divide the approximate one hundred-word sampling by the number of sentences.
4. Count the number of words of three syllables or more, but do not
   count (a) proper nouns, (b) compound easy words such as *book-
   keeper*, (c) verb forms made into three syllables by adding *ed*, *es*,
   or *ing*. Enter the total number of "hard" words.
5. Total #3 and #4.
6. Multiply the total in #5 by (.4) to obtain the approximate grade
   level of the reading material.

Another easy-to-use formula is the *SMOG Readability Formula* (see
McLaughlin, 1969). Directions for using it follow.

1. Count ten consecutive sentences near the beginning of the text,
   ten in the middle, and ten near the end. Count as a sentence any
   string of words ending in a period, question mark, or exclamation
   point.
2. In the thirty selected sentences count every word of three or more
   syllables. Any string of letters or numerals beginning and ending
   with a space or punctuation mark should be counted if you can
   distinguish at least three syllables when you read it aloud in context. If a polysyllabic word is repeated, count each repetition.
3. Estimate the square root of the number of polysyllabic words
   counted. This is done by taking the square root to the nearest perfect square.
4. Add 3.0 to the approximate square root. This gives the SMOG
   grade, which is the reading grade that a person must have completed if he or she is to understand fully the text assessed.

Before a textbook is selected from the bookroom or for purchase,
teachers should have a few randomly selected students (1) read it aloud to
discover if they can simply decode the prose, and (2) take a short true-
false or fill-in-the-blanks test to see how well they understand it. A book
labeled "Grade 7" may turn out to be difficult for the students.

Tested Strategies

Four tested strategies which may help teachers cope with the readability problem follow.

☐ Difficult textbooks can be managed if teachers give students an outline of the chapters with main and subtopics clearly indicated, explain possibly unfamiliar words, and perhaps provide summaries. Advance organizers and study guides, as noted earlier in this chapter, do not make a difficult book easy but they at least provide students access to it.

☐ Guide questions ease the student into difficult textbooks. When teachers identify the main points of each chapter and rephrase them as questions to be answered while reading, some of the difficulties are bypassed and learning is increased.

☐ Have students rewrite. Some difficult textbooks seem to have been written by committees. The reader cannot hear a "voice." Although the books may have actually been written by a single person, extensive revisions or editing may have made them so bland as to become uninteresting. Individual students may be encouraged to rewrite parts of the book, in their own speaking voice and directed at different kinds of readers (for example, younger students in lower grades, children on an Indian reservation, Russian students studying English as a second language in a Moscow school, or beings from another planet). A variation of this activity is to have students retell parts of the book assuming a different "voice." How would the paragraph be said by a cowboy? A hippie? A sports announcer?

☐ Difficult textbooks may be supplemented by easier ones. Through the years many teachers have advocated a multiple-text approach in which the basic (difficult) text is used in conjunction with textbooks treating the same topics but written for other grade levels, with trade books and magazine articles on the same topic, or with duplicated teacher (or student) revisions of the class book. The multiple-text approach helps solve the problem of the overly-difficult basic book while it also offers students other points of view, other styles and formats, and opportunities for the group to compare materials for accuracy, relevancy, recency, and possible bias.

"Desperate Remedies"

Desperate remedies for situations in which the book is clearly too advanced for students include:

☐ The teacher reads aloud. To be sure, this is avoiding the issue of *reading* (although some teachers have students follow along as they read) but it does insure *some* learning of content.

☐ Difficult books can be paraphrased by teachers. In fact, some teachers actually rewrite sections of the book. This unfortunate but unavoidable in some cases. Rather than penalize students for someone's poor judgment in book selection, such teachers believe the additional effort is justified.

BASIC STUDY SKILLS FOR STUDY-TYPE READING

Chapter 2 concluded with a list of basic study skills required in classroom listening. What specific skills are associated with reading and studying school assignments? At least twenty seem involved:

1. Defining one's own purpose for reading the assignment
2. Guessing the author's purpose for writing the chapter, article, or selection
3. Looking ahead to discover the author's plan of organization
4. Identifying unfamiliar concepts
5. Identifying the author's unstated assumptions
6. Using sound, structure, and context clues to get the meaning of unfamiliar words
7. Using a dictionary or glossary when necessary
8. Using an advance organizer or study guide when provided
9. Using a recommended study method, such as SQ3R
10. Recognizing the author's main points
11. Noting specific supporting details and examples
12. Distinguishing between new and old, and relevant and irrelevant material
13. Asking one's own personal questions of the text
14. Relating study material to one's own experiences and previous learnings
15. Predicting possible text questions
16. Judging the accuracy, recency, and possible bias of the material
17. Summarizing the author's ideas and information orally or in writing
18. Using the table of contents and index
19. Using maps, graphs, charts, tables, and pictures
20. Using headings and other typographical aids.

Idea Box
Reading Activities

To help students become more aware of the purposes for reading, have them tell the titles of the last three items they read recently outside of school (books, magazine articles, newspaper pieces, parts from manuals or guide books). Ask them to indicate *why* they read these particular items. Then suggest that they also note the reasons they think the authors had for writing them. Lead the group to see the variety of purposes readers and authors have for reading and writing.

To give practice in guessing an author's plan and purpose, distribute and read several first lines or paragraphs from different popular magazine articles. Have the students predict what direction the authors may go and what conclusions they may come to. Students may either read the actual articles later or be told how they were developed.

Students may prepare their own advance organizers. Have volunteers read ahead in the textbook and prepare brief outlines of main points or summaries to guide the other students when they reach those chapters. Some students may be encouraged to prepare more elaborate study guides of coming chapters (with outlines, summaries, guide questions, glossaries) for the rest of the class. These should be duplicated in advance and discussed by the student writers.

Encourage students to try out alternatives to the SQ3R method (such as PQRST, the Triple S Technique, OK5R, and OARWET). Allow them opportunities to discuss their responses to these study methods with the group, and to perhaps come up with original methods of their own.

To help students distinguish main points from supporting details and examples, have them prepare "digest versions" of chapters and related articles. The directions might be: Take this thirty-page chapter (or article) and cut it down as an editor might to a two- or three-page condensation for a digest-type magazine. The final products may be duplicated for use as advance organizers or reviews for future tests.

Have individuals or groups prepare test items. Instruct them to go through a chapter or assignment and list what they believe are the ten or twenty main points the author wants to highlight. Then tell them to turn each of the main points into a possible test question. With teacher assistance, a group of "editors" may go through the assembled questions and select items they believe best for a final chapter test.

To call attention to charts and graphs, suggest that students go through assignments to find places where an additional chart or graph would have helped them visualize the verbal content. Next, ask the students to draw such an aid for duplication and distribution for the entire class.

To make students aware of the value of headings and typographical aids, suggest that they select a chapter in a related textbook and show how they would redesign the book so that future readers would better understand the materials. They should consider: Which points should be highlighted by uppercase letters? Which points might be underlined? Placed in italics? What comments might be inserted in the margin to assist readers? In which places would "white space" highlight the author's points? Where might arrows be placed to help the reader move from point to point?

High school and college students often neglect the author's preface or introductory remarks. Suggest that students carefully read such material to discover the author's general purpose in writing the book, the scope and limitations as seen by the author, his or her acknowledged biases, and recognition given to other scholars. For books that do not have prefaces, encourage volunteers to write them.

To relate assigned reading to oral language activities, encourage volunteers to read ahead in the textbook and prepare their own "lectures" to present to the class. Student-lecturers must decide on main points, important supporting details and examples, plan of organization, and devices to keep listeners interested (such as listening guides, anecdotes, personal comments on the material).

Ask students to bring science or history textbooks to class. Call attention to the different kinds of type (such as boldface, italics, capitals, etc.) and different page arrangements (such as centered, boxed, marginal) that are used for the section headings. Note that the section headings often help summarize major points and are thus valuable study aids. Have students suggest other ways in which the author might have organized the material. Using poorly designed textbooks, spend some time in discussing ways in which the material might be better presented. The following questions may be asked: Where would *you* divide the chapter? What section heading would you write? What is the key information? How might you call attention to key information? What material might be boxed? Of what value is white space? How could the author or editor better make use of white space? What marginal notes would you put in if you were editing or writing this book?

With chapters from a textbook before them, have students rewrite the section headings as newspaper headlines. Select a chapter with ten or fewer distinct section headings and suggest that each be placed in bold type as a headline (for example, instead of "The struggle for self-government in the early colonies," students may write "Colonists Demand Say in Own Affairs"). From this activity students may go on to rewrite entire chapters as they might appear in a good modern newspaper.

Have students locate short articles in out-of-class reading (from *TV Guide, Reader's Digest, Scholastic, Downbeat, Popular Science* etc.) and show how these may be rearranged. Note that magazine editors are often limited by the demands of advertiser's space or the need to continue an article to pages in the back of the magazine. Suggest that students reorganize the material as they, personally, would like to see it. Discussions may be based upon such questions as: What do you think are the chief points of the article? What do you think ought to be highlighted? What seems less important? What pictures would you have used if you were editor? Such examinations may lead to similar analysis of textbook chapters, using the same or similar questions.

Some students (not necessarily younger ones) derive value from the "Stand-up Paragraph." Give the class a short article from a popular magazine to read. Have the class decide what the main ideas seem to be, and then have individual students stand in the front of the group and represent each main idea. Next, ask individual students to volunteer to represent important supporting details and stand up beside the "main idea person." When a line is complete in the front of the room, the group can decide if the main ideas are in correct logical or chronological order and, then, if the supporting detail students are lined up in correct sequence after the main ideas. An oral presentation of the article may be given, or the class may write the article from the line-up of students. This dramatic and visual approach to organization may later be applied to chapters in textbooks.

A useful variant of the SQ3R method is to have students examine the section headings of a textbook chapter, turn each into a question, and then (1) put the questions aside, (2) read the chapter, (3) close the book, and (4) go back to answer the questions. When students have completed the assignment, time may be spent on an examination of the ways in which different types of questions are answered. For example, "Will one word do the job? Is a completed sentence needed? Is the question really answered in the textbook? Is the answer factual or is it the author's opinion? Is the answer given in the book reasonable? Does it make sense to me?

A study technique that combines reading for main ideas and details leads to the following instructions to students:

1. Go through the entire chapter and note the section headings.
2. Write out these headings in your own words.
3. Read the chapter carefully, noting the details that are mentioned under each heading.
4. Close the book and go back to fill in under your headings all the details you can remember.
5. Reread the chapter to discover the details you did not remember and write them into your notes.

To develop elaborative or associational thinking skills, have students enumerate as many questions as they can that are *not* answered in a textbook chapter or article. Explain that a successful student uses his or her reading to stimulate creative thinking. Demonstrate this belief by having the entire class read a short article from a popular magazine and then noting on the chalkboard two or three questions raised in the teacher's mind but not answered in the article. Have students suggest questions that came to their minds as they read. List these on the board and discuss (1) reasons why the author did not elaborate on these points, (2) possible reasons why these questions came into the mind of one individual reader and not another, and (3) places where students might go to find answers to their questions.

To relate intake of ideas in reading with intake of ideas in listening, have individual students prepare brief, organized talks on topics that appeal to them. Suggest that each talk have at least three main ideas and definite details to support each. While volunteers give their talks, students in class should listen to discover the main ideas and supporting details, and jot these down for later discussion. Listeners may later compare their notes with those of the speaker's to learn whether they caught all the main and supporting ideas. Cassette tape recorders enhance the value of such exercises.

Précis writing is used less in schools today than a generation or two ago, but its value remains for many students. Using the instruction in recognizing main ideas and supporting details, students can be encouraged to write a précis on a chapter, a section of a chapter, an article, or a class talk. At first it may be necessary to explain the main idea, list important details for the group, and lead students into the process using simple material. Later, students may try the technique on more difficult material.

If a textbook does not have a glossary, have students prepare one for each chapter as they go along through the book. They may be done by individuals or small groups. The glossaries should be duplicated for use by all the students in the class.

References

Anderson, Richard C. "Control of Student Mediating Processes During Verbal Learning and Instruction." *Review of Educational Research* 40 (June 1970): 349-369.

Eanet, Marilyn G., and Anthony V. Manzo. "REAP—A Strategy for Improving Reading/Writing/Study Skills." *Journal of Reading* 19 (May 1976): 647-652.

Farquhar, William W.; John D. Krumboltz; and C. Gilbert Wrenn. *Learning to Study.* New York: Ronald Press, 1960.

Fry, Edward. "Readability Formula That Saves Time." *Journal of Reading* 11 (April 1968): 513-516, 575-578.

Gunning, Robert. *The Technique of Clear Writing.* New York: McGraw-Hill Book Co., 1952.

Harris, Albert J., and Milton D. Jacobson. "A Framework for Readability Research: Moving beyond Herbert Spencer." *Journal of Reading* 22 (February 1979): pp. 390-398.

Henry, George H. *Teaching Reading as Concept Development: Emphasis on Affective Thinking.* Newark, Del.: International Reading Association, 1974.

Herber, Harold L. *Teaching Reading in the Content Areas.* Englewood Cliffs, N.J.: Prentice-Hall, Inc., 1978.

Jewett, Arno. "Using Book Parts." In *Developing Study Skills in Secondary Schools.* Edited by Harold L. Herber. Newark, Del.: International Reading Association, 1965.

Karahalios, Sue M.; Marion J. Tonjes; and John C. Towner. "Using Advance Organizers to Improve Comprehension of a Content Text." *Journal of Reading* 22 (May 1979): 706-708.

McLaughlin, Harry G. "SMOG Grading— A New Readability Formula." *Journal of Reading* 12 (May 1969): 639.

Neisser, Ulric. *Cognitive Psychology.* New York: Appleton-Century-Crofts, 1967.

Newell, Allan, and Herbert A. Simon. *Human Problem Solving.* New York: Prentice-Hall, 1972.

Norman, Maxwell H., and Enid S. Norman. *Successful Reading.* New York: Holt, Rinehart and Winston, 1968.

Pauk, Walter. *How to Study in College,* 2nd. ed. Boston: Houghton Mifflin Co., 1974, p. 151.

Robinson, Francis P. *Effective Study,* 4th ed. New York: Harper & Row Publishers, 1970, pp. 32-33.

Staton, Thomas F. *How to Study.* Nashville, Tenn.: McQuiddey Printing Co., 1954.

Tadlock, Dolores Fadness. "SQ3R—Why It Works, Based on Information Processing Theory." *Journal of Reading* 22 (November 1978): 110-112.

Thomas, Ellen, and H. Alan Robinson. *Improving Reading in Every Classroom.* Boston: Allyn & Bacon, Inc., 1972.

Tutolo, Daniel J. "The Study Guide—Types, Purpose and Value." *Journal of Reading* 20 (March 1977): 503-507.

4

STUDY SKILLS IN MATHEMATICS, SCIENCE, AND LITERATURE

The previous chapters on listening and reading have suggested teaching strategies for introducing students to the use of basic study skills, along with ideas for providing them with practice in the use of these skills. Each concluded with a list of twenty study skills. This information was purposely generalized. It should carry over into most areas of the school curriculum and, with some modification by the teacher, be valuable for students at most grade levels. Teaching students to look for an author's or speaker's plan of organization or to identify main points in a talk or text is basic to all study, whether in social studies or science, whether in fourth grade or fourteenth. However, some special considerations arise when teaching in content areas where *text* (a mathematics problem, a science problem, a poem or story) is central to instruction. Mathcmatics, science, and literature are three such areas.

This chapter examines the study skills needed to succeed in these content areas, noting how the generalizations established under listening and reading may carry over into mathematics, science, and literature study.

STUDY SKILLS IN MATHEMATICS

Most study in mathematics focuses on the development of specific concepts and principles. Simple teacher guidance in solving countless problems is valuable only in that the effort leads to student success in generalizing the concepts and principles so that they may solve other problems. As many mathematics teachers have noted, "Students who learn how to solve an assigned problem but not how to solve others like it on their own are in trouble!" Therefore, teaching mathematics study skills must involve (1) helping students understand and use the language of mathematics (that is, the specialized terminology, the symbol system, and the graphics used), and (2) showing them how to perceive and use the patterns favored by the authors of mathematics textbooks. Seven general suggestions are given here.

Teach the Specialized Vocabulary

The SSCD approach to unfamiliar words presented in the preceding chapter works well for students (from fourth grade to college) when they read articles, stories, and most of their textbooks. It is useful in mathematics and needs to be taught and reviewed regularly. However, mathematics study involves many specialized words which must be understood by students; most have a single meaning and must be used precisely. Sound and structure clues may still be somewhat useful, but context clues and the dictionary are now indispensable.

Context clues abound in mathematics textbooks, chiefly because textbook authors deliberately plant them. Aware of the specialized nature of their technical vocabularies, authors of good mathematics textbooks provide definitions for difficult words in parentheses, italics, or boldface type, by examples, and through definitions and graphics. In the prereading session, teachers should call attention to new words and the ways they are used, thus reviewing previous instruction in the use of context clues. The idea of multiple meanings may be reviewed, too, by discussing those words which have a special meaning in mathematics and other meanings outside the field (for example, *cone, angle, point, field, group, mean, radical, plane, degree*). Before going through a problem on their own, students need to be reminded to watch for new words and old words used in new ways. They should list these words in their notebooks, and check to discover if the author has defined them within the context of the problem.

The "D" in SSCD is of paramount importance in mathematics study. The most skillful and best-intentioned authors cannot clear up all vocabulary difficulties in the text. Teachers need to identify "dangerous" words in advance, define them, and have students keep a record of them. Mathematics teachers need to review (or, in some cases, teach for the first time) use of the glossary, the index, the dictionaries, and the particular textbook's system of providing definitions (in a box, in color, through boldface or italics).

Student vocabulary lists, valuable in all school subjects, are especially important in mathematics. Teachers need to encourage students to keep a separate notebook for math words. These should contain all the words encountered through the course, with definitions and examples of their use in context. Time should be set aside regularly for in-class review, self-testing, and teacher-testing. As Armstrong (1967, p. 99) counseled students years ago, "Make the vocabulary of mathematics the first element of study in all mathematical subjects." The concepts and principles are approached only through the vocabulary, and the vocabulary words themselves often represent basic concepts and principles.

Show Students How the Symbol System Works

The language of mathematics is more than lexical items arranged syntactically; it includes a highly-evolved, arbitrary symbol system. To *read* mathematics implies not only understanding words in sentences but also understanding systematic symbol systems. In elementary school, the symbols may be dollar signs, decimal points, equal signs, and plus or minus signs; in high school and college, the range of symbols increases as students get into algebra, geometry, and calculus. Again, it is important for students to keep records in their notebooks of the symbols they encounter in the textbook and in class lessons. Their textbooks may include often-used symbols in a glossary or separate sections of the chapter, but keeping individual notebook records personalizes the learning. To some extent, it provides students and teacher with a control over the intake, recording, verification, and collection of the key symbols.

Experienced mathematics teachers often recommend that students, especially in elementary school, be reminded regularly that it is acceptable to read slowly and frequently shift attention from the text to their symbol lists (see, for example, Hater, Kane, and Byrne 1974). Some students feel obliged to move their eyes in a straight-forward manner, from left to right, across the lines, and down the page. They need to realize that in mathematics assignments it is necessary to reread, check the meanings of words, and verify their use of the symbols.

An effective way of making all students aware of the meaning and interrelationships among symbols and symbol systems is through *oral reading*. Robinson (1978, p. 235) notes,

> Seemingly, the very act of verbalizing gives help in the process of clarification. This type of oral reading—to help students focus with accuracy on the interrelationships among the symbol systems—should be very much like the oral reading that is recommended for proofreading—unit by unit—*but with active thinking taking place.*

Give Students Practice in Understanding Graphics

Graphics are as much a part of the language of mathematics as the special terminology or the symbol systems. They include figures, graphs, diagrams, tables, and charts. Graphics need to be taught as an intrinsic part of the language because most textbooks in the area use them as visual explanations of verbal material. They are used regularly to introduce main points, to reinforce previous points, and often as integral parts of important concepts and principles.

Some teachers approach graphics through graphs and tables, beginning with simple bar graphs in which students develop corresponding tables to complement each graph. Teachers should start with phenomena close to the lives of the students (number of books read by individuals in the class for fourth or fifth graders, or scores from athletic events for secondary school students) and have some groups present the information pictorially in some type of graph and other groups present the same information in a table. Then, teachers may have the class compare and contrast the final products. Other teachers explain and have students create similar graphs and tables as they are encountered in the textbooks. Most teachers who have successfully taught graphics make regular reference to diagrams, tables, graphs, and charts found in current newspapers and magazines.

An effective way of helping students relate pictorial and verbal presentations is to have them cover, with a card or paper, the verbal material accompanying a selected figure in their textbook and then write a verbal description of what the figure tries to communicate. After the verbal descriptions have been shared and compared with the textbook author's, students may then do the exercise in reverse (cover another selected graphic and, from the book's verbal description, draw a figure). These, too, need to be shared and compared with the figure in the book. Students should be encouraged to prepare their own graphics for textbook material, especially for verbal material not pictorialized in the book. Their work should be duplicated or posted as valid contributions to all students' understanding of the textbook.

Give Students Practice in Spotting Unstated Assumptions

The matter of unstated assumptions has been treated by mathematician George Polya in his suggestions for helping students read mathematical problems (Polya 1962). He presents the following "word" problem:

> A patrol plane flies 220 miles per hour in still air. It carries fuel for 4 hours of safe flying. If it takes off on patrol against a wind of 20 miles per hour, how far can it fly and return safely?

Polya points out that a student may "read" these sentences in a straightforward way and proceed to solve the problem. His or her success, however, is contingent upon the recognition of at least three unstated assumptions: (1) the wind is supposed to blow with unchanged intensity during the entire flight, (2) the plane travels in a straight line, and (3) the time needed for changing directions at the furthest point is negligible. Polya notes that all word problems contain such unstated assumptions and demand from the reader preliminary interpretation and abstraction. "This is an essential feature of the word problem which is not always trivial and should be brought into the open" (Polya 1962, p. 30). Such assumptions permeate mathematics textbooks from elementary school to college. Teachers need to watch for them constantly, and should encourage students to be vigilant as they read. Time spent in class identifying and examining unstated assumptions not only helps students become better math students, but may also help them in all school subjects. Such efforts may also help them become better critical thinkers long after they have completed their mathematics courses in school.

Demonstrate How Patterns Work

After examining various definitions of mathematics, Sawyer settled upon: "Mathematics is the classification and study of all possible patterns" (Armstrong 1967, p. 100). He defined a pattern, simply, as "any kind of regularity that can be recognized by the mind." The values of perceiving and exploiting patterns in reading, writing, studying, and thinking in general are discussed in Chapter 9 of this book. They may be intrinsic, as will be suggested, to certain mental operations and, consequently, important to all thinking and studying. Their study lies outside the province of this particular chapter; however, the importance of recognizing and using certain simple patterns regularly used by authors of mathematics textbooks needs to be examined here.

After surveying and studying a large number of popular mathematics textbooks, Robinson (1978, pp. 240–256) found three major patterns favored by most authors. Even beginning students should know these.

Concept Development Pattern

The concept the author wants to develop is usually set off by boldface, italics, boxes, or color. The goal of the author (and the teacher using the book) is to make the concept clear to student readers by having them work out the details of a practical problem which illustrates the concept. Robinson (1978, p. 243) suggests a six-step strategy: study the heading, read the definition(s), reread the definition(s), read the explanatory information and graphics, reread when necessary, and then reread the definitions. To this should be added: groups of problems illustrating the same concept should be worked on by the class so that students begin to see the basic concept from different points of view.

Principle Development

A mathematical principle (that is, a postulate, theorem, law, rule, or axiom) is a generalization growing out of a group of concepts. All are generally formal statements of a mathematical truth or assumed truth. The author usually expresses this larger generalization in boldface, italics, color, or capital letters; and usually provides solutions as illustrations of the principle immediately after its statement. Robinson notes that the following strategy works for many students: study the heading and introductory material, read the principle, reread the principle, read illustrations and sample problems, reread, compute, write, and/or draw as needed, and, finally, reread the principle. As in the case of the concept development pattern, students should do problems in groups to see how a basic law, rule, or axiom is derived from a multitude of separate examples.

Problem Solving

Because problem solving is often most troublesome to students (especially in the form of word problems), teachers need to attack this pattern in a variety of ways. Cooney, Davis, and Henderson (1975) present a set of guidelines for teachers to follow in helping students approach word problems. Robinson (1978, p. 252) has summarized these as follows:

1. Make sure students understand the problem.
   a. Do students understand the meanings of terms in the problem?
   b. Do they take all relevant information into consideration?
   c. Can they indicate what the problem is asking them to find?
   d. Can they state the problem in their own words?
2. Help students gather relevant thought material to assist in creating a plan.
   a. Assist them in gathering information by having them analyze the given conditions (and sometimes the assumed solution).
   b. Help them obtain information by analyzing an analogous problem.
   c. When they become discouraged by pursuing an unproductive approach, help them view the problem from a different perspective.
3. Provide students with an atmosphere conducive to problem solving.

4. Once students have obtained a solution, encourage them to reflect on the problem and the means of solution.
   a. If possible, have students verify solutions that have not been established deductively.
   b. Encourage them to seek and present alternate ways of solving a problem.
   c. Challenge them to investigate variations of the given problem.

Provide a Heuristic

Robinson's summary of guidelines to problem solving leads to the important matter of providing students with a general heuristic, or model of attack, they can use in all textbook assignments in mathematics. One is suggested in the format found for listening (in Chapter 2) and reading (in Chapter 3):

☐ Have students read through the problem, taking an overview to give them a general notion of why the class is doing the problems and the ways in which it fits into the context of the course.

☐ Explain new and possibly difficult words (such as *patrol plane*, *still air*, and *safe flying* in the problem on page 68).

☐ Set up a purpose and goal for "reading" (usually the answer to the question posed in the problem; in this case, "How far can it fly and return safely?").

☐ Have students read the problem.

☐ Ask them to self-test themselves and share their answers before revealing the correct answer.

While such an approach seems better than simply assigning the problem "cold," it clearly is not enough. It is worthwhile here to seek help from the mathematicians themselves.

Polya (1962, p. 122), for example, would agree that a format, approach, or model is needed: "The solution of many problems consists of essentially a *procedure*, a course of action, a scheme of well-interrelated operations, a *modus operandi*." He suggests certain prereading or presolving activities and the explanation of possibly difficult vocabulary items. As noted previously, he also calls attention to unstated assumptions within the text. He offers a seven-step "heuristic" for all problems, easy or difficult. The student asks:

1. What do I want?
2. What are the data? (or What do I have?)
3. What is the unknown?
4. How is it defined?
5. Is there an analogous problem?
6. What do I want in terms of the analogous problem?
7. How can I get it?   (Polya 1962)

Fehr (1955) offers a five-step approach based on his belief that *all learning requires association*. He states that learning to read and solve verbal problems means that students must be able to relate or associate the assigned problem with similar ones. He suggests that students:

1. Select significant words and phrases in a situation, show their importance to the situation, and attempt to define them.
2. Attempt to identify statements and implicit assumptions essential to the conclusion.
3. Attempt to evaluate the assumptions, accepting only those that past experience makes plausible and rejecting others.
4. Require evidence to support the conclusion.
5. Apply this method in establishing a mathematics structure   (Fehr 1955).

Reading specialists offer other valuable models or approaches that students may use in mathematics. PQ4R, for example, is a variant of SQ3R, developed particularly for math problems (Maffei 1973).

The approaches to classroom listening and reading given for general use in all school subjects combined with those of Maffei, Robinson, Polya, Fehr, and specialists in mathematics education lead to ten suggestions for helping students read school mathematics assignments:

1. Make sure students read through the assignment first and understand what they are seeking.
2. Explain all difficult words and phrases (both mathematical terms and ordinary English words students may not know).
3. Encourage students to *visualize* as much as possible (by using graphs, charts, diagrams, and pictures).
4. Do several easier sample exercises (either taken from the textbook or created for the purpose).
5. Associate the materials encountered in the assignment with previous learnings and other experiences from mathematics, from other school subjects, and from the students' own lives.
6. Call attention to basic arithmetic fundamentals involved (review and reteach if necessary).

7. Emphasize the basic principles in the problem or assignment.
8. Have students make up similar problems to demonstrate that they understand the principle.
9. Encourage students to teach one another the principle using their own examples and word problems.
10. Demonstrate how the homework (if any) is to be done.

A true heuristic, it must be noted, does not lie in suggestions for teachers such as these. Rather, it is a *student's* internalized procedure or approach (or, to use Polya's synonyms, a "course of action, a scheme of well-interrelated operations, a *modus operandi*"). The teacher—and this is true of all the study skills described in this book—can only explain, suggest, and provide much meaningful, relevant, guided practice in the use of the heuristic or, especially in the case of more mature students, several heuristics. The key word here is *much*.

STUDY SKILLS IN SCIENCE

Certain typical assignments in school science textbooks bring into focus at least two problems common to all instruction in study skills. Students are sometimes "assigned" a passage similar to the one below with instructions to "Read and be prepared to discuss it tomorrow."

> The most visible objects on the disc of the sun are clusters of spots, known as sun spots or simply spots. These range in size from tiny flecks visible only through a telescope to large areas which may be seen by the unaided eye. One sun spot group has been estimated to be as large as the circumference of the earth multiplied by 140 times. All have two portions, a darker one near the center called the umbra and a lighter one called the penumbra. The umbra appears darker than it really is because of the relative brightness of the surrounding area. Some penumbra have several umbra within them. Observers have traced the positions of sun spots throughout the year and have noticed two kinds of movement. Sometimes they move in straight lines and sometimes in slight curves. This is due to the inclination of the sun's equator to the plane of the earth's orbit.

A passage such as this, treated separately or as the first paragraph in a larger assignment in the book, may be better approached by using the generalized format suggested in Chapters 2 and 3:

1. Give students an overview of the selection.
2. Set up a purpose for reading.
3. Explain new terms.

4. Provide a study guide with an outline or study questions.
5. Encourage notetaking or other pen-in-hand responses to the reading.
6. Allow time for student sharing of notes and answers at the end.

The SQ3R study approach or one of its variants would also provide a more effective alternative to "Read and be prepared to discuss it tomorrow." However, reading assignments of this type, whether in science textbooks or in other school subjects, highlight two major problems for teachers of study skills. Both are rooted in assumptions that textbook authors, and some teachers, too frequently make: (1) all students share a common scientific, academic, or experiential background; and (2) all students want to read the assignment. Both problems are central to all instruction in study skills—and, indeed, to all schooling.

Do all students, even in relatively homogeneous communities and schools, share the same backgrounds? The student readers for whom the sample paragraph was written are, in many respects, more alike than different (particularly in terms of chronological age, physical attributes, general predispositions, needs, cultural backgrounds, and so forth). Yet countless subtle (and not so subtle) differences distinguish one from the other: for example, one student has looked through a telescope at the local science museum, another has traveled to Hong Kong and has a clearer notion of the earth's size, one has no idea of a disc, another is the daughter of a physics professor, still another has never developed the concept of relativeness when applied to light.

This single paragraph rests upon many "unstated assumptions" on the author's part: that *all* student readers (1) can conceive of nonvisible objects, (2) will believe anything can be seen on the sun's surface, (3) understand the concept of circumference, (4) can conceive of a distance multiplied 140 times, (5) know that telescopes are used to study the sun, (6) understand *inclination*, (7) know the terms *equator* and *orbit*, (8) will distinguish *umbra* from *penumbra* on the printed page, and (9) will know that movement here refers to movement of the spots. Clearly, before teaching the *content* of the assigned reading, the teacher must go back and first find out what students bring to the reading, and then teach to fill in gaps in individual backgrounds. The suggestions in Chapters 2 and 3 that teachers clarify difficult terminology and concepts in preteaching sessions and Herber's (1978) warnings about "assumptive teaching" 1978 seem to be of even greater importance to teaching science from a textbook.

The author of the passage on sunspots assumes a common background which readers may not have. He also assumes that the students *care* to read his paragraph. Do all student readers really care about sun spots? About astronomy? About science? About school? These questions lead to a key issue in all teaching (see Chapter 12); it is simply high-lighted in the examination of this possible science assignment. Fortunately for teachers, some students do want to read this assignment; some will do it to earn good grades, some want to avoid punishment for *not* doing it, some are anxious to please parents and teachers, some believe it will help them gain college admission, and some are truly interested in sun spots, astronomy, science, and academic pursuits. However, as all teachers know, some students will not be motivated to read the passage. They do not care. The final chapter of this book discusses motivation and the student's self-concept of himself or herself as a learner. Here, some specific suggestions are offered in reference to the paragraph cited. If the teacher is convinced of the importance of this particular assigned reading, then the teacher has to give students reasons for reading, preferably derived from the assignment itself and not based on extrinsic forms of motivation (that is, getting good grades, avoiding punishment, pleasing adults, etc.). Some approaches might be:

☐ Read the beginning paragraph and ask: What do you think the author is leading up to? What will he write next? What seems to be the point of the paragraph?

☐ Relate the reading to the readers by asking such questions as: Have *you* ever looked through a telescope? When? Where? Did you look at the sun? Did *you* see sun spots? Have you ever looked at the sun through dark glasses? What else could you have used? Why must you protect your eyes? Did you see a sun spot?

☐ Relate the reading to other media by asking: Have you seen a photograph of a sun spot? Did it have an umbra? Umbrae? A penumbra? What are the differences?

☐ Extend the reading experiences by asking such questions as: Why are scientists interested in sun spots? Could they affect *your* life? In what ways?

☐ Focus on the scientific method by asking such questions as: How do scientists reach conclusions? How do they really *know* sun spots move? Why do they say movements shift because of inclinations in the sun's equator? What is an hypothesis? How do we all use the scientific method in daily life? Have *you* used it recently? When? In what way?

To make study skills in science "come alive" for students, teachers need to show photographs; draw pictures; have students create pictures and models; arrange appropriate field trips; personalize the material; constantly relate the science learnings to the interests, concerns, and needs of students; and provide regular opportunities for them to involve themselves in the material by sharing personal experiences. One effective way to make study skills come alive is to teach students how the scientific method works. Even elementary school students may be shown how scientists gather data, make hypotheses, and test them out. They can be shown that the "dry" expositions of their textbooks are actually the results of exciting quests for truth. This may seem old advice, recapitulated over and over again in professional literature; nevertheless, it remains true. The ideas and information in the textbook remain for many students "a lot of black marks on white paper" until their teachers adjust the material to the experiential backgrounds of students and relate it, by one means or another, to their lives.

The assumptions of many textbook authors and some teachers that all students share the same background and that all have a natural desire to complete assignments are not, of course, peculiar to science study. Both lead to student failure in all school subjects, at all grade levels. They are spotlighted here under science because science textbooks and assignments based on them seem especially open to criticism: *too much is assumed* about students' prior knowledge and present interests.

Two important recommendations are implied in this discussion:

1. Teachers need to fill in gaps in the background knowledge of students for every assignment.
2. Teachers need to relate, as much as possible, the content material to the lives of their students.

At least four other suggestions for improving science study skills may be made.

Encourage Students to Keep Master Lists

One master list, kept from the first day of the course and in a personal notebook, should include all technical and specialized words in the scientific vocabulary of the science textbook, with definitions and page references in the text. A second master list should include all theories and laws that are encountered in the book, again with page references and explanations. A third list may contain the formulas, equations, and devices presented in the textbook and in class. Lists will differ, of course, for different grade levels and for different areas of science. They will provide students with a ready means of review and reference, and they may be used by students for self-testing or by the teacher as a source for test items at the end of a unit or marking period.

Encourage Students to Develop Graphs and Models

Simple sketches, diagrams, illustrations, graphs, charts, tables, photographs, and other visual aids should be used by the teacher in explaining textbook material; they should also be developed *by students.* Perception and understanding of relationships are more clear for students when they prepare their own visuals. They can present phases, steps in sequence, quantities, enumeration, proportions, and measurements pictorially and, in the process, better understand key learnings. Student productions should be kept in individual notebooks and regularly displayed or duplicated for others in the class. If "a picture is worth a thousand words," a model may be worth a million. Models by students should be an intrinsic part of all classroom learning. They should be made, displayed, examined, and discussed. Again, this may seem old advice, but student development of models and all types of graphics remains one of the best avenues to improved study skills in science.

Encourage Students to See Patterns

In his study of recent science textbooks, Robinson found six major patterns predominating: enumeration, classification, generalization, problem solution, comparison and contrast, and sequence (Robinson 1978, pp. 166–189). Patterns used by textbook authors have been discussed briefly in the preceding section on mathematics study skills and will be discussed in greater detail in Chapter 9 of this book. Here, it may be enough to note that teachers should call attention to the major patterns used in their textbooks and give students practice in identifying and using the patterns to better understand material in science. The major patterns and a brief description of each follow.

Enumeration.   In this basic pattern, the author states the topic and follows it with a list of characteristics, features, descriptions, or attributes. The reader's task is to identify, understand as best he or she can, and remember each item.

Classification.   Here the topic is divided by the author into two or more parts, often with subparts under each. The reader needs to see the relationships of the parts and subparts to the whole topic.

Generalization.   The author's main purpose here is to state a generalization (a principle, hypothesis, conclusion) and support it with evidence in the form of examples and details. The reader's task is to distinguish between the main idea or generalization and the supporting evidence.

Problem-solution.   In his examination of science textbooks, Robinson (1978, p. 180) found this pattern taking five forms: (1) the problem may be clearly stated, followed by a solution, also clearly stated; (2) the problem may be clearly stated but followed by several hypothetical solutions; (3) the problem, clearly stated, may be followed by no solution(s); (4) the problem may be presented in the form of a question with the solution(s) in the form of an answer, or (5) neither problem nor solution(s) is given and the reader must infer the pattern. Because this pattern is widely-used in science textbooks, teachers need to provide much class guidance in recognizing and taking advantage of it.

Comparison and contrast.   In this pattern, the author tries to make one idea, event, or piece of information clear to the reader by pointing out ways in which it is like and/or unlike another the reader already knows. As will be shown in Chapter 9, the device is a potent way of learning and, to a remarkable extent, lies at the heart of all learning. Students need assistance in seeing how the pattern works to use it most effectively.

Sequence.   Here the textbook author presents an explanation of the steps in a process or an experiment. The student's task is to understand each step in sequence, isolate it from attendant information, and see the interrelationships among the steps. The pattern is relatively easy to follow in most textbook writing, but it is difficult in science because students are often unused to the precision. Clearly, teachers need to provide much in-class guidance in the recognition and best use of the sequence pattern.

Remind Students of the Goals of Scientific Inquiry

Science study skills are often thought of as acquisition skills; that is, skills needed to take in new ideas and information. This point of view is understandable: teachers feel that students need to have a substantial backlog of information before they can use it. There is an irony in this point of view, however, because science is essentially inquiry—using the known to discover the unknown. Teaching the study skills of acquisition is only a first step. In the heart of all science study lies an attitude toward knowledge and learning (the learner "feels" that he or she can arrive at general principles or laws by collecting data, hypothesizing, and testing out) and the use of fairly well-established techniques for discovering general principles or "truths" (by gathering data, hypothesizing, and testing out).

Central, then, to all study skills instruction in science should be the "scientific method." Teachers, whether teaching fourth grade or fourteenth, need to regularly teach students how the method works, as well as develop attitudes conducive to scientific inquiry. (For further discussion, see Romey 1968; Sund and Trowbridge 1973; or recent professional books on science teaching, such as Collette 1973.)

STUDY SKILLS IN LITERATURE

Literature teachers are all too aware of the affective dimension in their teaching: "We teach values, attitudes, appreciations and are concerned primarily with emotions, feelings, and the aesthetic aspects of *our* material." Some disdain a "skills approach" to great novels, stories, poems, and dramas: "Literature is not to be studied," they say, "but to be savored, enjoyed, experienced!" It is difficult to argue against this point of view when one is surrounded by colleagues, parents, and friends who do not read great (or *any*) novels, stories, poems, or dramas, who are "turned off" by the *study* of literature in school.

Should literature be studied in school? The question and possible answers have been discussed at length in professional literature (see, for example, Rosenblatt 1968; Sauer 1961; or Frye 1964). The point that needs to be made in the present context is that values, attitudes, appreciations, and the aesthetic aspects of literature are found within a cognitive framework. Authors present words, phrases, images, ideas, and symbols that trigger emotional responses within syntactical and larger discourse arrangements that must be at least partly understood intellectually before the possible affective impacts may occur. This suggests that literature teachers do indeed have to teach appropriate study skills in their area. Student readers must have at least minimal intellectual understanding of the material before literature may effect its special powers.

Four general suggestions for approaching study skills in literature are given here. They are based on observations of successful teaching and on research findings. They point the way toward an organized approach to the formal study of literature as distinct from the equally important programs in wide reading for enjoyment found in many schools. (For a comprehensive review of research in literature teaching, see Purves and Beach 1972.)

Teach Literary Concepts As Higher Level Reading Skills

One reason the formal study of literature has alienated many students is that such study is often vague, anfractuous, and ultimately unsatisfying to the learner because it focuses upon *knowing about* (concepts, titles, authors, periods, trends), not *knowing how* (to interpret, to evaluate, to manage specific skills in other contexts outside the literature class). Too often, teachers use literature as a springboard into discussions of other topics or as a vehicle for learning about specialized matters that have little or no relevance to the lives of many students.

One way to make literature study meaningful to students and provide an organizing basis for the literature program is to "translate" the traditional topics and concepts of the program into higher level reading skills which may then be used by students in nonliterary reading and in other aspects of their lives. Plot, character, setting, theme, and other topics may be turned into skills of immediate and wider usefulness. *Plot*, for example, may be treated as: (1) following a sequence of events, (2) recognizing rising action and high point, (3) recognizing sources of tension, (4) identifying foreshadowing clues, and other specific reading skills. In the same way, *setting*, instead of serving as an often vague focal point for a lecture, may be treated as a set of teachable (and testable) reading skills, such as: (1) recognizing clues indicating place, (2) recognizing clues indicating time, and (3) visualizing physical places and people. *Characterization*, often the foggiest topic in some classes, may be broken up into discrete skills, such as: (1) recognizing ways in which an author reveals character traits through speech, and (2) recognizing ways an author reveals character through actions (Devine 1978).

The values of such a skills approach to literature include the following:

☐ Vague, teacher-dominated lessons and discussions are constrained or curtailed. (The teacher's primary goal is now to teach students *how to read* a story, poem, or play, not to talk about authors' lives, periods, trends, and other essentially peripheral matters.)

☐ A skills-based program provides for more effective testing. (The objectives of measurement are not to discover how much information students have about the works but how well they can apply the newly-acquired skills to *other* works.)

☐ The skills are transferable out of the literature class. (Recognizing ways in which an author reveals character through his or her speech, for example, is a skill used daily by students as they assess strangers and friends by their spoken language; following a sequence of events may be transferred to history or science class; and so on.)

☐ Such an approach gets more directly at underlying mental processes. (Students are encouraged, for example, to give evidence to support their inferences about plot or characters.)

Give Practice in Inference-Making

The fourth justification given above leads to an important recommendation for literature teachers. Readers often make inferences about plot, characters, and aspects of literature (as they do about people and events in their lives) without seeking evidence to support their inferences or much understanding of the mental processes involved in inference-making. Literature classes provide a natural place for the development of many thinking skills, especially those associated with inference-making. Teachers can explain that an inference is an "educated guess," only as good as the evidence available to the inference-maker, and that there are good and poor inferences, and good and poor inference-makers. Instead of simply *telling* what the setting of a story or poem is (or *assuming* that students already know), some teachers ask students to read the beginning. Students are then asked: What clues has the author given to help you infer, or guess, the time and place?

Instead of telling students what a character is like, one teacher gives out 3 × 5 cards, tells students to write a statement about a character in the story ("The character has his mind on something else"), and asks them to support their inferential statement with evidence from the text ("He doesn't hear what the boy tells him" and/or "He drives past the red house"). The teacher then explains that the statements are inferences and are only valid when supported by evidence. The class is then led into a discussion of inference-making in "real life," gathering examples of good and poor inference-making from the students' own experiences. To relate this instruction to formal literature study, the teacher later draws three columns on the chalkboard, headed "Character's Speech," "Character's Actions," and "Speech and Actions of Others." The instructor leads students to see that an author reveals information about a character by what he or she says, what he or she does, or the ways others in the story behave and talk about the character. Some research evidence indicates that teaching inference-making skills in literature class leads to an improvement of thinking skills, especially those associated with inference-making (Sandberg 1970).

Some questions teachers may ask to improve inference-making skills are:

☐ What is the time of the story? The place? What evidence in the text leads you to your answer? What clues has the author given that make you think it happened when and where it did?

☐ What kind of a person is X? What did the person *say* that leads you to this answer? What did he or she *do* that makes you think so? What do other characters in the story say about this person? How do they act toward him or her? In what ways do their speech and actions support your answer?

☐ What do you think will happen next? What evidence in the story leads you to your answer? Can you find other foreshadowing clues? Do your predictions about events in life usually come true? Upon what evidence do you base "real-life" predictions? What is the last inference *you* made? On what evidence was it based?

For further discussion of the cognitive dimension in literature study, see Elkins 1976.

Encourage Students to Anticipate

Much of the delight associated with reading or listening to literature comes from anticipation. It is the curiosity to discover "what comes next" that encourages readers to turn pages and listeners to pay attention. Teachers may exploit this natural interest by (1) reading aloud or having students read silently a designated section of the story or novel, (2) stopping to itemize what has happened to that point, (3) encouraging students to predict what will happen, (4) having students read or listen to check out their predictions, and (5) allowing time for students to share their discoveries. This kind of classroom literature study is important because it encourages students to anticipate, predict, and discover the accuracy of their predictions, which increases the pleasures of literature. It is also important because research evidence indicates that student readers need much guidance in looking ahead, checking out their guesses about characters and story outcomes with evidence from the text, and discovering "what really happens" in a story. Squire and others who have examined student readers' "internal" response to literature while reading have found that readers often fail to understand what is happening in a story because of their preconceptions about characters and plot, stereotypes they carry into the reading from other reading and media experiences, and their tendency to see happy endings even when none exist (Squire 1964; Purves and Beach 1972).

Use a Study Guide

Teachers of other content areas regularly note the value of study guides (Tutolo 1977; Thomas and Cummings 1978; Herber 1978). Literature teachers need them to help their students focus on the particular study skills needed to better understand stories, novels, plays, and poems. Clearly, an SQ3R-type of structure is inappropriate in reading materials where anticipating "what comes next" is of paramount importance. A guide for a story or poem includes many features discussed in Chapters 2 and 3. A few are suggested below.

Prereading activities include:

1. Establishing a purpose for reading (such as a question to be answered, an inference to be checked out, or a problem to be solved)
2. Clarifying possibly unfamiliar concepts (about the genre, style, author's assumptions, specific ideas used by the author in the work)
3. Explaining possibly unfamiliar words (by reviewing the SSCD approach or by providing a teacher-made glossary).

During-reading activities include:

1. Answering specific factual questions given by the teacher
2. Searching for examples to illustrate a particular literary concept (such as "Authors often tantalize by foreshowing clues; find three in the story.")
3. Practicing a higher-level reading skill used in literature ("Recognizing ways authors reveal character traits through speech is an important skill; as you read, find three examples of dialogue which show the hero is shy.")
4. Filling in a plot diagram provided by the teacher
5. Developing a time line of events in the story
6. Jotting down, at stipulated points, predictions of how the story will end
7. Noting questions the reader wants answered
8. Noting points in the work that indicate the author's point of view or attitudes
9. Testing out points in the story or poem by relating and comparing them to the reader's own experiences in life.

Postreading activities include:

1. Checking the purpose for reading
2. Reviewing understanding of concepts
3. Verifying and using new vocabulary items
4. Sharing responses to the work
5. Suggesting alternative endings
6. Sharing notes taken while reading
7. Applying the main skill emphasized by the teacher in this lesson to another story or poem

STUDY SKILLS IN MATHEMATICS, SCIENCE, AND LITERATURE

Chapters 1 and 2 concluded with lists of basic study skills used in classroom listening and in reading school assignments. All of these skills are involved in successful study in mathematics, science, and literature.

Are any especially appropriate to these three content areas? Are any additional skills required in these areas? The following three lists are suggested to supplement the two "master lists" given in the first chapters.

Mathematics

1. Identifying unfamiliar words and terms
2. Using sound, structure, and context clues to get the meaning of unfamiliar words
3. Using the glossary or dictionary to define new words
4. Being aware of multiple meanings, especially of ordinary words used in specialized ways in mathematics
5. Learning new symbol systems
6. Using graphics (tables, charts, figures, diagrams)
7. Identifying "unstated assumptions" in word problems
8. Recognizing commonly-used patterns found in mathematics textbooks (concept development pattern, principle development pattern, and the problem solving patterns)
9. Identifying the main question or problem to be solved
10. Knowing several heuristics or plans of attack
11. Using one of the heuristics or plans of attack (such as PQ4R)
12. Identifying basic principles
13. Restating word problems in one's own language
14. Visualizing the features of a problem when appropriate
15. Relating new problems to previous learnings in mathematics.

Science

1. Identifying unfamiliar words and terms
2. Using sound, structure, and context clues
3. Using the glossary or dictionary
4. Identifying the author's or teacher's assumptions about the extent of one's previous learning
5. Relating new material to what one already knows
6. Recognizing inferences and generalizations
7. Finding evidence to support inferences and generalizations
8. Keeping lists of new words, theories, formulas, equations, and other new learnings

9. Using graphics
10. Recognizing patterns commonly used by authors of science textbooks (enumeration, classification, generalization, problem solving, comparison and contrast, sequence).

Literature

1. Following a sequence of events
2. Anticipating outcomes
3. Recognizing clues to setting
4. Identifying parts of plot (introduction, rising action, high point, falling action, conclusion)
5. Recognizing foreshadowing clues
6. Recognizing ways in which an author reveals a character through his or her speech, his or her actions, the speech and actions of others, and/or direct statements.
7. Noting mood and tone
8. Recognizing theme
9. Noting use of symbols
10. Making and finding support for inferences about character, plot, setting
11. Identifying unfamiliar words and using appropriate techniques to arrive at meaning
12. Noting unfamiliar concepts and materials
13. Relating the work to one's own life
14. Distinguishing genres in literature
15. Recognizing common literary devices (personification, simile, metaphor, etc.).

Idea Box
Mathematics

Have students, individually or in groups, preview the word problems in the next section of their textbooks to discover the basic arithmetic fundamentals required for solution. Then have volunteers take time in class to quickly review for the whole group the necessary fundamentals before they work on the problems.

Encourage individual students, or small groups, to develop timed games to review basic fundamentals. These may be patterned after baseball, football, or a game "in season." Teams, scoreboards, judges, and timers may be selected, and class time is used to review "basics" in a game context.

Have students teach one another. Once a concept, principle, or process has been taught to the whole class, divide the group into pairs for *team teaching*, in which each student in the team teaches the other and then becomes the student and is taught.

Encourage students to update word problems in the textbook. Assign each student one word problem from the book to rewrite so that the problem is more interesting to the class. A textbook problem such as, "Tom lives 3/4 of a mile from a tennis court. If it takes him 6⅔ minutes to go 1/3 of a mile, how long will it take him to walk to the court?" may be rewritten by students as "Harry (a student in the class) lives 3/4 of a mile from the gas station where he works (he does). He takes 6⅔ minutes to walk a third of a mile, so how long will it take him to get to work?" Students may later substitute different numbers and different situations.

Sometimes explanatory material is loaded with concepts that are not explained on the pages although they were explained previously in the book. Have volunteers preview the material, identify the concepts, and explain them to the class before they read the assignment.

Have students identify key concepts in the assignment and explain them to the class in their own words. Encourage them to illustrate the concepts with examples from their own experiences.

Group of students may develop a Student Guide to the textbook chapter or section, in which they (1) locate all difficult terms and list them alphabetically with definitions and/or synonyms, (2) provide guide questions to help readers, (3) suggest additional examples to help clarify the text, and (4) give short self-tests for students to administer to themselves. Guides may be duplicated and distributed.

Encourage individual students to explore the history of mathematics. They can (1) locate and read appropriate material, (2) prepare bibliographies for class distribution, (3) write research papers, and/or (4) make oral presentations to the class. The study of mathematics becomes more alive for some students when they can see it in historical perspective and share their findings with others.

Suggest that students locate and take a sample of the Scholastic Aptitude Test to discover how well they understand basic skills. Using material from published tests or review handbooks, students may develop their own diagnostic tests of arithmetic fundamentals to be duplicated and shared with the class.

Have students review their own books for the three basic patterns (the concept development pattern, the principle development pattern, and the problem-solving pattern) and share their findings with the class. They can indicate which patterns are most often used by the author, what each looks like, how each is best managed, and/or which seems easiest.

Science

Using a given paragraph from their textbooks, have the students find the key words and phrases, the most important single idea, and the examples that support that idea. When the class becomes proficient at this kind of analysis, an entire chapter or section of a chapter can be studied by (1) having the class read the entire assignment; (2) assigning each student, in a sequence, one paragraph to analyze; and (3) sharing the next day the findings in consecutive order.

Have students read through the assignment to "make connections." Remind them that learning takes place when the learner can relate to the material in a personal way. Each student then reads and notes the points in the assignment that he or she can connect in some way with his or her own life. Time should be set aside so that each person may share "personal connections" and tell why they help understanding and memory.

Students may rewrite sections of their books—for younger students, for other kinds of readers, in other styles, or for other purposes. For example, you might ask, "What would this page sound like on a children's television program? How could it be rewritten best for a small child? How would you rewrite it as a newspaper story?"

Whenever the opportunity arises in the course, teachers should encourage students to prepare models (with cardboard and paper, wood, wire, string, pipe cleaners) to help them—and others in the class—better understand the textbook. The possibilities are unlimited and need to be exploited.

To develop an appreciation for the ways scientists work, have each student locate and read a biography of a famous scientist. They may write one-page reviews of the books on ditto masters so that all the reviews may be duplicated, bound together as a booklet, and distributed to the class. Or, more simply, time may be set aside for sharing sessions for students to tell about their books.

After discussing the scientific method in class, students may tell about instances in their own lives when they have used it or a variation of it. These, too, may be written, bound, and distributed to the class.

To make students more aware of patterns used by textbook writers, have them analyze their own textbooks to discover which patterns are favored by the author(s): enumeration, classification, generalization, problem solving, comparison and contrast, or sequence. Allow time for discussion of student findings.

Encourage individuals or small groups to develop a Science Dictionary. All important terms in the chapters may be itemized, alphabetized, and defined. These may be duplicated or posted.

Literature

To help students relate a poem or story to their own lives (and to teach theme at the same time), have them individually write, in a single sentence, what they believe the main point of the work is and tell how it relates to their own lives. Students may share their ideas orally or by binding their papers together in a booklet for the class to share.

Because the oral dimension of literature is so often neglected in the average English class, students should frequently be encouraged to prepare (individually or in groups) readings from selections in the anthology. These may be presented before the class "live" or tape-recorded. Other students may search the school or local public library for recordings by poets, authors, or actors to play for the group.

Many stories lend themselves easily to dramatization. Suggest that interested students prepare scripts of stories to act out in class. The dramatic presentations provide the teacher with opportunities to review many basic literary concepts, by asking: "What is the setting? What props will be needed? What is the high point of the plot? Which aspects of the character's personality are highlighted here? How? Through his or her speech? Actions?"

After teaching literary concepts as higher level reading skills, the teacher may focus on one skill (such as recognizing clues to setting) and have individuals or a group make up a "test" to discover how well students in the class can use the skill on unfamiliar stories. Students may read the opening paragraphs of stories to the class and ask their classmates to indicate (1) the place, (2) the time, and (3) the clues they used to arrive at their answers.

Most skills involved in reading literature are useful in other contexts, such as television and film viewing. Select three key skills and have the students watch the same TV show or film to discover how effectively they can apply the skills. For example, after studying how an author reveals character, the students can note how TV and film scriptwriters reveal character traits (through speech, action, and the speech and action of others).

Have students make inferences about a character on a popular television program and then come to class prepared to give the reasons why they made the inferences. This kind of inference-making may then be related to that which students make as they read stories and poems in their anthologies.

Find stories that do not have clear-cut endings, and have the students tell what the endings might be. They should be prepared to defend their ideas with evidence found in the stories.

Have students develop glossaries of literary terms with examples illustrating each term taken from the literature they have read in class. These may be duplicated and distributed.

References

Armstrong, William H. *Study is Hard Work.* New York: Harper and Row, Publishers, 1967.

Collette, Alfred T. *Science Teaching in the Secondary Schools.* Boston: Allyn and Bacon, 1973.

Cooney, Thomas J.; Edward J. Davis; and K. B. Henderson. *Dynamics of Teaching Secondary School Mathematics.* Boston: Houghton Mifflin, 1975.

Devine, Thomas G. "Teaching Literary Concepts as Reading Skills." *Connecticut English Journal* 10 (Fall 1978): 5-7.

Elkins, Deborah. *Teaching Literature: Designs for Cognitive Development.* Columbus, Ohio: Charles E. Merrill Publishing Co., 1976.

Fehr, Howard F. *Teaching High School Mathematics.* Washington, D.C.: National Education Association, 1955.

Frye, Northrop. *The Educated Imagination.* Bloomington, Ind.: Indiana University Press, 1964.

Hater, M. A.; R. B. Kane, and M. A. Byrne. "Building Reading Skills in the Mathematics Class." *The Arithmetic Teacher* 21 (December 1974): 662-668.

Herber, Harold L. *Teaching Reading in Content Areas.* Englewood Cliffs, N.J.: Prentice-Hall, Inc., 1978.

Maffei, Anthony C. "Reading Analysis in Mathematics." *Journal of Reading* 16 (April 1973): 546-549.

Polya, George. *Mathematical Discovery: Understanding, Learning, and Teaching Problem Solving.* New York: John Wiley and Sons, Inc. 1962.

Purves, Alan C., and Richard Beach. *Literature and the Reader.* Urbana, Ill.: National Council of Teachers of English, 1972.

Robinson, H. Alan. *Teaching Reading and Study Strategies: The Content Areas,* 2nd ed. Boston: Allyn and Bacon, Inc., 1978.

Romey, William D. *Inquiry Techniques for Teaching Science.* Englewood Cliffs, N.J.: Prentice-Hall, 1968.

Rosenblatt, Louise M. *Literature as Exploration,* rev. ed. New York: Noble and Noble, 1968.

Sandberg, Nancy B. "An Evaluation of a Technique to Develop the Skill of Supporting Inferences about Character in Reading Narrative Fiction." Ph.D. dissertation, Boston University, 1970.

Sauer, Edwin. *English in the Secondary School.* New York: Holt, Rinehart and Winston, 1961.

Squire, James R. *The Responses of Adolescents While Reading Four Short Stories.* Champaign, Ill.: National Council of Teachers of English, 1964.

Sund, Robert B., and Leslie W. Trowbridge. *Teaching Science by Inquiry in the Secondary School.* Columbus, Ohio: Charles E. Merrill, 1973.

Thomas, Keith J., and Charles K. Cummings. "The Efficacy of Listening Guides: Some Preliminary Findings with Tenth and Eleventh Graders." *Journal of Reading* 21 (May 1978): 705-709.

Tutolo, Daniel J. "The Study Guide—Types, Purpose and Value." *Journal of Reading* 20 (March 1977): 503-507.

5

STUDY SKILLS AND THINKING PROCESSES

A reexamination of the lists of basic study skills which concluded the three previous chapters (Classroom Listening, Reading to Study, and Study Skills in Mathematics, Science, and Literature) leads to an important question: *Are these study skills or descriptions of thinking processes?* Certainly, items such as using the index, taking notes, and using graphs, charts, and tables refer to *study skills,* as the term has been ordinarily used. The lists also included (or implied) such items as defining purpose, recognizing main points, noting inferences, making predictions, anticipating outcomes, seeing relationships, relating the known to the unknown, and identifying unfamiliar concepts. Are these study skills or *thinking skills?*

Because the question is central to this entire book, this chapter first examines the question, its implications, and possible answers. It then presents one kind of thinking (critical thinking) and the study skills (in critical listening and critical reading) associated with it. The chapter concludes with a list of study-thinking skills and an Idea Box of suggested teaching-learning activities.

STUDY SKILLS AND THINKING

When a teacher sets out to show students how to listen to a lecture, how to read a chapter in a social studies textbook, or how to do a word problem in mathematics, many of the teaching considerations are quite basic and down-to-earth. Students need to be reminded to follow the listening guide the teacher has distributed, or make references between the printed text and a graph in the book, or note the definitions of technical terms printed in boldface type in the book's margins. The potential for acquiring the new information and ideas is enhanced for students if they make maximum use of aids provided by the teacher or textbook author. However, when a teacher wants students to better understand or "make sense of" the assignment, the teacher moves beyond simple, basic study skills and becomes involved with the not-so-simple thinking processes of the students and the author or lecturer. *Study* is no longer a matter of using an index or taking advantage of typographical aids; it is a matter of defining purpose, noting inferences, seeing relationships, identifying main points, predicting, anticipating, relating, and so on. It is *thinking*.

Helping students to "think through" assignments becomes a major goal of the study skills program. Unfortunately, stating the goal may imply that teachers have answers to several key questions about thinking which, indeed, have not been answered to the complete satisfaction of all psychologists and philosophers. Some of these questions are raised below. Some answers—from the point of view of a study skills specialist—are suggested. Both questions and suggested answers need to be given some thought by teachers who want to help their students manage school assignments more effectively.

What Is Thinking?

"Many are of the opinion," wrote the Gestalt psychologist Wertheimer, "that men do not like to think; that they will do much to avoid it; that they prefer to repeat instead. But in spite of many factors that are inimical to real thinking, that suffocate it, here and there it emerges and flourishes. And often one gets the strong impression that men, even children, long for it" (Wertheimer 1959, pp. 1-2).

But what is thinking? What takes place in such processes? What happens if one really thinks? What are the features, the steps? How do they come about? What are the differences between good and bad thinking? Can good thinking be improved? "For more than two thousand years," Wertheimer noted, "some of the best brains in philosophy, logic, in psychology, in education, have worked hard to find real answers to these questions," but "there is something tragic in the history of these efforts" (Wertheimer 1959, p. 2). Indeed, answers remain elusive.

Part of the problem, as Russell pointed out, is that *thinking* is an omnibus term. It is hard to define without using terms such as *mind*, *consciousness*, and *judgment*, and these terms shift their meanings easily and are themselves difficult to define satisfactorily. As he noted, "When a philosopher is philosophizing, a poet contriving a sonnet, a housewife balancing a budget, a child painting a picture of a bus, an infant crying for his cereal—in all these activities some sort of thinking is taking place"; and, in each case, some process or sequence seems a dominant factor (Russell 1956, p. 4). For his study of children's thinking, Russell accepted, with some qualifications, this definition of thinking: "a determined course of ideas, symbolic in character, initiated by a problem or task, and leading to a conclusion.'' That definition, with some refinements that will be developed in the following pages, is accepted for this discussion of study skills and thinking processes because it makes clear that thinking may be distinguished from intelligence and learning.

The definition also leads to two considerations important for teachers of study skills: thinking seems to include six general stages or steps, and it may be described under six overlapping headings. The six stages are summarized as:

1. The students' environment somehow stimulates mental activity. Objects or persons in the environment, perceptions, memories, his or her physical or emotional state, or combinations of these create tensions and stimulate thinking.
2. Some direction for the thinking is established. From all the possible directions to move, the student, for one reason or another, begins to think in one way, neglecting alternatives.
3. The student then searches for related materials. The search may involve reading about a topic, discussing it with friends, exploring memory for similar past experiences, and organizing related information and ideas.
4. He or she develops possible hypotheses or tentative conclusions. As materials are explored in the third stage, some are eliminated as irrelevant, others are organized and reorganized until the student settles in on possible explanations or hypotheses.
5. The hypotheses are critiqued. The tentative explanations are analyzed and criticized until only the most viable remain.
6. The student then tests out the hypotheses or explanations that have survived the fifth stage. This may be done deductively by checking examples with a general rule or principle, or inductively in an experiment of some sort.

These six steps in thinking are not true of all thinking, at all times, in all places. They do, however, provide a guide for teachers in setting up activities and exercises designed to develop key study skills. Many of the suggestions made in previous chapters (such as students needing to establish a purpose for reading or listening, anticipate outcomes, make predictions, evaluate information, etc.) are clearly related to the stages as presented here. Dewey (1933), who first analyzed stages in thinking, seemed to focus primarily on problem solving-type thinking. The six stages previously mentioned, based on Russell's later analysis (Russell 1956, pp. 15–17), help explain the steps as found in different kinds of thinking.

The following six kinds of thinking overlap one another but may be described separately:

Perceptual thinking.   This kind of thinking is less directed toward a goal or conclusion and most affected by the environment. The student is shown a photograph of a sun spot and may "think" *sun* or *spot.* This is not higher level thinking, but it does involve selection of certain items from many presented.

Associative thinking.   This occurs when one object or idea triggers the memory to link it to other objects and ideas. *Sun* may stimulate the student to think of *summer, baseball, escape.* Such thinking is not directed consciously toward a goal but is influenced by the student's memories of past experiences and dominant interests at the moment.

Inductive-deductive thinking.   This thinking occurs when a student tests out an idea either by checking to discover if examples "fit" a given rule or principle (deductive) or to discover the principle by an experiment (inductive). Both are goal-directed and may be defined in terms of the six stages previously listed.

Problem solving.   This type of thinking is best defined in terms of the six stages: the student senses a problem, defines it, gathers relevant data, forms hypotheses, critiques the hypotheses, and tests out the best ones.

Critical thinking.   This occurs when the student evaluates the data he or she collects. Some of it may be irrelevant to the problem, some of it biased, and some of it false. Critical thinking, which is examined more fully later in this chapter, clearly overlaps the other five kinds of thinking described here.

Creative thinking.   This thinking takes place when the student goes beyond the routine solution of a problem to a fresh discovery or new invention. It is related to both associative thinking and problem solving and is often labeled imaginative or divergent thinking.

Breaking down thinking into six kinds or types is not acceptable to all students of thinking. Some psychologists see problem solving as central; others believe the breakdown is artificial or simplistic. Many information-processing theorists look at thinking from a different point of view (see, for example, Neisser 1967; Newell and Simon 1972). The distinctions are made here because they are useful to teachers of study skills who want to isolate specific mental processes associated with kinds of thinking in order to teach them as individual study skills.

What Are Thinking Processes?

Both Wertheimer and Russell use the term *processes;* many more recent writers on the subject of thinking regularly refer to *mental processes* or *higher mental processes.* What is a mental, or thinking, process? As is the case with much of the literature in the area of thinking, a student of the subject often finds a semantic quagmire—terms are used in different contexts, reused in others, but never satisfactorily defined. Recent specialists in information-processing theory discuss *information-processing skills* and seem to be using the term synonymously with mental processes (see Block and Dworkin 1976). Because the term and its attendant concept are important to the theoretical framework developed in this book, it is defined here, speculatively, as "a mental operation involved in thinking." Inference making, discussed in the last chapter under Literature, thus becomes a set of discrete processes such as recognizing an inference, noting evidence upon which the inference is based, evaluating the inference, distinguishing between valid and nonvalid inferences, and, finally, making an inference. The operations represented by these gerund phrases are mental constructs; that is, they are never observed in themselves but only assumed to exist by observers who note the behaviors (usually language behaviors) of the thinker (making, recognizing, evaluating, etc., the inferences).

At each of the stages in thinking, there seem to be certain mental processes at work:

☐ Stage 1 probably includes recognizing a problem or recognizing the source of a problem.

☐ Stage 2 may include noting possible approaches to the problem or selecting an approach.

☐ Stage 3 probably includes such mental processes as distinguishing between relevant and irrelevant material, organizing material, sequencing material, noting main points, relating the new to the old, and relating the unknown to the known.

☐ Stage 4 may include anticipating endings, predicting events, making inferences, judging inferences, organizing and reorganizing material, and distinguishing between relevant and irrelevant material.

☐ Stage 5 includes such critical thinking processes as distinguishing fact from opinion, evaluating sources of information, noting bias in sources, and recognizing emotional appeals.

☐ Stage 6 would include those processes associated with "testing out" and inductive-deductive thinking.

For each kind, or type, of thinking, certain mental processes seem to also be functioning:

☐ Perceptual thinking seems to involve recognizing main points, distinguishing relevant from irrelevant material, and noting sequences.

☐ Associative thinking includes relating the new to the old, seeing relationships, and recognizing patterns.

☐ Inductive-deductive thinking involves relating evidence to rule or generalization, noting proof, and distinguishing between relevant and irrelevant material.

☐ Problem solving includes defining purpose, gathering data, and predicting outcomes.

☐ Critical thinking includes organizing data, evaluating it, and judging sources.

☐ Creative thinking involves seeing (new) relationships, anticipating outcomes, and predicting events.

Can Thinking Processes Be Taught?

Although actual research evidence in this area is minimal, some research findings indicate that when specific higher mental processes are taught as related language skills (for example, recognizing inferences) and as listening-reading skills (recognizing a speaker's or an author's inferences), behaviors are changed (Devine 1969; Lundsteen 1969; Lundsteen 1970). Most writers on the subject of thinking have suggested that when thinking processes are isolated and taught as skills, habits, or techniques, general thinking improves. Some have been able to collect evidence from varying studies to support their assumption (see, for example, Russell 1956, pp. 330–390); others (see, for example, Wertheimer 1959) have structured coherent approaches which incorporate many of the processes and operations.

Thinking processes are evidently not innate. Just as success in skiing or piano playing comprises the relative mastery of sets of specific learned skills, successful problem solving or critical thinking seems to comprise relative mastery of sets of specific, learned thinking skills or processes.

Strategies for teaching these skills have been in the educational literature for many years. For example, as long ago as 1920, Parker offered suggestions to teachers for developing specific thinking skills, or processes, in problem solving:

1. Get students to define the problem clearly.
2. Aid them to keep the problem in mind.

3. Get them to make many suggestions by encouraging them
   a. to analyze the situation into parts,
   b. to recall previously known similar cases and general rules that apply,
   c. to guess courageously and formulate guesses clearly.
4. Get them to evaluate each suggestion carefully by encouraging them
   a. to maintain a state of doubt or suspended conclusion,
   b. to criticize the suggestion by anticipating objections and consequences,
   c. to verify conclusions by appeal to known facts, miniature experiments, and scientific treatises.
5. Get them to organize the material by proceeding
   a. to build an outline on the board.
   b. to use diagrams and graphs,
   c. to take stock from time to time,
   d. to formulate concise statements of the net outcome of the discussion (Parker 1920).

Since the 1920s a variety of strategies have been developed: "provoked" situations (Stauffer 1969), "spontaneous" situations (Duckworth 1969), even strategies designed specifically for "adolescent slower learners" (Weber 1974).

It is a basic premise of this book that thinking processes may be taught: "Since strategies for sound thinking are learned they can be taught" (Stauffer 1977, p. 245). Later in this chapter, critical thinking is broken down into a set of teachable and testable processes, and strategies for teaching them are suggested. It may be true that the research evidence in this area is not all in yet, but there is enough evidence and enough theoretical consensus to encourage teachers to confidently try to develop thinking processes. Learning how to study does involve use of certain thinking skills, and strategies exist for teaching these skills.

How Is Thinking Related to Intelligence?

Despite the firmness with which many teachers, parents, and others hold to the belief that thinking and intelligence are connected, the relationship is not thoroughly understood. Part of the problem lies in the fact that many of our popular beliefs about intelligence fall into the category of tribal myths, old wives' tales, and unsupported assumptions (see any recent study of IQ, such as Block and Dworkin 1976). Intelligence is not a well-defined concept. For many, it is defined as what the tests measure, and those tests are increasingly less accepted as valid measures (see, for example, Karier 1972; Bane and Jencks 1973; Chomsky 1972; McClelland 1973; Layzer 1976). It has been noted that (1) there is no scientific basis for the claim that so-called IQ tests do indeed measure intelligence,

(2) the IQ tests actually consist of "arbitrary stunts," (3) emotional responses to the tests influence the scores, (4) correlations with school success are nonvalidatory because school success itself is not a reliable index of intelligence, and (5) even if the tests measure ability, they probably measure a rather narrow kind of scholastic ability (Block and Dworkin 1976, pp. 2–3). As some psychologists have pointed out, "There is no consensus among psychometricians about general intelligence" (Block and Dworkin 1976, p. 465). Others recommend that the term *intelligence* be dropped altogether (McClelland 1973). Many note that there is no reason to believe IQ is an index of capacity to acquire higher cognitive skills (Layzer 1976).

It may be that intelligence is simply the sum total of the efficient uses one makes of the various thinking processes. A highly intelligent person successfully uses many of the thinking skills or processes (or "habits" or "techniques") described in this chapter; a less intelligent person uses fewer successfully. It may be, too, that in time intelligence will be measured by criterion sampling. As McClelland has noted, "If you want to know how well a person can drive a car (the criterion), sample his ability to do so by giving him a driver's test,"—not a paper-and-pencil test for following directions or a test of general intelligence (McClelland 1973). If teachers want to know how well a student thinks, they should test specific thinking processes or skills; if they want to know how well a student "thinks through" a mathematics problem or a poem, they should test the specific study-thinking skills involved in reading a word problem in mathematics or a poem in English class.

How Is Thinking Related to Reading?

Many reading specialists seem always to have assumed that reading and thinking were almost synonymous. Even at the basic decoding level, readers must do what Russell calls "perceptual thinking" (Russell 1956, pp. 65–100); beyond decoding, most reading skills resemble thinking skills. One teachers' manual for a junior high school basal reading series notes:

> The student who reads with understanding is prepared to react to a selection in a number of ways, each of which may be conceived as a reading skill of a higher order than literal comprehension. In certain instances students will need to go beyond the facts, accepting or rejecting information and making distinctions between fact and opinion, cause and effect. In other instances students will want to create new ideas out of the materials read, to make inferences about characters, and to predict outcomes. The reading act is not complete without such thinking and interpreting (Devine 1967).

This same teachers' manual presents a list of reading skills which clearly resemble descriptions of higher mental processes in thinking (for example, drawing conclusions, making inferences, anticipating events and predicting outcomes, and distinguishing between cause and effect).

Through the years, many reading specialists have noted the relationship between thinking and reading and other language arts. As Durrell wrote, almost forty years ago: "When the various skills involved in reading and composition are finally analyzed and put into systematic sequences to improve ease of mastery, the result will be found to be a series of steps to improved thinking" (Durrell 1943, p. 110). More recently, Stauffer (1969) has developed specific strategies, DRTA's (direct reading-thinking activities), for teaching thinking skills through reading, and Herber (1978) has created Reading and Reasoning Guides (in English, social studies, mathematics, and science) designed to improve thinking-reading in content areas.

TEACHING STUDY SKILLS IN CRITICAL THINKING

Critical thinking is the kind students do when they subject incoming information and ideas to scrutiny. As new information comes to them they must (if they are to "think straight" and not be completely baffled by the world around them) assess it carefully for accuracy, examine it from differing angles, evaluate its sources for bias and distortion, and judge it according to some norms or standards. *Critical thinking*, like *thinking* itself, has unfortunately become an omnibus term, used indiscriminately by some authors to describe almost all facets of thinking. This overgeneralizing is somewhat understandable because, in fact, critical thinking permeates the other five kinds of thinking (perceptual, associative, inductive-deductive, problem solving, and creative) and it is found at all six stages (from initial sensing of the need for mental activity through the testing out of a hypothesis).

The skills involved in critical thinking, like thinking processes themselves, are probably not innate. As Russell (1956, p. 287) has noted, "Most children do not learn to think critically by themselves; they need help in becoming critical thinkers." There is research evidence that some skills associated with critical thinking, especially some related to critical listening, can be taught successfully. Devine (1961), for example, demonstrated that ninth-grade students could be taught to recognize inferences, to distinguish facts from opinions, to recognize bias, to distinguish between emotive and report language, and to judge sources. Lundsteen (1963) found that fifth- and sixth-grade students could be taught to detect purpose, evaluate propaganda, and evaluate arguments. Adams (1968) successfully taught high school students to recognize emotional appeals and other propaganda devices.

Critical thinking skills, especially as found in listening and reading contexts, seem especially important for students today. In a democratic society where freedom of speech assures equal rights to the honest advocate and the demagogue, it is possible for skillful but unprincipled speakers and writers to shape public opinion, influence voters, and affect behaviors. Professional persuaders, whether politicians, advertisers, pleaders of causes, even professional educators, can bombast students and adults with words, some of them capable of misleading, distorting, confusing, or corrupting. As the philosopher Brameld wrote two decades ago (when the mass media was a good deal less far-reaching than it is today):

> Distortion of the facts about group conflicts, allegiances, and conditioners becomes increasingly a "fine art," practiced on a mass scale by radio and television commentators, in newspapers and motion pictures, and in public education   (Brameld 1956).

Critical reading has attained a place of some prominence in at least some school curriculums. Teachers have developed materials and strategies for improving critical thinking through reading (see, for example, Stauffer 1969; King, Ellinger, and Wolf 1967). Critical listening is still not a concern in many school programs. This is regrettable, as Johnson pointed out:

> As speakers, men have become schooled in the arts of persuasion, and, without the counterart of listening, a man can be persuaded—even by his own words—to eat foods that ruin the liver, to abstain from killing flies, to vote away his right to vote, and to murder his fellows in the name of righteousness. The art of listening holds for us the desperate hope of withstanding the spreading ravages of commercial, nationalistic, and ideological persuasion   (Johnson 1949).

Critical Thinking As Critical Listening-Reading

Probably forty or more discrete higher mental processes are involved in critical thinking (such as recognizing inferences, distinguishing fact from opinion, and noting bias). Many of these are also involved with other kinds of thinking (inductive-deductive, problem solving, or creative thinking). As they stand, these higher mental processes are *mental constructs*, postulated by philosophers or psychologists, and not directly observable or teachable. Each of these processes, however, is reflected in some specific language operation or skill. Recognizing inferences, for example, may be translated as a specific critical listening skill (recognizing a speaker's inferences) or a specific critical reading skill (recognizing a writer's inference). Teachers can talk and think about higher mental processes as mental constructs but not really teach them. Once reworded as specific listening or reading skills, they can be taught in the classroom as study skills in listening or reading.

Eight critical thinking processes are listed below. Each may be turned into a corresponding critical listening or critical reading skill. Lists such as this vary from authority to authority, but there is considerable consensus on these eight items: all are central to critical thinking. Strategies for teaching them as reading-listening skills are available. They may be taught directly in separate lessons and exercises, or as part of ongoing instruction in all subject matter areas. Suggestions for teaching follow.

Recognizing Purpose

A key critical thinking skill in general becomes a crucial study skill in school. Students at all levels need practice in discovering a speaker's or an author's purpose in a lecture, chapter, speech, article, or assignment. Less successful students are often ''less successful'' because they have never been asked to look at and critically examine the purpose of a talk or selection. One way to help students begin to think about purpose is (1) to present a few paragraphs side-by-side (from a school textbook, a newspaper article, or even a technical handbook) and list three or four statements of purpose, only one of which is correct; and (2) to discuss in class the reasons why only one is correct. When students begin to see that authors (and speakers) usually have some reason for a communication, they can begin themselves to select passages and suggest possible author-speaker purposes for class analysis. Once such preliminary steps have been taken in class, students need to be asked regularly (so that in time the questions are to some extent internalized): Why did the author write that? Why did the speaker say that? What were his or her reasons? Could the author or speaker have had a secret reason? What is the main point the person is trying to get across to me? What is *my* reason for reading or listening to this particular selection? These questions need to be posed for all study material, and at all grade levels.

In teaching students to recognize purpose, teachers should probably have three overlapping goals: wanting students to note (1) the obvious, ''public'' purpose; (2) the less-public, sometimes ''hidden'' purpose; and (3) the student's own personal purpose for reading or listening. Students need practice in using this basic critical reading-thinking skill on a variety of materials—their own textbooks, letters-to-the-editor, advertisements, newspaper articles, reviews of records and films, library books, even stories and poems. It is a pivotal competence for the successful student.

Distinguishing Relevant from Irrelevant Information

While students learn to recognize purpose (the speaker-writer's "public" one, the possibly "hidden" one, and their own), they also need to distinguish between ideas and information that truly belong to the topic and those that creep in because of the speaker-writer's careless preparation, sloppy thinking, or deliberate intention to mislead. Elementary school students can learn that, if the author's purpose is to explain the causes of the common cold, the author should not discuss the energy crisis or Alaskan glaciers—unless there is a reason (hidden? careless?) for the introduction of the apparently irrelevant material. High school and college students need to be reminded that a chapter, article, or lecture on family life in Early America or the oil cartel should focus on the topic, and, if it does not, they have a responsibility to discover the reasons for the introduction of extraneous material.

One approach to this skill is to give students lists of items, most of which relate to an obvious topic, and have them identify and delete the irrelevant items ("Cross out words which do not belong: home plate, pitcher, short stop, typewriter, mitt, bat, diamond, outfield, third base, racket"). Elementary school students may develop their own lists to stump the class. Secondary school students may be encouraged to collect paragraphs from their reading which seem to include irrelevant sentences, and then share them with the class and explain why they think the sentences were included. (Some students may be introduced to the *non sequitor*—an inference or conclusion not based on evidence provided—and encouraged to discover examples in their outside reading.) Because this skill relates directly to most thinking and most language arts activities in all content areas, it may be taught in a listening or reading context and in composition lessons. As they develop their own reports, students may be taught the importance of deleting irrelevant material from the preparatory notes and outlines before they write research papers and class reports.

Evaluating Sources

Students need to learn that all speakers and authors are not necessarily competent to speak or write about their chosen topics. One approach to this skill with elementary school students is to present them with jumbled lists of topics and "authorities" and have them match person with topic (for example, boxing, rock music, hockey, and nutrition in one column, and, jumbled in the next, Mohammed Ali, Billy Joel, Bobby Orr, and the name of the school nurse in the other). Similar lists may be presented later with more specific topics and people (repairing a fuse box, explaining the causes of skin rash, interpreting a paragraph from an automotive manual, etc., and the school custodian, school nurse or physician, a shop teacher, etc.).

Secondary school students may discover the credentials of speakers and authors by answering: What are this person's qualifications? Has he or she wide experience in the field? Appropriate educational background? Does the person possibly have a hidden reason for speaking or writing on the topic? They may also be introduced to appropriate reference books in the library: the various volumes of *Who's Who*, encyclopedias, almanacs, biographical dictionaries, and so on. Students at all grade levels need to be reminded regularly that printed texts are not sacred documents ("I read it in a book, so it must be true!"), that they were written by human beings and, consequently, are sometimes incorrect, sometimes biased, and sometimes deceitful.

Noting Special Points of View

To help students recognize conflicting points of view, have them examine actual or teacher-prepared letters-to-the-editor on a specific topic and then lead them to see how the writers' views differ. Then have students write (or tell about letters they might write) on a topic from the points of view of various people. For the editorial topic, "Our school should provide a smoking room for students," students may write from the points of view of a local physician, the city fire chief, the football coach, a teacher who has given up smoking, a candidate for class president, a lobbyist for the tobacco industry, or the owner of a local store. Students may later present round-table discussions in which each person presents a different viewpoint on a controversial subject, and then analyze the discussion and similar discussions they have noted on radio or television. High school and college students may prepare questions on a topic that is apt to arouse conflicting viewpoints. They can ask several people in the community to respond, and then present the results to the class with their analysis of how answers were shaped by the respondee's occupation or age.

Discussions of point of view need to be related to previous discussions of sources and purposes: What are the author's or speaker's real purposes? Could the person be biased? How might his or her background influence point of view?

Recognizing Bias and Slanted Language

To help students recognize bias, start with simple statements such as "I saw Johnny walk out of the yard with the bike tire," and in contrast "I saw him slink out of the yard hiding something behind his back." Students can be led to see that certain words indicate the speaker's or writer's bias toward Johnny. The following are effective ways to explain the emotional connotation of words:

1. Draw a cartoon of a large person on the chalkboard.
2. Note that the only neutral word to describe the figure is *overweight*, but that many synonyms exist in the language for *overweight*.
3. List on one side of the figure all the "positive," or favorable, synonyms students can suggest (for example, *chubby, robust, plump*).
4. List on the other side all the "negative," or unfavorable, synonyms they can suggest (such as *fat, gross, obese*).
5. Explain that a writer or speaker can "slant" his or her language, either purposely or unconsciously, by choice of synonyms. (If a speaker calls the figure "fat and gross," listeners may assume that the speaker is biased against the figure; if "plump and chubby" is used, they may assume the speaker is biased in favor.)

This same kind of lesson may be repeated with *underweight* (positive synonyms: *slim, slender, svelte*; negative: *skinny, scrawny*), and later with other cartoon figures and other words.

Students may then be given jumbled lists, such as the following, and asked to place terms into appropriate columns, headed Favorable, Neutral, and Unfavorable:

1. strong man, absolute ruler, dictator
2. community, people, mob
3. leader of the people, party leader, rabble-rouser
4. go-getter salesperson, energetic salesperson, high-pressure salesperson
5. progressive, modern, crackpot
6. time-tested, old, outmoded
7. venerable, old, antiquated

When students begin to realize that words have connotations or emotional overtones and that the deliberate or unconscious use of certain words in speech or print tends to slant the language and, consequently, influence listeners or readers, they may be asked to contrast passages, such as the following, and asked: What seems to be the purpose of each? The "public" purpose? The "hidden" purpose? How should a person interpret each? Which words are "charged"? Which reveal the speaker's or writer's bias? What is his or her bias?

1. After Congressman Philips wasted as much time as possible, he finally stumbled through his speech.

   After Congressman Philips weighed every aspect of the important controversy, he rendered his momentous decision.

   (Which is biased for the Congressman? Which against? Which words indicate the writer's bias?)

2. Harry ("Killer") Kane, the notorious gambler, was questioned by the police about a gangland slaying.

   Mr. Harold Kane, well-known in local racing circles, was asked by local authorities to comment about recent events in the city.

   (Which is biased for Kane? What words are "loaded"? What else may *police* be called? In what ways do these words show bias?)

3. Danny's shifty eyes darted suspiciously around the room until he located his accomplice.

   Danny's eyes moved brightly across the room until he located his friend.

   (Which is biased in Danny's favor? Which words give away the writer's feelings about Danny?)

4. The embassy official courageously maintained his innocence.

   The embassy official refused to admit his guilt.

   (Which statement is biased against the official? Which specific words indicate the writer's bias?)

Recognizing Emotive Language

Students need to be reminded frequently that the language they read and hear is not always a straightforward presentation of ideas and information. Speakers and writers often either express their own emotions along with the ideas and information or try to arouse emotions in listeners and readers. One way to help students recognize emotive language is to have them focus on specific words that carry an emotional "charge." For example, have the students write down all the words they can think of that are used synonymously with *law enforcement agent* or *officer*. Then direct them to place these under three columns headed Favorable, Neutral, and Unfavorable. Lead students to see that their words on all three lists refer to the same referent but that each carries a special "extra meaning," often one with strong emotional overtones.

An excercise for elementary and middle-school students asks them to mark words on a list, such as the following, with a plus (for favorable to the student), a minus (for unfavorable), a zero (for no strong feelings):

winter	supermarket	war
school	chemistry	snakes
cats	election	pioneer
sneakers	bus	jet
freedom	corn	blood

Allow time for students to share their responses and tell the reasons why each one has favorable or unfavorable associations. Ask such questions as: In what ways have your own past, personal experiences influenced your reaction to a word? Are the feelings in the word or in you? Why is it, then, that most people react negatively to a word like *snake*? This kind of exercise and discussion should not be limited to younger students because, as many college teachers will testify, older students are often handicapped in their thinking by superstitions about words and failure to distinguish among words, referents, and *their* intellectual and emotional responses to words.

Students at all grade levels should be encouraged to collect and analyze examples of emotive language. Teachers need to point out that emotive language is often acceptable and important to civilized life (in poetry, novels, drama, sermons, love letters, friendly letters, and personal writing of all kinds) but that it has less justification in political, economic, business, and professional communication.

Students should be introduced to the propaganda devices outlined by the Institute for Propaganda Analysis in the 1930s (Russell 1956, p. 296):

1. The Glittering Generality (giving something a good label so that it will automatically be accepted without examining evidence)
2. Name Calling (giving something a bad label so that it will be automatically rejected or condemned)
3. Transfer (carrying the authority and prestige of something respected and reversed over to something else in order to make the latter acceptable)
4. The Testimonial (linking the prestige and good will associated with a famous person in, for example, sports, religion, or entertainment, to a product or activity so that some will hopefully "rub off" on the latter)
5. Plain Folks (making a person, a politician, appear as just an ordinary person rather than the unordinary one he or she really is)
6. Card Stacking (presenting only the favorable facts and suppressing the unfavorable).

Students may then be given practice in detecting the devices through exercises such as the following:

1. "Fraternities have no more place in our public schools than a Hitler Youth Cadre." What is it? (Name Calling)
2. "This plan is un-American." What is it? (Glittering Generality)
3. "You should vote for our candidate. He has been associated all his life with fighting for our freedoms." What is it? (Transfer)
4. "All the great rock guitar players use this amplifier." What is it? (Testimonial)
5. "Our candidate grew up on a farm just up the road from us and got up every morning like the rest of us to go to school and work." What is it? (Plain Folks)
6. "This plan means lower taxes, more benefits to voters, and less bureaucracy." What is it? (Card Stacking)

Distinguishing Fact from Opinion

Surprisingly enough, many adults cannot distinguish between factual statements (verifiable by someone else) and those that express opinions, feelings, and preferences. Teachers can help students make the distinction by giving pairs such as these and asking students to determine which can be verified and which simply gives the writer's opinion:

1. John is industrious.

   John works in a supermarket after school.
2. Ted is punctual.

   Ted has not been late for school in three years.
3. Mary is careless.

   Mary lost both her history book and her bus ticket yesterday.

Students may be given exercises such as the following:

Draw a line from the opinion statement to the factual statement needed to support it.

Dave received all A's this year.	The dance was dull.
The thermometer reading was 79°.	The weather was balmy.
Steve doesn't speak to me.	He is a good student.
Bill hasn't done any homework.	He is a snob.
Everyone left before the dance was over.	He is lazy.

After each sentence is a blank space. In the blank write F for Fact or O for Opinion.

"This business of letting 18-year-olds vote is a lot of nonsense._____ I'll admit some kids are mature and sensible but most young people today are babies._____ They have no sense of responsibility. Look at the insurance rate for instance. The insurance companies had to make a special rate for young drivers._____ Drivers in the 16- to 18-year-old bracket have more accidents than drivers in the 21- to 25-year-old bracket. _____ Actually, the voting age should be 25 instead of 21._____"

Students will—and should—argue about the difference between fact and opinion. The distinction is not clear-cut, even for logicians. The point of the exercises and discussions is to encourage students to look twice, evaluate, judge, critique, *think*. After classroom exploration, students may be encouraged to bring examples into class from television, advertising, newspapers, radio, even textbooks. The goal of such discussion and instruction is to help students think critically about incoming ideas and information.

Recognizing and Evaluating Inferences

Once students realize the basic difference between fact and opinion, they may take the next step and identify inferences. One approach to the three levels of statements is through an anecdote such as the following:

> A strange man came into our room, stomped over to the window and said, "There are black clouds in the sky." He paused and said, "It'll rain soon." Then, as he exited, he said, "This part of the country has lousy weather."

The "strange man's" three statements may be placed on the chalkboard for student analysis through such questions as: Which can actually be verified or checked by one of us? Which, therefore, is really factual? Which is simply an expression of his opinion or feeling? Which is his prediction, or educated guess? Students may be led to see that an inference is usually someone's prediction or guess, and it is only as good as the guessor-predictor and the information (facts) he or she has available. If the man in the story observed correctly, maybe his inference is good; if he is a stranger to the area and has little knowledge of local weather conditions, his inference may not be a good one.

Such an introductory lesson may be followed by exercises such as the following:

Directions: Label each statement F for Fact (it may be verified), O for Opinion (it tells about the person's beliefs or feelings not the thing discussed) or I for Inference (it is the speaker's "educated guess" based on the facts).

1. I always received an "A" in math.   _____

    I received an "A" in algebra.   _____

    I will do "A" work in tenth-grade
    geometry.   _____

    I am a good math student.   _____

2. Susan refused to go to the dance with me.   _____

    Janet said she was busy when I asked her
    to go.   _____

    I'll never get a date for the prom.   _____

    I am not popular with girls.   _____

3. I am in tip-top condition.   _____

    I haven't been ill since I was in
    kindergarten.   _____

    When I was four, I had the measles.   _____

    I don't need Blue Cross.   _____

Students should be encouraged to locate inferential statements they find outside of school and bring them to class for analysis. Guide questions for discussions may include: What factual statements are needed to support the inference? Who seems to be making this "educated guess"? What do you know about the inference maker? Is he or she experienced in the field? (See Study Skills in Literature in Chapter 4 for additional material on inference making.)

Critical Thinking and School Assignments

Teachers who have successfully taught critical thinking through lessons in critical listening and/or critical reading note that one reason for the effectiveness of such instruction is the material. They regularly took examples from newspapers and magazines; they also sent students to their radios and television sets to locate examples of emotive language, inferences, bias, or propaganda devices, such as the Band Wagon or Glittering Generality. "It's hard to fail," one teacher commented, "when the classroom material is fresh and relevant to the lives of the kids!" Can the initial interest be transferred to school assignments? Many teachers say, "Yes!" The secret, they say, is to encourage students to look critically at all sources of information and ideas. This means textbooks, teacher-made study guides,—even announcements from the principal's office.

One way to encourage critical thinking, listening, and reading is to build into all classroom assignments and school activities the following questions. They can be structured into prereading or prelistening activities and/or into follow-up activities for lectures and readings. They can be duplicated for student notebooks or posted in a prominent place in the classroom. They provided a constant reminder to students and teachers that thinking is only as effective as the quality of information and ideas the mind has to work with.

Critical Thinking Guide

1. Has the speaker-writer used loaded or emotionally-charged words? What are they?
2. Is he or she a good source of ideas and information on this subject? Have you checked his or her credentials? What are they?
3. Which statements are clearly factual? Clearly opinion? How can you tell?
4. Does the speaker-writer seem to be deliberately trying to arouse your emotions? What are some examples of his or her emotive language?
5. Which statements are clearly inferential? Is there evidence in the talk or writing to support these inferences?
6. Has the speaker-writer referred to experts by name or are the references based on hear-say evidence ("They say" or "Research proves")?
7. Is the speaker-writer biased? How do you know?
8. What assumptions are implied by his or her statements? What are they?

Idea Box
Critical Thinking

Encourage students to search their memories to each recall an instance of problem solving in their own lives. Ask volunteers to share their examples, noting the reasons why the problems came to their attention and the steps they took to solve them. Introduce secondary school students to the "Six Steps in Problem Solving" (in this chapter) and ask them to recall (and tell about) the steps in relation to their problems.

Can animals solve problems? Interested students may tell about their observations of animals actually solving problems. Ask volunteers to check available sources of information (starting with the *Readers' Guide to Periodical Literature* in the library) and report to the class on known cases of animals "thinking." Further discussion may be based on the question: If animals can think, too, what really distinguishes man from animals?

Are there really different kinds of thinking? Give the class the six types of thinking (given in this chapter) and ask them to give examples of each taken from their own lives: When did you last do associative thinking? Critical thinking? Creative thinking? Tell about it.

After discussing "loaded words" in class, have students collect examples from the conversations they hear around them of people using emotionally-charged words. These may be listed on the board or posted as a class reminder of the widespread use of emotive language.

Warn students of the "They say" problem in thinking. Explain that too frequently people base their thinking on information that does not come from a respectable source. Speakers and writers often introduce important information by noting, "They say," "It is reported," or "Research indicates." Have students find examples from outside of class and discuss the dangers of this kind of communication.

Have students discuss the difference between *thinking* and *intelligence*. Lead them to see that intelligence is actually a rather vague concept about which psychologists do not agree, but that thinking seems to be a set of skills almost anyone can learn. Discuss the steps found in problem solving and/or the specific skills found in critical thinking, and note that ordinary people can, indeed, learn to think more effectively by following specific steps and using certain skills. Obviously, all classes at all times are not prepared for such discussions, but teachers need to regularly note that people *can* think better.

Collect and share "thinking games." Before class or in those minutes before the final bell, bring in simple games and encourage students to put their thinking caps on! Easy games include sequences (Continue: 1, 2, 4, 7, 11, __, __, __; or 4, 5, 7, 11, 19, __, __, __; or 6, 3, 9, 6, __, __, __) and simple arithmetic problems (such as: If it takes one hour to saw a cut through, how long will it take you to cut a ten-foot log into one-foot chunks?).

Collect short mysteries, from fiction or real-life, and share them with students. Several have been collected in paperback books; others are regularly found in magazines. The format is usually the same: Here are the circumstances; this is the evidence; who stole the jewels? Students can also be on the watch for these verbal puzzles to contribute to a classroom collection.

Students need to see how other people, perhaps famous ones, have used their thinking skills. Elementary and middle-school students may do "Reading Quests" in which they search the biographies of scientists, artists, political leaders, or famous philosophers to discover examples of men and women thinking effectively. It is difficult for students to value or appreciate an activity they know little about. Their reading discoveries should be shared in class, talked about, and regularly referred to by the teacher. Secondary students may develop research projects in which they locate examples of problem solving and effective thinking on the parts of mathematicians, scientists, scholars, and others.

Have five students volunteer as witnesses for a trial involving an automobile accident. First, give a brief oral account of the accident, and then have the volunteers individually draw a chart on the board showing how they "saw" the accident. Divide the remaining students into two groups, attorneys for the defense and for the plaintiff. They must decide which student-witnesses they would accept for the actual trial.

To demonstrate the dangers of hear-say evidence, many teachers have used this classroom activity. They take one student outside the room and read a brief anecdote from a card. That student, in turn, takes a second student outside and repeats the anecdote from memory. The third student repeats the story to a fourth, and so on through twelve students. Finally, the teacher reads from the card the original version for the class to compare with the version they heard from the twelfth student. So many changes occur from first to twelfth version that students are more skeptical of oral evidence in the future.

Prepare a short dramatic incident in the classroom. Two students, for example, may volunteer to act out a dispute over possession of a ring (or another object) in the rear of the room before the class begins. Have each student in the class write a one-paragraph description of the incident and later read it aloud to the total group. Lead the class to see how discrepancies creep in to most accounts and how perceptions differ because of the observer's position in the room and one's state of mind at the moment of the event. Encourage the group to apply what they have learned in the discussion to media reporting in general.

Social studies textbooks, in particular, should be scrutinized by students. Encourage them to apply the skills they have learned in critical thinking to chapters studied in class. Ask the following: Where did the author get this information? Is his or her source to be trusted? Which statements are facts? Opinions? Inferences? Do you detect any bias? Might an author lie deliberately? Unconsciously? What protection do you, as the reader, have against misinformation and bias in textbooks?

Show students that asking questions can help solve problems. Give them this problem:

> A man owned a fox, a duck, and a bag of corn. One day he was on the bank of a river, where there was a boat large enough for him to cross with only one of his possessions. If he left the fox and the duck alone, the fox would eat the duck. If he left the duck and the corn alone, the duck would eat the corn. The river was too rough for the duck to swim. How did he get safely across the river with all three possessions?

This situation, along with many others, is found in Weber's book on teaching so-called "adolescent slower learners" (Weber 1974, pp. 128–129). He guides students this way:

Can he take the fox first? (Duck will eat corn.) If he takes the corn first? (Fox will eat duck.) Therefore, he takes the duck first. Then he takes either the fox or the corn. But on the other side he will be faced with a similar problem. Let us assume he takes the fox. This would leave the fox and the duck on the other side while he fetches the corn. What to do? If he brings the fox back, he will be no farther ahead: therefore, bring the duck back, leave it and take the corn over where it will be safe with the fox. Then he comes back to get the duck.

Artificial? Yes. Ideally, problems given to students should be rooted in their own immediate lives. But teachers who have successfully developed thinking skills in "adolescent slower learners" note that it is important to provide much initial success with easier games and problems in order to build confidence and give their students the feeling that "they, too, can think well."

Have students write short paragraphs giving the viewpoint on urban renewal of each of the following people:

1. Mr. A, a life-long resident of the area scheduled to be torn down in order to build new apartments
2. Mr. B, a nonresident builder who plans to construct the apartment house
3. Mr. C, who will lose his grocery store in the area
4. Mrs. D, a member of the planning board which recommended the demolition
5. Miss E, a columnist who writes a consumer column for the local newspaper.

The letters may be written directly on ditto masters, duplicated, and used for class analysis.

Encourage students to prepare advertisements for products they invent. Suggest that they first write a straightforward descriptive advertisement containing *only* factual statements, and then write a typical modern advertisement which uses opinion statements, emotive language, and positively-charged words. Allow time for sharing and analyzing the student products and advertisements. Ask students to identify the "tricks" they use to persuade consumers.

To help students understand points of view, have them select a topic from the current news and write two letters to a newspaper, each taking a different stand. These may be shared and discussed. Questions may include: In what ways does a writer indicate his or her position? In what ways is bias shown? What are the reader's defenses against misinformation?

Have more mature readers read "The Principles of Newspeak" in George Orwell's *1984*, and share with the class their definition of Newspeak, examples in the novel, and examples found in contemporary writing. Have them explain what Orwell meant by "Newspeak was designed not to extend but to *diminish* the range of thought."

Encourage high school and college students to investigate some of the popular books on *semantics*. As a class or individual project, suggest a library search to discover (1) what *semantics* is, (2) how its study may improve thinking, (3) ideas from the books to share with the class, or (4) comments about the field from nonsemanticists. Many students through the years have been excited by this field of study and attribute their concern about thinking to some of the popularizations found on library shelves.

Present students with a list of the basic propaganda devices (the Glittering Generality, Name Calling, Transfer, Testimonial, Plain Folks, and Card Stacking, described in this chapter) and have them find examples of each from (1) newspapers, (2) magazines, (3) radio, (4) television, and (5) ordinary conversations. Interested classes may type their examples on ditto-masters for publication as a class guide to "Propaganda Awareness."

Introduce high school and college students to the *sham enthymeme*. Explain that it results when one part of a syllogism, usually the major premise, is omitted. Start discussion with easy examples, such as: "The government controls the use of harmful drugs today; therefore, the government can control the growth of nuclear power plants." (The major premise has been deleted: "Government control is equally effective in drug control and nuclear plant development.") Encourage students to find similar examples from their out-of-class reading and, if possible, in their textbook study.

After discussing the differences between statements of fact and opinion, have students bring to class some *statements that are always true.* They will find, of course, that it is difficult to locate such statements. Teachers may use the discussions to develop many points about thinking in general and critical thinking in particular.

Initiate a "Search for Falsehoods." If students are interested in the area of fact versus opinion, suggest a class investigation of falsehoods in our contemporary society. Students may search television, radio, newspapers, magazines, and other sources to discover persistent falsehoods that permeate the media. These should be analyzed and discussed, and possibly duplicated or posted.

Introduce high school and college students to the persistent kinds of false argumentation:

1. *Post hoc ergo propter hoc* reasoning ("after this; therefore, because of this") occurs when the thinker assumes that because A came before B, A must be the cause of B.
2. *Begging the question* happens when something is assumed proved although the proof is not demonstrated (for example, "The unfair practice of requiring all students to take English should be discontinued at once!" assumes without providing proof that the practice is unfair).
3. *Faulty dilemma* presents only two sides of an argument when actually there are more than two (for example, before Hitler came to power, he told voters they had to choose between National Socialism and Communism, but they really had several other alternatives).
4. *Ignoring the question* happens when the speaker or writer continues the argument while ignoring the basic issue involved (as when one small child says, "Well, you kicked me" when told "You hurt my arm").
5. *Argumentum ad hominem* is found when the speaker or writer sidetracks the argument by making accusations against a person (such as, "Don't vote for him no matter what he says about taxes—his wife was an alcoholic!")

After these have been explained in class, ask students to locate examples of each in advertisements, letters-to-the-editor, or magazine articles.

References

Adams, Francis J. "Evaluation of a Listening Program Designed to Develop Awareness of Propaganda Techniques." Ph.D. dissertation, Boston University, 1968.

Bane, Mary Jo, and Christopher Jencks. "Five Myths about Your IQ." *Harper's Magazine* 246 (February 1973): 28–40.

Block, N. J., and Gerald Dworkin, eds. *The IQ Controversy.* New York: Pantheon Books, 1976.

Brameld, Theodore. *Toward a Reconstructed Philosophy of Education.* New York: Dryden Press, 1956.

Chomsky, Noam. "Psychology and Ideology." *Cognition* 1 (1972): 11–46.

Devine, Thomas G. "The Development and Evaluation of a Series of Recordings for Teaching Certain Critical Listening Abilities." Ph.D. dissertation, Boston University, 1961.

Devine, Thomas G. *Manual for Teaching Discovery through Reading.* Boston: Ginn and Company, 1967.

Devine, Thomas G. "A Suggested Approach to Controlled Research in Language-Thinking Relationships." *Journal of Research and Development in Education* 3 (Fall 1969): 82–86.

Dewey, John. *How We Think*, new edition. Boston: D. C. Heath Co., 1933.

Duckworth, E. "Piaget Rediscovered." In *Piaget Rediscovered: Report on Cognitive Studies and Curriculum Development.* Edited by R. Ripple and U. Rockcastle. Ithaca, N.Y.: Cornell University Press, 1969.

Durrell, Donald D. "Language and Higher Mental Processes." *Review of Educational Research* 13 (April 1943): 110–114.

Herber, Harold L. *Teaching Reading in Content Areas.* Englewood Cliffs, N.J.: Prentice-Hall, Inc., 1978.

Johnson, Wendell. "Do You Know How to Listen?" *Etc.* 7 (Autumn 1949): 3.

Karier, Clarence. "Testing for Order and Control in the Corporate Liberal State." *Educational Theory* 22 (Spring 1972): 154–180.

King, Martha L.; Bernice D. Ellinger; and Willavene Wolf, eds. *Critical Reading.* Philadelphia: J. B. Lippincott, 1967.

Layzer, David. "Science or Superstition? A Physical Scientist Looks at the IQ Controversy." In *The IQ Controversy: Critical Readings.* Edited by N. J. Black and Gerald Dworkin. New York: Pantheon Books, 1976, pp. 194–241.

Lundsteen, Sara W. "Teaching Abilities in Critical Listening in the Fifth and Sixth Grades." Unpublished dissertation, University of California, Berkeley, 1963.

Lundsteen, Sara W. "Research in Critical Listening and Thinking: A Recommended Goal for Future Research." *Journal of Research and Development in Education* 3 (Fall 1969): 119–133.

Lundsteen, Sara W. "Manipulating Abstract Thinking as a Subability to Problem Solving in a Problem Solving Context of an English Curriculum." *American Educational Research Journal* 7 (May 1970): 373–396.

McClelland, David C. "Testing for Competence Rather than for 'Intelligence.' " *American Psychologist* 29 (January 1973): 107.

Neisser, Ulric. *Cognitive Psychology*. New York: Appleton-Century-Crofts, 1967.

Newell, Allan, and Herbert A. Simon. *Human Problem Solving*. Englewood Cliffs, N.J.: Prentice-Hall, 1972.

Parker, S. C. "Problem-Solving or Practice in Thinking." *Elementary School Journal* 21 (1920): 16–25, 98–111, 174–188, 257–272.

Russell, David H. *Children's Thinking*. Boston: Ginn & Co., 1956.

Stauffer, Russell G. *Directing Reading Maturity as a Cognitive Process*. New York: Harper and Row, 1969.

Stauffer, Russell G. "Cognitive Processes Fundamental to Reading Instruction." In *Cognition, Curriculum, and Comprehension*. Edited by John T. Guthrie. Newark, Del.: International Reading Association, 1977, pp. 242–254.

Weber, Kenneth J. *Yes, They Can! A Practical Guide for Teaching the Adolescent Slower Learner*. Toronto: Methuen, 1974.

Wertheimer, Max. *Productive Thinking*, enlarged edition. New York: Harper and Row, 1959.

6

STUDY SKILLS AND VOCABULARY DEVELOPMENT

Much mental activity is gloriously nonverbal! Images, ideas, and memories float through the mind, sometimes patterning in expected ways, sometimes surrealistically juxtaposing. Recollections of people, events, and objects, visions of the near and distant future, sounds, the wishes, lies, and dreams of the poet—all clash, harmonize, terrify, or assuage —and all without words!

The mental processes examined in Chapter 5 (inferencing, generalizing from evidence, and evaluating critically) are contingent upon language, upon verbal patterning, and upon words. Most of it can be analyzed, considered, interfered with, and influenced by instruction in schools.

It may be that all mental activity can be arranged, for examination, on a continuum, with the nonverbal (reveries, dreams, and image-making) at one end, the highly verbal (syllogistic reasoning, organizational thinking, logic, and critical thinking) at the other, with perhaps associational thinking and problem solving somewhere in the middle.

A book on study skills must recognize that the nonverbal extreme of the continuum exists, and that students' wishes, lies, and dreams are important. However, it must also be recognized that nonverbal mental activity must remain at the periphery of a study skills program. Most school learning is highly verbal, and study skills instruction needs to focus on the verbal dimension of learning; on listening, reading, organizing, synthesizing, reporting; on using textbooks, taking notes, writing research reports, and taking tests. Because these activities are verbal, a study of study skills must focus on words.

Previous chapters have examined words as they related to listening and reading. As has been noted, students need techniques to deal with new words as they encounter them (the SSCD method, for example), and much direct instruction in vocabulary as an intrinsic part of listening and reading lessons. Later chapters suggest ways to help students with words as they organize, synthesize, give meaning to new material, and, finally, prepare reports and take tests.

This chapter stops at midpoint in the book to review much of what is known about vocabulary development, and it suggests ways of improving instruction. It first reviews key aspects of general vocabulary development, then looks at ways to build word power, and concludes with suggestions for certain approaches to vocabulary building. Underlying all three discussions is the belief that teachers must teach words. Vocabulary study is of paramount importance in a study skills program. Without systematic instruction in words, study skills lessons lose much of their effectiveness.

WORD STUDY IN SCHOOL

Children acquire their vocabularies, of course, as they acquire their language. Words come to them along with the sound system and syntactic patterns. Indeed, the phonological, syntactic, morphological, and semantic systems cannot be separated (except for research and study); all are bound inextricably. Schooling does affect language behaviors. Students, for example, may learn different dialects (especially social-class dialects), new ways of patterning sentences (although fewer than many teachers would like to believe), and how to manage the printed versions of spoken language. Of all ways in which schooling influences language development, those related to vocabulary growth seem the least subtle. Students learn words they would not ordinarily learn from television, radio, or out-of-school conversations. They begin to observe semantic variations; hopefully, they have opportunities to experiment with new words and try them out in meaningful settings. It may be that word study is one area in which schools can have their greatest potential impact.

Vocabulary and School Success

Despite decades of research and theorizing, intelligence is still not thoroughly understood. As suggested earlier in this book, it may be that intelligence, as we know it, is a combination of learned skills (thinking and study skills), motivation, and self-image. Intelligence, as the term is currently used in schools and society, may simply be what intelligence tests measure. However, one characteristic of intelligence (as it is understood and measured today) is fairly clear: it is somehow related to the quality and quantity of one's word stock. Vocabulary is tied somehow with intelligence. As Dale and O'Rourke (1971) note, a student's vocabulary level is a good index of his or her mental ability. Students who perform well in school, on our present intelligence tests, and perhaps in life, do have larger vocabularies. High scores on vocabulary tests do correlate highly with school grades, scores on IQ tests, and scores on reading tests. The question of whether students with large vocabularies have them because they are born with high intelligence or whether they have high intelligence because they have had school and life experiences which led to large vocabularies is not answerable—and it may never be.

In a study skills program, teachers need to discuss the importance of vocabulary development, pointing out to students that their own vocabularies reflect the nature and quality of their lives, indicating what they have studied, where they have been, and the subtleties and refinements of their minds: "A good mind means a good vocabulary and a good vocabulary means a good mind. Which comes first? Which causes the other? It is more accurate to say that they are interactive—each is an inseparable part of the background and abilities of the learner" (Dale and O'Rourke 1971). With more sophisticated classes, time may be spent well in discussions of the very issues raised here; with all classes, attention needs to be given regularly to discussions of the importance of knowing words, not only to succeed in school but to control language, thinking, and, to some extent, life.

The Importance of a Planned Program

Much vocabulary acquisition takes place in the ordinary course of living. People meet new words and concepts and somehow figure out the speakers' and writers' meanings. Children pick up their entire vocabularies by casual encounters, guess work, and random reinforcement. Teachers could allow the vocabulary development of their students to happenstance, hoping that as students heard and read new words in and out of class they would infer, reinfer, and, in time, shape informal definitions and rough meanings. Unfortunately, many teachers rely on random encounters, trusting that time and experience will provide their students with a working knowledge of the words they need to know.

Research findings indicate, however, that formal instruction in vocabulary is markedly more effective than informal, unplanned growth. Studies through the years lead to the belief that time spent in class teaching vocabulary is well spent. Students, under the guidance of an informed teacher, can learn and remember words faster than on their own. Direct instruction *is* more effective than incidental acquisition (Harrington 1979; R. Savage 1979).

Direct instruction in vocabulary may be built into each individual lesson, sequenced carefully throughout the year in a program independent of the daily lessons, or a combination of separate lessons and an independent program. The first approach has been described in Chapter 3. It includes at least five steps:

1. The teacher first previews the reading assignment or oral presentation for the class and identifies those words that may be unfamiliar to many in the group.
2. Then the teacher teaches those words directly before the class
   reads or listens to the lecture.
3. A word approach method, such as SSCD, is demonstrated and/or
   reviewed for the "new" words (Are there *sound* clues? *Structure*
   clues? *Context* clues? Do we need the dictionary?)
4. The words, with synonyms or brief definitions, are either written
   on the chalkboard or duplicated and given to each student.
5. After the reading or oral presentation, time is spent in reviewing
   the words and their meanings, using them in talk and writing, and
   rechecking the ways the words were used in the lesson.

In a sequenced program independent of such a daily lesson approach,
workbooks, commercially-developed materials, lessons, and/or exercises
are selected and used throughout the year. Implicit in this second approach are (1) much preyear planning by the teacher, team, or department; (2) availability of duplicating resources and funds to purchase commercial material; and (3) some teacher sophistication about vocabulary
development. For example, a program might include instruction in the
most useful prefixes and suffixes or those Latin or Greek roots underlying
many English word "families." The teacher needs to know what is important to teach and how to prepare effective exercises and learning
activities. Time, resources, and knowledge are necessary for the preparation of such a year-long program. (Suggestions for developing and implementing a program are found in the following pages.)

It may be that the most effective vocabulary program includes both
strands: attention to words in each lesson, and a sequenced, year-long set
of exercises and activities. Students need both.

Making Students Aware of Their Many Vocabularies

Even more advanced students are often unaware that they have at least
four vocabularies. At the beginning of the school year and at regular intervals, students need to be reminded that they have vocabularies in listening, reading, speaking, and writing, and that these differ in size and
quality. They should have opportunities to discuss the quality and extent
of each and be led to see that each is influenced by a variety of factors.

Speaking vocabulary, for example, consists of "unrehearsed" words
actively used daily. It is affected by time. Speakers have to speak quickly
so that listeners' attentions do not wander. They do not have time to
search for fresh or exact words; consequently, ordinary speech is limited
in vocabulary range. Writing vocabulary, on the other hand, may be

larger (because writers have time to pause, think, and use a dictionary), but is constrained by the problem of spelling. Listening and reading vocabularies tend to be larger because students have been exposed to the language of more experienced and skillful writers and speakers; students have had to develop the ability to infer meanings. Context provides clues to meaning and, especially in reading, there is time to guess. It may be that students' reading vocabularies are larger because readers do not have to worry about spelling or pronunciation and do have time to make and verify inferences about word meaning (Deighton 1971).

Students need opportunities to discuss kinds of vocabularies. Discussion may make them more aware of words in general, the importance of vocabulary to their own lives, and the value of increasing their own speaking, reading, writing, and listening vocabularies. Regular use of the SSCD method increases this awareness. When students meet an unfamiliar word, they can be reminded to sound it out ("It may already be in your listening vocabulary, but you've never *seen* it before"), look at the structure ("It may contain a root or affix you have written out in a different word or seen in print elsewhere"), and check the context ("It may be a word in your listening vocabulary but used differently here"). Regular reference to kinds of vocabulary sharpens student awareness of words and, more important, their own relationship to words.

Teaching About Words in General

Specific vocabulary instruction is enormously valuable in a study skills program, but even more important is the creation of interest in words and language. The goal of all formal vocabulary teaching should be the growth of interest in words; lessons in roots, affixes, or word lists are subordinate to its development. As Pauk (1974) tells students, "The first step in improving vocabulary is to develop a genuine interest in words." The problem is how to do it. Successful adult students are often characterized not only by an interest in words but by excitement, even passion, for words. How did they develop their enthusiasm?

One explanation is that they were influenced by teachers (in and out of school) who loved words for their own sake. They were stimulated and challenged by teachers who focused their attention on definitions, meanings, or etymologies of words casually encountered. Pauk tells the following story:

> For me, the critical incident was a remark I heard when very young. While talking about the perennial topic of weather, a man said, "It will stop raining by this afternoon, and we'll have sunny skies. I'm an optimist." I suddenly became aware that one's thoughts and personality could be expressed in interesting, thoughtful, and precise terms. Although I did not

know the definition of *optimist* until later that day when I looked it up in the dictionary, I knew immediately that here was a man who was not perfunctorily uttering clichés. This man was thinking as he was speaking. And to think, I realized, a person has to have a good vocabulary (Pauk 1974).

One enthusiastic teacher of vocabulary recalls a high school teacher who challenged his use of *liberal* during a chat on the school steps during lunch one day: "Liberal? Adam Smith was a liberal. Roosevelt has been called a liberal. What's the word really mean?" Such casual encounters with people who care about words evidently rub off on students. Those who are fortunate enough to associate in early life with word lovers, or those who care about words, often become word addicts themselves.

How can such interest be incorporated into a study skills program? Many successful teachers of vocabulary have introduced students to dialect study and the history of English.

Introducing the Study of Dialect

People are sometimes shocked to discover that *they* have a dialect. Many teachers, beginning in middle schools, have explained to their students that, when people live in close physical proximity, they tend to speak alike, and that linguists are able to draw isoglosses (or lines) on a map showing where one dialect area ends and another begins. Students may be shown that linguists use three sets of differences that signal changes from one dialect to another. These are:

1. Sound difference (for example, speakers from coastal New England drop their *r* sounds from "Park the car in Harvard Yard," but put them into places where a consonant is needed to separate two vowel sounds, "The idear of it appalled me!").
2. Grammatical differences (for example, many southern speakers use a plural *you*, "you all," because Modern English does not have one).
3. Word differences (a long, slender loaf of bread with cold cuts, tomato, and lettuce is called a "submarine sandwich" in some dialect areas, and in others a "hoagie" or "hero sandwich").

Teachers who have successfully taught lessons and units in regional dialects say that such study tends to make students more sensitive to the language they see and hear around them, and it also makes them more conscious of words, word meanings, and changes in meanings and words. While such study is particularly appropriate in English and language arts classes at all levels, it may also be introduced in other subject-matter areas. Fortunately, teachers do not have to take courses in linguistics to introduce their students to this dimension of language; several excellent books and pamphlets are available (see, for example, Shuy 1967; Reed 1977).

Teaching the History of English

One of the most effective ways to make students sensitive to words is to introduce them to the history of their own language. Unfortunately, most students (and many teachers) know little of the background of the language they speak daily. Yet, the subject is not difficult to teach and learn and, as many successful language users testify, it is a powerful incentive to vocabulary development.

Students may be taught, for example, that English began with the invasion of the British Isles by Germanic tribes about 450 A.D. when the colonizing Roman legions were called back to protect Rome and left England unguarded. These Angles, Saxons, and Jutes filled a gap left by the original inhabitants, speakers of Celtic, who escaped to mountains of Scotland, Wales, and Ireland. This "Old English," a language with inflectional endings for nouns, verbs, adjectives, and pronouns, much like Modern German, remained the language of England for several centuries until the invasion of the Norman French. These descendents of Viking tribes who had taken over northern France spoke a dialect of Latin called Norman French. Their language was imposed on the original Germanic invaders. Because the rulers had to talk to the ruled, both languages merged together. The inflectional endings were lost and sentence position became important (as it is in Modern English) to indicate subject, predicate, and indirect and direct objects. The vocabularies of the two languages, however, remained more or less intact, giving Modern English two or more words (synonyms) for about everything. Students are usually interested to learn that the original Anglo-Saxon words are generally more direct and down-to-earth (words such as *hate, love, mother, father,* plus all swear words and those pertaining to the "natural functions"), while the Norman French words tend to be fancier, more highfalutin, pompous, or pretentious (especially those words associated with the military, law, government, or religion).

With this kind of basic introduction, students may be led to see that English became a "borrowing" language, which took, during the Renaissance, thousands of words directly from Latin and Greek, and later from Modern German (*frankfurt* and *poodle*), Italian (*piano* and *soprano*), Indian (*tobacco* and *wigwam*), and other languages.

Students may learn in formal class presentations or in casual discussions in class about the Anglo-Saxon invasions, the Norman Conquest, Renaissance word borrowings, and the later development of Modern English. Several books on teaching English and language arts provide teachers with the background they need (see, for example, Sauer 1961, pp. 21–35; J. Savage 1977, pp. 72–74); many scholarly books in the field are readable and extremely useful (see, for example, Baugh 1957; Jesperson 1956; Pyles 1964). The subject is intrinsically fascinating for most students at all grade levels and, once introduced by the teacher, can become an area for independent study, student reports, and class research. Books such as *Words and Their Ways in English Speech* (Greenough and Kittredge 1961) and pamphlets such as *Interesting Origins of English Words* (1961) open the door to etymology. When students see the historical backgrounds of words like *bonfire, education, candidate, rock-and-roll,* or *television,* their study of the more formal aspects of vocabulary is enriched.

BUILDING WORD POWER

Clearly, it is impossible to teach students all the words in the language or all about vocabulary study. English currently has more than 600,000 words. Lists of books *about* the language and its vocabulary may extend to hundreds of pages. Students would—and should—be intimidated by this mass of information.

What students need, and what can be given to them in a study skills program, is *word power*—the power to deal with a new word or a new meaning when they meet it. Acquiring a vocabulary is a life-long process. What teachers can do is provide students with specific strategies for dealing with unfamiliar words and their meanings.

Specific strategies in building word power through the use of structural and context clues are available and need to be used regularly in the classroom. Research and decades of successful classroom experience indicate that word power can be developed in students by approaches such as these:

1. Teach students key root words from which many other words have developed.
2. Teach common prefixes and suffixes which assist them in getting at the meanings of unfamiliar words.
3. Give regular practice in using context clues.

Each of these three approaches needs to be examined in some depth.

Teaching Word Roots

In English, as in other languages, words were coined in the past by combining "old" words with useful affixes and with other existing words (for example, the verb *know* took on the noun-signalling suffix *-ledge* to become the noun *knowledge,* the adverb *back* became attached to *yard* to become *backyard).* The process continues into modern English and will presumably continue into the future. Most students vaguely realize that they can find words within words. Some play word games that make the process clear ("How many separate words can you find in *intercollegiate football?);* most have had helpful instruction in elementary school reading programs. Examination of new words for roots or base words needs to continue through all grades for students to become truly skilled at using this form of word power.

In early grades it may be enough to regularly call attention to words within words *(baseball, homerun, fieldhockey).* Certain key roots may later be used to develop "word families" *(ball* leads to *football, ballplayer, ballgame, foulball).* Once students have become aware of the possibilities of exploration, they may be introduced to formal lists of common roots and be encouraged to develop games and individual exercises in word building. One list for board discussion and class activity follows:

Root	Meaning	Examples
agri-	field	agriculture
		agronomy
anthro-	man	anthropology
		anthropologist
astro-	star	astronaut
		astrophysics
bios-	life	biology
		biosphere
cardio-	heart	cardiac
		cardiology
chromo-	color	chromotology
		chronometer
demo-	people	democracy
		democratic
derme-	skin	epidermis
		epidemic
dyna-	power	dynamic
		dynamite
geo-	earth	geology
		geography
helio-	sun	heliotrope
		heliocentric

Root	Meaning	Examples
hydro-	water	hydroplane hydrochemistry
hypno-	sleep	hypnosis hypnotic
magni-	great	magnificent magnify
mono-	one	monoplane monolithic
ortho-	straight	orthodox orthodentistry
psycho-	mind	psychology psychometry
pyro-	fire	pyromaniac pyrotechnics
terra-	earth	terrace terra firma
thermo-	heat	thermometer thermofax

Students may be encouraged to (1) add to the example column from their memories or by checking the dictionary, (2) watch for new words in their reading and listening that have these roots, or (3) create new words not in the dictionary based on these roots.

The list may be adjusted "upward" or "downward" to fit a given class. The important point about any such list of roots is not that these are *the* valuable roots to be learned by all students, but that any list may serve as a springboard into activities to make students more aware of word parts and more confident of their ability to figure out unfamiliar words.

The next list, on the other hand, has some claim to be valuable in its own right. According to one authority (Brown 1952), these fourteen words may be used to get the meanings of over 14,000 English words!

Word	Prefix	Common Meaning	Root	Common Meaning
precept	pre-	before	capere	take, seize
detain	de-	away, from	tenere	hold, have
intermittent	inter-	between	mittere	send
offer	ob-	against	ferre	bear, carry

Word	Prefix	Common Meaning	Root	Common Meaning
insist	in-	into	stare	stand
monograph	mono-	alone, one	graphein	write
epilogue	epi-	upon	legein	say, study
aspect	ad-	to, towards	specere	see
uncomplicated	un-	not	plicare	fold
nonextended	non-	not	tendere	stretch
	ex-	out of		
reproduce	re-	back, again	ducere	lead
	pro-	forward		
indisposed	in-	not	ponere	put, place
	dis-	apart from		
oversufficient	over-	above	facere	make, do
	sub-	under		
mistranscribe	mis-	wrong	scribere	write
	trans-	across, beyond		

With lists on the chalkboard, on wall charts, or duplicated for student notebooks, students may be encouraged to produce word "families" or "constellations." One is given here for upper level classes and may serve as a model (suggested by Pauk 1974):

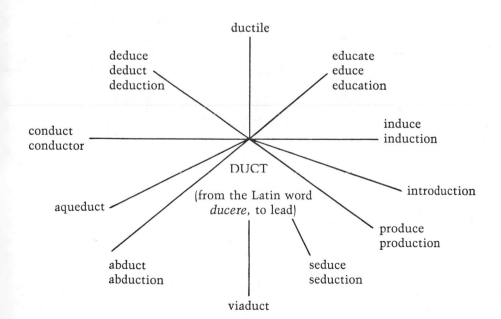

A comprehensive list of common roots and derived words may be found in *Techniques for Teaching Vocabulary* (Dale and O'Rourke 1971). The authors advise teachers not to teach words and roots in isolation. They say to always give students practice in using the words they discover or produce. Their advice to students is worth reproducing here:

> To be a good reader, writer, speaker, or listener, you have to know and like words. To be successful with words you have to be curious about words and the roots of words. You must notice how words are used in sentences and how words themselves are made up, what their parts are.
>
> How closely do you look at words? Have you noticed the root *disc* in *discuss*? the *vision* in *television*? the *sign* in *signature*? Knowing how words are related can help you build a large, useful vocabulary.
>
> Have you noticed that many words belong in one family? such words as *paragraph*, *telegraph*, *autograph*, *biography*? Did you know all these *graph* words refer to writing?
>
> Have you noticed the words that belong to the *phon* family? *Earphone*, *headphone*, *phonograph*, and *symphony* all refer to sound.
>
> Why be content with learning one word at a time if you can learn two, three, or four? (Dale and O'Rourke 1971).

Teaching Affixes

Just as the purpose in teaching roots is not to have students learn all possible roots but to have them become aware of the value of root knowledge in figuring out meanings of unfamiliar words, so the reason teachers need to give practice in using prefixes and suffixes is to further develop word power. Again, a first step may be through lists.

Give students a list of basic common prefixes and have them come up with examples of words containing these prefixes. Then they can be encouraged to search their school assignments and out-of-class reading for other examples. One "starter" list of prefixes follows:

Prefix	Meaning	Examples
anti-	against	antitank
auto-	self	automatic
bene-	good	benefit
circum-	around	circumscribe
contra-	against	contradict
hyper-	over	hypertension
hypo-	under	hypotension
inter-	between	interval
macro-	large	macroscopic

Prefix	Meaning	Examples
micro-	small	microscopic
multi-	many	multimillionaire
neo-	new	neolithic
pan-	all	Pan-American
poly-	many	polygamy
post-	after	postgame
pre-	before	pregame
proto-	first	prototype
pseudo-	false	pseudonym
retro-	backward	retrospect
semi-	half	semiretired
sub-	under	submarine
super-	above	Superman
tele-	far	television
trans-	across	transcontinental

A variety of games and exercises may be developed in which students collect examples (such as negative prefixes un-, in-, im-, a-, or an-). Class lists may be posted in earlier grades of examples using ex-, ante-, super-, sub-, or the number prefixes such as mono-, bi-, di-, duo-, tri-, quad-, tetra-, penta-, and so on. Students may be encouraged to add to the lists or create original words using the prefixes. Students should also be allowed to create their own self-tests, word games, and puzzles for common prefixes (such as anti-, ambi-, cent-, holo-, iso-, omni-, and so on).

Several years ago, Stauffer (1942) identified fifteen prefixes that accounted for 82 percent of the words listed in Thorndike's *A Teacher's Word Book of the Twenty Thousand Words Most Frequently and Widely Used in General Reading for Children and Young People*. These prefixes were: *ab, ad, be, com, de, dis, en, ex, in* (into) *in* (not), *pre, pro, re, sub,* and *un*. A variety of games and exercises may be developed for teaching and reviewing these important prefixes. For example, Mason and Mizer (1978) suggest that students be given sentences which are meaningless because the wrong prefixes are substituted in certain words. Students are then asked to correct the improper prefixes so that the sentences make sense:

1. Black smoke came from the inhaust pipe.
2. Mac played subfessional football.
3. He was destitute from the exstitute.

Suffixes usually serve grammatical purposes, indicating verbs (-ed, -s, -ing), nouns (-or, -er, -ment), adjectives (-er, -est), and adverbs (-ly). Some teachers feel that this grammatical terminology may help learners; others feel that it may hinder. In either case, one suggestion stands: it is best to let students make their own generalizations about the purpose the suffix serves by inferring meaning from their own examples. The teacher can start with three or four words students use (*quickness, brightness, sickness*) and build lists, later suggesting the purpose of the suffix (in this case it turns an adjective into a noun).

Some useful suffixes to teach, either directly or inductively, are:

Suffix	*Meaning*	*Examples*
able	can be done	readable
ade	thing made	lemonade
ana	collection of	Americana
ancy	state of	truancy
ard	person who	drunkard
arian	person who	librarian
ate	to make	fascinate
ation	process	visitation
ency	quality of	frequency
er, or	person	actor
esque	in the style of	statuesque
gram	something written	telegram
ic	to form nouns	magic
ical	to form adjectives	comical
ion	state of	ambition
ish	to form adjective	clownish
ism	a belief	realism
ist	a person who	guitarist
ize	to make	civilize
ent	full of	fraudulent
less	without	fatherless
ment	state of	puzzlement
or, ore	person who	donor, commodore
ory	place where	laboratory
ry	collection of	jewelry
some	like	bothersome
ster	one belonging to	gangster
ous	in the nature of	tempestuous
ward, wards	course or direction	homeward
wise	manner	counterclockwise
wright	workman	playwright
y	inclined to	dreamy
yer	person who	lawyer

Teaching Use of Context

Most authorities agree that listeners and readers get most of their understanding of words through observation of context, and that teaching students to use context clues is the best single way of developing word power. The young reader who meets *podiatrist* in the sentence, "The woman's feet hurt so she went to a podiatrist," will guess the word's meaning from its use. Then, if the reader has learned about structural clues, the guess can be verified by checking the root and suffix. Context clues do not always work (in "The boy spoke with alacrity," the reader cannot tell whether *alacrity* means sympathy, bitterness, or speed), but a vocabulary program without attention to context could lead to an overformalized study of roots and affix lists. The study of context clues keeps word study in a meaningful focus.

Fortunately, writers and speakers—consciously, unconsciously, or because they cannot help it—plant context clues in their writing. Such clues have been studied by several authorities (see Deighton 1971; Dale and O'Rourke 1971; Johnson and Pearson 1978; Ives, Bursuk, and Ives 1979). The following classification is frequently found in the professional literature (Hook 1965):

1. Experiential clues (John disliked his roommate; therefore, everything the guy did *infuriated* him.)
2. Comparison-contrast clues (Tom was lazy but his brother was *diligent*.)
3. Synonym clues (The team yelled, jumped, shrieked, and turned cartwheels. Such *animation* was rarely seen in that school.)
4. Summary clues (Chad refused to do homework. He lacked respect for teachers. He was always disobedient. Finally, *disciplinary* action had to be taken by the principal.)
5. Association clues (After studying the front and sides of the new gym building, she walked to the back of the *edifice*.)
6. Mood or situation clues (The rapidity with which he moved across the room, quickly reached the lock, and flung open the door indicated his *agility*.)
7. Previous contact clues (Her action *symbolized* peace. The reader here recalls previous statements such as the dove symbolizes peace, or the scales symbolize justice.).

Such contextual clues to meaning are summarized and classified in a variety of ways. One recent book on teaching reading and study strategies (Robinson 1978, pp. 95–100) notes that meaning may be indicated by:

1. Direct statement (*Glandular fever*, or infectious mononucleosis, is a serious disease.)

2. Example (*Methadone* is an example of a synthetic drug.)
3. Synonym (To *malign* is to slander an innocent person.)
4. Experience (The basketball game was a *fiasco*, with our team scoring 21 points to their 104.)
5. Description (The *griffin* was a mythological monster with an eagle's wings, head, beak, and a lion's body, legs, and tail.)
6. Comparison (Day after day, day after day,/We stuck, nor breath of motion;/As *idle* as a painted ship/Upon a painted ocean.)
7. Contrast (When the light brightens, the pupils of the eye contract; when it grows darker, they dilate.)
8. Reflection of intent, mood, tone, or setting (The starchiness in his voice and the scowl on his face warned us that father was in a *captious* mood. Absolutely nothing suited him! Dinner was too late—the meat was too cold—the coffee was too hot!).

Robinson notes that in the *experience* clue the background, both linguistic and experiential, the reader brings to the sentence becomes the contextual aid; readers must recall their own experiences for keys that will unlock meaning. In using clues of *intent, mood, tone,* or *setting,* the reader infers a feeling that harmonizes with the overall context. In some ways, he notes, this is the easiest because it is at the affective level and usually does not depend on deep thought (Robinson 1978).

Linguists and reading specialists note that in addition to these essentially *semantic* clues, writers and speakers provide certain *syntactical* clues—because of the structure of the language. For example, the *syntactical pattern* of a sentence and the functions of words in it helps readers and listeners arrive at decisions about meaning. When meeting *corpulent* in "The corpulent man could not fit easily into the child's chair," readers and listeners know—because of their built-in sense of the structure of English sentences—that it is adjectival and cannot be a noun functioning as subject for the sentence. *Inflectional clues* (such as *-ed* or *-ing* on verbs or the possessive or plural *s* on nouns) also help limit meaning by indicating the part of speech. A whole group of *markers* also assist the readers and listeners: articles, such as *a, an, the,* indicate nouns; auxiliaries, such as *was* or *had,* signal verbs; prepositions show phrases; and clauses are noted by clause markers, such as *when, because,* or *if.*

Linguists also note that in addition to syntactical clues such as found in sentence patterns, inflectional endings, and markers, speakers and writers use the *anaphora,* which is a syntactic signal influenced by meaning. In its simplest form, it is found in pronouns and their antecedents: "Money can be a dreadful thing. It leads to personal disaster for many people." In some instances, the anaphora confuses readers and listeners because the antecedent is found some distance back in the flow of discourse and they are unable to identify it. It may be said that the anaphora is a devious syntactic-semantic context clue and, by its very nature, needs to be taught in a vocabulary program.

Students at all levels need practice, day after day, in using semantic and syntactic context clues. Teachers should preview reading assignments and select those words which may be unfamiliar to most students in the class and give practice, in advance of reading, in using context clues. This daily teaching may be supplemented by brief exercises in which students are directed to find clues in teacher-prepared material. Workbooks and commercially-prepared materials are valuable, but exercises written by the teacher for a particular class have a special timeliness and pertinence lacking in "canned" material. An example culled from newspapers, school textbooks, television, even school bulletins means more to students than one found in a workbook. After practice, students themselves can learn to make exercises for the class or for one another.

APPROACHES TO VOCABULARY BUILDING

What can individual teachers do to improve their students' vocabularies? Several strategies have been suggested or implied in the previous pages. Four approaches to vocabulary building are examined next.

Direct Teaching of Vocabulary

Many teachers and authorities advise against direct teaching of vocabulary through word lists, exercises, and drills. They cite scattered research evidence to indicate that learning words through reading and real-life situations is more effective. On the other hand, other teachers (and equally prestigious authorities) recommend direct teaching, drill, and reinforcement. They, too, cite scattered evidence from research to support their position. A disinterested look at the research, however, reveals no clear-cut pattern (see, for example, Deighton 1959; Dale and Eichholz 1960; Petty 1968; and other references at the end of this chapter). One cannot *prove* that incidental learning (no matter how structured) or direct teaching is superior. One finding is worth noting (and perhaps, citing over and over again!): any kind of vocabulary training seems better than none at all.

One example of direct teaching of vocabulary is to simply list new words on the chalkboard or distribute lists and have students memorize the words and their definitions. Direct teaching of vocabulary for many teachers in the past (and in some schools today) consists of memory work, drill, and testing. Teachers base lists on their own research or on vocabulary textbooks, give assignments, review in class, and drill and test again. Critics insist such practices are "deadly" and nonproductive, yet many adults regularly use words in conversation that they recall learning in a classroom many years before *from a list*. For many, the method clearly works.

Latin and Greek roots may also be taught directly. Tell students, for example, that ten Latin and two Greek roots lie at the heart of over 2,000 English words! Write these on the chalkboard or duplicate them, and have students memorize them:

Roots	English Examples
Latin	
facio (do, make)	facilitate
duco (lead, bring forward)	educate
tendo (stretch)	tendon
plico (fold)	complicate
mitto (send)	transmit or remit
pono (place)	postpone
teneo (hold, have)	tenacity
fero (carry)	transfer
capio (take, seize)	capture
specio (see, observe)	spectator
Greek	
logos (speech or thinking)	logical
grapho (write)	phonograph, autograph

Send students to their textbooks and newspapers to locate English words with these roots. Have them copy the sentences in which they found them, and then review them in class. Drill and test, have students make up their own sentences with words containing the roots, and then drill and test again. This is direct teaching—at its best and/or worst—but it can work!

Another example of direct teaching important affixes is by writing some on the board or duplicating them for student notebooks:

Prefixes		Examples
ab-	(away from)	abnormal
ad-	(toward)	advance
com-	(with)	command
de-	(from)	devolution
dis-	(apart)	disengage
en-	(in)	enact
ex-	(out of)	export
pre-	(before)	preschool

Prefixes	*Examples*
re- (back)	regain
sub- (under)	submarine

Suffixes	*Examples*
-tion (expression action)	revolution
-er (one who does)	leader, teacher
-or (one who does)	actor, director
-ent (indicating quality)	different
-ity (state of)	timidity
-ure (act or state)	exposure
-ous (having)	poisonous

Tell students that the more affixes they know, the better they can master new words. Encourage them to memorize lists, then drill them, give examples, and test. Send students out to find more examples. Again, drill and test. Make up fill-in-the-blanks exercises, and then have students make exercises for one another. Drill and test once more.

To give practice in using context clues, list words from assignments and have students guess at the meanings by using clues they find in the text. Have them bring to class sentences containing new words they have encountered in outside reading. Then encourage the group to define the words using only context clues. Make up simple exercises of words found in magazines (presented in context) for students to define through context. Use context clues exercises in workbooks and other commercially-prepared materials. Advocates of direct teaching regularly say: "Never allow a week to go by without some drill work in the use of context clues, and students will eventually learn this important skill! Avoid drill and regular practice and some students may learn the skill on their own, but it is better not to leave learning to chance!"

This is an old-fashioned teaching at its worst, according to many. But, enthusiasts for the approach say, "Good or bad, it is better than no vocabulary teaching at all." They note: "When critics of this kind of teaching can demonstrate beyond reasonable doubt that all teachers at all grade levels are teaching vocabulary more effectively by other methods, the direct teaching approach can be abandoned. Until then, there is certainly a place for it in schools."

Teaching Vocabulary Through Games

Games may "sweeten" drill. Through the years many teachers have developed a variety of games and play strategies to accomplish the same goals as those of direct teaching and drill. Many drills and reinforcement exercises are easily turned into games that stimulate and excite students at all levels. Descriptions are found in many of the professional books in language arts (see, for example, Smith 1972; J. Savage 1977) and in the professional journals (such as *The Reading Teacher*, *Language Arts*, or the *Journal of Reading*).

Savage, for example, suggests:

1. The Minister's Cat, in which children think of adjectives in alphabetical order: The minister's cat is an *affable* cat, the minister's cat is a *brave* cat, the minister's cat is a *cuddly* cat.
2. Swifties, in which an action word or an adverb is chosen for the context of a sentence: "There goes Moby Dick," Tom *wailed*. "I have no hair," the man *bawled*. "Look at the pig," Jack *squealed*.
3. The Alliteration Game, in which students supply alliterative adjectives to accompany alphabetical lists of nouns, *aggravating alligator*, *bashful baboon*, *cackling crows* (J. Savage 1977, pp. 81–82).

Such games may be based on formal word lists. They may be adopted for most grade levels. They certainly enliven drill and more structured exercises.

Word building games may be created from class work in roots and affixes. For instance, give students a common root and encourage them to add prefixes to the beginning and suffixes to the end to discover how many other words may be built upon the root. A variety of competitions and team games may be developed around word building. For example, ask: How many words can you make from the prefix *non-*? Or *re-*? How many with the suffix *-ment*? or *-on*? How many with two or more roots?

Cunningham (1978) describes the Mystery Word Match. To play this game, the teacher divides the class into two competing groups. Each takes a turn asking a question about the mystery word. Guessing the word after the first question is worth ten points. One point is subtracted for each negative answer. The team that guesses the word is awarded the number of points it is worth at that time. The teacher draws lines on the board to indicate the number of letters in the mystery word, writes the clue words on the board, and has students make sure they can pronounce them. The meanings of the words are also discussed and students use each in original sentences.

The game is carried out by the students to discover which parts of the clue words are used in the mystery word. Students may ask: Does the mystery word begin like _____? End like _____? Have a middle like _____? In the following example, the three words on the board are: *absolute*, *rebel*, and *attention*.

Teacher: Bill's team won the toss and can go first. The mystery word is worth 10 points.

Bill's	
team member:	Does the word begin like *attention*?
Teacher:	No. Joe's team for 9 points.
Joe's	
team member:	Does the word end like *attention*?
Teacher:	Yes, it does. (Writes *tion* on the last four lines.) You may go again.
Joe's	
team member:	Does the word begin like *absolute*?
Teacher:	No, it does not. Bill's team for 8 points.
Bill's	
team member:	Does the word have a middle like *absolute*?
Teacher:	Good for you. (Writes *solu* on appropriate lines.) Go again.
Bill's	
team member:	Does the word have a beginning like *rebel*?
Teacher:	Yes, it does. (Writes last two letters in to get <u>*resolution*</u>.) The team may confer and name the word. (The team decides on *resolution*, and the teacher records 8 points for Billy's team. The game continues with the next mystery word.)

Cunningham (1978) notes that the game helps adolescents in a remedial reading class to decode polysyllabic words. As can be seen, it also forces students to consider word parts (common roots and affixes) in a play situation, having much the same value as an exercise or drill, yet providing fun. Some of the Mystery Word Game Starters Cunningham suggests are:

Mystery Word	*Starters*
ineffective	attentive, informal, effecting
unofficial	unfortunate, office, specialty
expressive	repulsive, experience, impressing
inactive	reactor, restorative, reinstate
informal	inattentive, fortunate, abnormal
contestant	condensation, pretest, informant
university	diversity, unicycle, immunity
revolution	convocation, solution, renovate
respectful	inspector, remember, beautiful
refreshment	reevaluate, astonishment, freshness

Games are not only for elementary school students or remedial readers. Many high school teachers also make drill palpable—and sometimes exciting—with games. Virginia Ross, of Marshfield (Massachusetts) High school, uses Fun Words. After studying common Latin and Greek roots, she gives students a list of made-up words such as pyro/homi and asks them to figure out the meaning (*fireman*):

1. SOL/FLOR
2. MEDI/ANNU
3. CARN/Sphere
4. ANNU/LIBR
5. SUB/HYDRO
6. AQUA/CYCLE
7. STELL/ICHTHYO
8. SEMI/MORT
9. SOL/THEO
10. AQUA/PORTER
11. BI/CHRONER
12. TERR/ZOO
13. THERMO/CAPIT
14. BIBLIO/BIO
15. GEO/ANTHROPO

Using the Dictionary to Teach Vocabulary

"Incidental" learning usually refers to that which is unplanned by the teacher. Events occur in the classroom (or out of it) which lead students to an understanding, a new meaning, or an insight not structured into the teacher's plan book. In the case of vocabulary development, it refers to those wonderful occasions when people add a word to their vocabularies without being taught it! Much vocabulary learning occurs this way. Unfortunately, it is too casual and random. Teachers need some devices to take advantage of these occurrences. One device is the personal dictionary.

Teachers encourage students to note on 3 × 5 cards or slips new words they encounter, check the dictionary for an appropriate definition, and write it and the sentence in which the word occurs on the card or slip. Class time should be regularly set aside for discussions of these "finds." At intervals (once a month or each marking period) students compile their findings alphabetically in their own dictionaries. The incidental aspects of learning are thus controlled and formalized to some extent.

Teachers who use the personal dictionary approach to vocabulary building note that: (1) it is more personal (in that words are the students' own discoveries and not the teacher's), (2) words are often more relevant to the lives of the students (because they locate them in their own reading), (3) the approach gives the teacher opportunities to discuss several related topics (such as the nature of definition, parts of speech, the importance of context), and (4) it leads to more formal study of dictionaries.

Instead of individual notebook-type dictionaries, some teachers use Word Banks or Word Boards. Word Banks are maintained by an entire class. As each student finds interesting new words, he or she writes the appropriate information (definition, sentence in which found, part of speech) on a card that goes into a file box (or "Bank"). These are kept through the entire year, referred to regularly in class, and located in a prominent place in the room. Students are encouraged to go to the Word Bank when writing papers or preparing oral presentations to draw on its wealth. Word Boards serve many of the same purposes, but they restrict collecting zeal because they place limits on the size of the collection. Students usually tack their cards or slips alphabetically on a large board posted in the room. Unlike the filebox bank, the board is visible at all times and may be referred to frequently in class discussions. Because the number of words collected is limited by available space, some teachers suggest focusing on certain kinds of words, such as descriptive words, science terms, words with multiple meanings, emotive words, or, in high school classes, high-level abstractions.

Space restrictions limit Word Boards to certain kinds of words. Students' hobbies, special interests, or part-time jobs may serve—productively—to limit personal dictionaries, particularly with secondary school students. In many classes, teachers encourage students to develop rock or jazz dictionaries, alphabetical lists (with definitions) of automotive terms, technical terms in specialized fields, or slang dictionaries. All such variations of the personal dictionary make word study more meaningful and enhance vocabulary growth.

Teaching Vocabulary Through Personal Experience and Reading

Common sense indicates that the best way to learn new words is to actually have the experience associated with the words. For example, teaching the word *optometrist* (or the difference between *optometrist* and *ophthalmologist*) may be accomplished through drill or games. The student who visits an optometrist to have her or his eyes tested for eyeglasses is more apt to "know" and remember the word (as the student who needs more specialized attention from an ophthalmologist will be more able to define and remember *ophthalmologist*). *Resolution* may be added to the vocabularies of students who play the Mystery Word Match, but, if they have joined together in the Student Council to pass a resolution related to important school affairs, they will better understand and remember it. Clearly, teachers cannot control all the possible learning experiences of all students. Planned experiences may help them with *democracy* or *tyranny*. Field trips to museums of science may help them learn *laser, planetarium,* or *telescope.* Life experiences may give them meanings for *depression, elation,* or *angst.* Teachers cannot structure such learning. Can they facilitate it in any way?

Many teachers have long recognized that one of the best ways to encourage word learning in life is to encourage word learning in personal reading. Because wide, personal reading is to some extent a substitute for wide, personal experience, many teachers try to make students more sensitive to words they meet in their own reading, assuming there will be a carry-over into real life experiences. For example, the reader who is struck by *bifurcate* in his reading (and uses structural and context clues, and perhaps a dictionary, to arrive at its meaning) may think twice about the word when he hears it in conversation or on television. The student who is curious about *contemplate* in her novel may be curious enough, when she hears it, to check its meaning in a dictionary and contemplate the experience in which the word occurred. Much out-of-class reading of novels, biographies, magazines, and other so-called recreational material can serve as vicarious experience—for life in general and for vocabulary building in particular.

An unfortunate paradox is found here. The very teachers, parents, and school administrators most anxious to develop study skills are often the least reluctant to relinquish school time to wide, personal reading or encouragement. One regularly hears of teachers reproached for spending a period on silent ("nonstudy") reading: "Teachers should be teaching study skills not just sitting there watching the kids read!" However, evidence does exist indicating that students may, indeed, be stimulated to read more. (For a dramatic instance, see Fader and McNeil 1968; for a review of more formal research, see Purves and Beach 1976.) Activities to stimulate wide, "nonstudy" reading include:

1. Setting class time aside each day or week for silent reading of library or paperback books chosen by the students themselves
2. Establishing regular schedules for student-teacher conferences about personal reading
3. Arranging class and individual trips to school and local libraries
4. Stimulating personal library "searches" to discover answers to individual student questions (see Chapter 8)
5. Arranging library research projects for students to locate books to further inform them about topics studied in the course (see Chapter 8)
6. Promoting the purchase of books for private collections through book clubs, local book distributors, and school Book Fairs
7. Arranging competitions and various kinds of contests to provide wide reading of nonschool materials

8. Enticing students to books by appropriate displays, field trips, talks in class by librarians, authors, and others from outside the school
9. Relating personal reading to film and television experiences
10. Relating personal reading to hobbies, sports, and individual interests
11. Sharing discoveries and opinions about outside reading by students and by the teacher
12. Giving course credit for time spent outside of class in personal reading.

Such a list may be extended. The point is that student vocabularies expand as students read. The more they read, the greater their individual word collections become. Any classroom activities that promote wide, personal reading promote vocabulary development.

Idea Box
Vocabulary Development

A sensory approach is effective with younger (and sometimes older) students. In personal dictionaries, Word Banks, or class Word Boards, tell students to focus on words that describe sounds, tastes, smells, sights, or touches. For touch, for example, ask each student to put his or her hand into a Mystery Bag as it is passed around the group and write down one word to describe the touched object (a rock, piece of fruit, tool). List these on the board, discuss them, and add some to the collection of useful or interesting words.

One effective way to remember new words is to picture them. Have students draw illustrations or cartoons to help them remember words on class lists or in their personal dictionaries. These may be posted, shared, or discussed.

Another way to remember new words is to relate them to personal experiences. Suggest that students examine class word lists and think of experiences they have had which they can link to particular words. Allow them opportunities to tell about these memory connections, and then self-test to discover if personal associations help as "memory joggers."

Have students invent mnemonic devices to remember new words. Point out that the memory is often aided by irrational mental connections ("We remember *stubborn* if we think of a child who kicked a chair when refusing to do what he was told and *stubbed* his toe" or "We can remember *loquacity* if we think of 'locking the tongue' of a person who talks too much"). Note that many of the most effective memory devices are sometimes crazy and highly personal. Students may report to the class on their personal devices and share ideas for remembering new words. A class list of devices may be posted or duplicated.

All students of words report that once they have learned a new word they repeatedly encounter it in their own reading. Suggest that students keep journals and report to the class their vocabulary findings. A log entry might indicate the new word and designate each fresh encounter with the new word, perhaps with a note on the place where the student "refound" the word.

To test out the SSCD approach in nonschool situations, have students keep a journal or log in which they enter new words found outside of class. Beside each word, they should note the technique they used to unlock its meaning: Were sound clues sufficient? Did structure clues help? Which ones? Was context useful? Did the dictionary help?

Have students invent new words. Explain how *snide* came from *sneer* and *rude* to fill a need for a word that did not exist. In presenting their words, students should be able to spell them, tell how they created them, define them, and defend them as worthwhile additions to the English vocabulary.

A vocabulary technique used by students of a foreign language is equally useful for building English vocabulary. Have students enter the correct spellings of English words on one side of a 3 x 5 index card and a dictionary definition on the other side. Suggest: "As you are riding to school, waiting for buses, or otherwise finding time is wasting, flip through your cards and learn the meanings of new words." The words may come from lists distributed by the teacher, from students' in-class or home reading, or from their personal dictionaries. Students may test themselves on their stock of cards or test one another. They may prepare more formal tests for end-of-course self-grading.

Send students on Etymology Searches. Show them how they can trace word histories, using dictionaries found in the classroom. Ask: where did we ever get words like *bumpkin, potato, cigarette, bicycle*? Have them suggest words for investigation. If the school or local library includes an edition of the Oxford English Dictionary, teachers can show students how the editors tracked down most English words and give examples of how they were used at different times in history. Ask: What was the original meaning of *nice*? *knave*? *glamour*? *piano*?

Have students select a passage from a textbook or article and trace (as best they can) the originating language of each word. Ask: How many came from Anglo-Saxon? From Norman French? What have these words in common? How many came from Latin? Greek? Portuguese? Spanish? Chinese? American Indian languages? What do you infer from your discoveries?

English has a larger word stock than any other modern language. After discussing the history of English and its tendency to borrow from other languages, have students start Synonym Banks. They may list twenty ordinary words they personally use frequently, and then start collections of synonyms for later use in their own writing and conversation.

Have students create their own word games for the class. These may range from Vocabulary Bees to crossword puzzles. Suggest that individuals check the school or local library to locate books which contain ideas for word games and share good ones with the group.

Note that all speakers have favorite words which they use frequently in their speaking vocabularies. Have students keep records of words favored by teachers, politicians, television actors, or sports figures. Allow time to share these discoveries and suggest synonyms for the much-used words.

Abstract words present problems to all thinkers. Introduce secondary school and college students to the Abstraction Ladder. (Start with a bottom step such as Matilda, the chicken, and show how each higher step becomes increasingly abstract and removed from reality: Matilda becomes chicken which becomes *poultry*, which becomes farm *product*, then *profit*, and finally *wealth*). Show students that words higher up on the ladder are difficult to "pin down" because they represent high-level mental abstractions divorced from reality. They can develop ladders of their own and search for examples of abstract words in their own reading and listening.

Younger students can be shown that high-level abstractions may be brought down to earth by using a model, such as Charles Schulz's "Happiness is a Sad Song." Ask them to complete sentences such as, Sadness is _____; Happiness is _____; Excitement is _____; Peace is _____; Misery is _____.

Introduce high school and college students to the study of semantics. Several good popular books are available to explain the history and developments of semantics as a linguistic, philosophic, and practical field of study. This is a topic for individual or class library research.

High school and college students might be interested in compiling (individually or as a class) a list called *Fifty (or Five Hundred) Words Every Educated Person Should Know*. These may be culled from textbook or general reading and selected because of their frequency and value. After discussion and editing, final lists may be duplicated for all students in the class.

New words come into the language daily. To demonstrate this truism to students, have them seek out words that have come into the language since they were born. They will be amazed at the number. College students might be challenged to trace down recent words such as, *auto cheia, anerobic, balletic, contranomers, dishikis, erk, ligotype, naifs, rebarbatively, stagflation*, and others.

Because the dictionary is such a valuable tool in vocabulary development, specific instruction is needed in *how to use* a dictionary. With copies on everyone's desk, demonstrate exactly what a dictionary can do for a student. Attention should be directed to (1) pronunciation (students should be told how to use the pronunciation clues, for example); (2) the part of speech; (3) etymology (students need information in how to use the abbreviations indicating language derivation and knowledge of how and why words could come from another language); (4) antonyms and homonyms; (5) meanings (they need to know that a dictionary only reports the way a word is used and does not make up meanings); and (6) multiple meanings. Many students reach college without ever having had minimal instruction in the use of the dictionary. This situation could be altered by (1) formal lessons by the teacher at regular intervals, (2) class assignments which lead students to regular use of the dictionary, and (3) individual projects which send students to seek out specific information from its pages.

Linguists often complain that schools fail to teach *about* dictionaries. Students (and many adults) credit dictionary makers with virtues they do not claim for themselves and, perhaps worse, assume all dictionaries are alike. To give students better undedrstanding of the dictionary as a tool (and, in the process, continue to promote interest in words and vocabulary development), set up frequent assignments which send students out to examine *several* dictionaries. Discuss with the students that "Webster" is a name that *any* dictionary maker can use legally (the original American dictionary by Noah Webster is long out of print and the name is, like the *coke* of *Coca Cola*, not a brand or trade name), and that each modern dictionary is put together by different dictionary makers, that all are different, and that some are better than others. One way to do this is to select a word that appears in a lesson and have students check several different dictionaries to compare definitions. Tell students to report on publication dates, editors' credentials, size and price of dictionary, and so on. Lead students to see that certain dictionaries are better for certain purposes (for example, the *American Heritage Dictionary* gives birth and death dates of famous people, often includes pictures, and tells whether a word is acceptable or not in Standard English; the *Oxford English Dictionary* gives almost complete word histories, with numerous examples of how words have actually been used at different times in history). Dictionary explorations may begin in the early grades and should certainly continue through college. Teachers at almost every level should consider one-to-four week units on the history, development, uses, and shortcomings of dictionaries.

To help students see the difficulties of defining words, have them select more words than they currently use and, without looking at a dictionary, try to write a definition. These may be written separately at first and then collected and duplicated for class examination. Help students to distinguish between classes and items in a class, between general and specific words, between logical and stipulative definitions, between easily defined and almost impossible-to-define words. For more sophisticated students such lessons may serve as an introduction to logic and semantics, but for all students these lessons can help sharpen awareness of words and word meanings. Most students can see the difference between defining specific words (*sugar, automobile, fingers*) and abstract words (*love, wealth, anger*). This approach may be used to teach about emotionally charged words, the difference between connotation and denotation, and the use of metaphor in definition (for instance, the *leg* of the table, the *arm* of the chair). Teaching definition is an area where students truly see the relationship between language and thinking.

Try the Word a Day technique. Suggest that each student take a turn in bringing in a word for the day. The student writes it on the board, gives a definition, and tells where the word was discovered and why it was chosen. Students in the class keep a record (on a posted list or in their notebooks) and try to use the word at least three times during the course of the day. At the end of the week or month, the class may test itself to discover how well each person remembered.

Some words are overused by people of all ages. Class time may be well spent in discussing such words (*nice, interesting,* etc.) and preparing lists of alternatives. Using a dictionary or pooling their word knowledge, students can list other substitutes for the overused words. Post these lists or keep them handy in notebooks, and try to choose the more "interesting" alternatives in speech and writing.

Call attention to multiple meanings through contests to discover who can find the most meanings for given words. *Run*, for example, seems to have well over 100 different meanings! Start board lists of common words that may be dangerous because they have so many meanings for different listeners and readers.

References

Baugh, Albert. *A History of the English Language*, 2nd ed. New York: Appleton-Century-Crofts, 1957.

Brown, James I. *Efficient Reading*. Boston: Houghton Mifflin, 1952.

Cunningham, Patricia M. "Decoding Polysyllabic Words: An Alternative Strategy." *Journal of Reading* 21 (April 1978): 608–614.

Dale, Edgar and Gerhard Eichholz. *Children's Knowledge of Words*. Columbus: Bureau of Educational Research and Services, Ohio State University, 1960.

Dale, Edgar, and Joseph O'Rourke. *Techniques of Teaching Vocabulary*. Palo Alto, Calif.: Field Educational Publications, Inc., 1971.

Deighton, Lee C. *Vocabulary Development in the Classroom*. New York: Bureau of Publications, Teachers College Press, Teachers College, Columbia University, 1959.

Deighton, Lee C. "Vocabulary Development." In *The Encyclopedia of Education*, Vol. 9. New York: The Macmillan Company and The Free Press, 1971, pp. 460–469.

Fader, Daniel N., and Elton B. McNeil. *Hooked on Books: Program and Proof*. New York: Berkley Publishing Corporation, 1968.

Greenough, James, and George Lyman Kittredge. *Words and Their Ways in English Speech*. New York: Macmillan, 1961.

Harrington, Richard. "The Effect of Vocabulary Exercises on Vocabulary Acquisition of Eighth Graders." Ph.D. dissertation, Boston University, 1979.

Hook, J. N. *The Teaching of High School English*. New York: Ronald Press, 1965.

Interesting Origins of English Words. Springfield, Mass.: G. and C. Merriam Co., 1961.

Ives, Josephine P.; Laura I. Bursuk; and Sumner A. Ives. *Word Identification Techniques*. Chicago: Rand McNally College Publishing Co., 1979.

Jesperson, Otto. *Growth and Structure of the English Language*. New York: Doubleday Anchor Books, 1956.

Johnson, Dale D., and P. David Pearson. *Teaching Reading Vocabulary*. New York: Holt, Rinehart and Winston, 1978.

Mason, George E., and John M. Mizer. "Twenty-two Sets of Methods and Materials for Stimulating Teenage Reading." *Journal of Reading* 21 (May 1978): 735–741.

Pauk, Walter. *How to Study in College*. Boston: Houghton Mifflin Co., 1974.

Petty, Walter T., et al. *The State of Knowledge about Teaching Vocabulary*. Urbana, Ill.: National Council of Teachers of English, 1968.

Purves, Alan C., and Richard Beach. *Literature and the Reader: Research in Response to Literature, Reading Interests, and the Teaching of Literature*. Urbana, Ill.: National Council of Teachers of English, 1976.

Pyles, Thomas, *The Origins and Development of the English Language*. New York: Harcourt, Brace and World, 1964.

Reed, Carroll E. *Dialects of American English*, rev. ed. Urbana, Ill.: National Council of Teachers of English, 1977.

Robinson, H. Alan. *Teaching Reading and Study Strategies: The Content Areas*, 2nd ed. Boston: Allyn and Bacon, Inc., 1978.

Sauer, Edwin. *English in the Secondary School.* New York: Holt, Rinehart and Winston, 1961.

Savage, John F. *Effective Communication: Language Arts Instruction in the Elementary School.* Chicago: Science Research Associates, Inc., 1977.

Savage, Ronald C. "An Investigation of the Process-Orders Involved in the Analysis of Content-Technical Words by Students in Grades Six Through Nine." Ph.D. dissertation, Boston University, 1979.

Shuy, Roger W. *Discovering American Dialects.* Urbana, Ill.: National Council of Teachers of English, 1967.

Smith, James A. *Adventures in Communication: Language Arts Methods.* Boston: Allyn and Bacon, 1972.

Stauffer, Russell G. "A Study of Prefixes in the Thorndike List to Establish a List of Prefixes That Should Be Taught in the Elementary School." *Journal of Educational Research* 35 (February 1942): 453–458.

7

NOTETAKING, HOMEWORK, AND STUDY GUIDES

Study skills in listening, reading, vocabulary, and thinking may be significantly improved if students learn how to effectively take notes, complete class and homework assignments, and use study guides. Research and observations of successful classroom practices lead to suggestions for helping students in these three important areas.

Chapter 7 first examines research and practice in the teaching of various responding and notetaking skills, then current views and practices in assignment-giving and homework are presented, and, finally, the use and improvement of study guides is explored.

NOTETAKING AND RESPONDING SKILLS

Students are frequently discomposed, if not perplexed, by the barrage of incoming new information and ideas. In listening to classroom talk and lecture, in reading school assignments and textbooks, in evaluating material in speech and print, in using the library and preparing research papers, students often ask, "How can we keep track and make sense of it all? Are there ways of sorting it out so that we can remember and use it?" The frustrations are understandable; so much material assaults students that breakdown in collecting and processing incoming information is common to all, and is a frequent cause of difficulties in learning.

Techniques for "catching on paper" significant points of a speaker or author seem vital to later making sense of material. Four approaches to notetaking and other responding skills are described here, with suggestions for teaching.

Notetaking

Observations of many teachers and students through the years indicates that passive listening or reading leads to minimal learning. The listener's facial expressions may signal awareness and reflection; the reader's eyes may move (dutifully) along the lines of print; the degree and quality of mental activity may be high or low. Teachers cannot always tell from watching. They have noted, however, that successful students usually "do something" as they read or listen: they underscore, circle words and phrases, list, and/or jot down reactions.

To make students aware of the value of notetaking, many teachers begin simply by talking about responding-with-pen-in-hand. They point out that the human memory—at best—is a fragile thing, wonderous but often undependable, and that even the best students cannot remember all they hear, see, or read because so much new material comes into the mind it is impossible to retain it all. Teachers then discuss ways to maximize the quality of the intake process, either by listing these on the chalkboard or by eliciting them from the group. They try to make students realize that they should "do something" as they read, such as writing down key ideas, or writing down, as in a shopping list, the main points as they occur in the talk or printed message, or jotting down what they think are the key words or phrases.

Discussion of notetaking is important; actual practice with teacher guidance is crucial. When students are aware of the importance of physical response in study, they need short practice sessions in which they listen and read-with-pen-in-hand and open notebooks. Five- or ten-minute sessions each day at the beginning of the school year are basic to the development of this study habit. At the end of the sessions, students may share their notes, describe their personal notetaking styles (Full sentences? Phrases? Key words?) and take teacher-prepared (or, later, student-prepared) quizzes to discover which style works most effectively for them.

A variant of pen-in-hand techniques has been tried with junior high school students (Bizinkauskas 1970). The teacher utilized tape recorders, first discussing the importance of some kind of notetaking, and then giving students opportunities to record into their tape recorders key words, phrases, sentences, and ideas. He discovered, as have several other researchers (see, for example, Palmatier 1968; 1973; 1974) that although one specific technique—in this case, the tape-recorded "notetaking"—was not dramatically more effective, notetaking of one kind or another is better than passive reading (or listening).

The findings of formal research studies seem to generally support the four principles governing notetaking set up by Courtney (1965):

1. Rather than massive direct quotes, notes should be in the student's own words to avoid rote-learning.
2. There should be a consistent format for recording the information, perhaps including a variety of personalized abbreviations or symbols.

3. All notes must be properly labeled for topic, time, and referent.
4. Although all notetaking is selective, it must be sufficiently complete to be intelligible at a later time.

Underlining

Underlining, or underscoring, is generally limited to study reading situations and to classes where students own their own textbooks. Teachers below college level may duplicate a lecture, particularly at the beginning of the school year, and have students follow the talk in print, underlining key words, phrases, or ideas. They may also distribute duplicated copies of articles, sections of books, or passages from important chapters, and show students how to underscore. Underlining, however, is used more in college than in elementary or secondary school, and, indeed, is the most used study technique for many college students (Policastro 1975).

Students who use the technique should be shown that it is only one step from passivity. Better to underscore than to read passively, yes, but the practice, for many students, becomes such a casual response that any potential value it may have diminishes. A stroll through a college library often reveals dozens of undergraduates underlining (in yellow markers) almost every line (sometimes *every* line) of print on the pages before them; they seem merely to be forcing their eyes along the line of print by following the flow of ink. In explaining the dangers inherent in the underlining method of textbook notation, teachers in the Academic Study Skills Program at Ramapo College (New Jersey) emphasize the following three points:

1. Students usually underline too much. The average textbook runs about 400 pages. If just 20 percent of each page were underlined, it would result in eighty pages of rereading (while turning all 400) for a review or in preparation for an exam.
2. The underlined section will often lose some, if not all, of its significance when reread at some future time. The student then has to reread surrounding material in order to reconstruct the original meaning, requiring extra time and effort.
3. Underlining is a comparatively passive activity and has the effect of psychologically deferring the active (learning) process to some future point. Often a student will underline something which is assumed (rightly or not) to be important, though not fully understood, with the intention of rereading the item at a more "opportune" time in order to discover the complete meaning   (Policastro 1975).

Probably better than underlining are *marginal comments* and *coding systems.* Students may be shown that their responses in the margin are more valuable because they are more personal. Questions asked of the author, rephrasing of difficult sentences, and the copying of dictionary definitions of unfamiliar words indicate that the reader is more engaged in the process of learning than when tracing yellow lines across the page. Some teachers encourage students to develop their own coding systems. Students use different colored markers to indicate main ideas and supporting evidence, circles around new terms when introduced by the author, arrows from idea to idea to show relationships, boxes to contain related ideas, triangles to mark the development of ideas from a main idea sentence to include all supporting example and detail sentences, marginal numbers to indicate chronological patterns, stars to show the relative importance of ideas to the reader, question marks to point out unsupported references, hearts and flowers to mark emotional language, and so on.

Simple underscoring is better than passive reading. In turn, marginal comments and/or a personal coding system involve the reader even more directly in the author's presentation.

Outlining

In many ways, outlining is the most useful of all recording techniques, but it has been given a bad name in some schools by overuse and misuse. Outlining assumes students have reached a point in their development when they are able to select key ideas and distinguish them from supporting evidence and example, distinguish the relevant from the comparatively irrelevant, follow sequences of ideas, recognize chronological patterns and cause and effect relationships, and use other high-level organizational skills. Some teachers in the past have insisted upon outlining before students were ready.

In the early stages, teachers need to give classes a well-developed outline of the lecture or chapter to be studied, and then carefully explain, both in advance and after listening or reading, the ways in which the material follows the outline. For elementary and junior high school students, this means that teachers need to use material that is simply organized (for example, material with three main ideas, each followed by three examples, or a simple how-to-do-it process in which each step along the way is clearly presented in order). Students at this stage need the outline before them and much teacher guidance. Only after students realize that a speaker or author follows an outline should teachers ask students to outline themselves—and then only after an intermediate step has been completed. This intermediate step consists of the class examining incomplete outlines in which students are given (1) an almost complete outline with three or four supporting details left blank for them to fill in while listening or reading, (2) an outline with main topics but all supporting details to be filled in, and (3) an outline with supporting details and examples but all main idea topics to be filled in.

The ability to recognize organization in a talk or written message is rarely a "natural accomplishment" nor essentially a quality of native intelligence (Courtney 1965, p. 78); it is an ability that can be taught. Fortunately, many strategies for teaching organizational skills are available and are presented in Chapter 9. Outlining, as a basic study skill in notetaking and recording, relies on a variety of perceptions and understandings which may best be taught through lessons in writing and reporting. Outlining ability in general seems contingent upon the development of certain higher mental processes most effectively approached by specific lessons in organizing, patterning, and planning. They are discussed in Chapter 9.

One danger inherent to outlining as a recording technique needs to be noted: all material encountered by students is not necessarily organized. Most talk—in and out of the classroom—is spontaneous, random, and full of irrelevancies; much published writing is disorganized, episodic, and poorly edited. Students need to see that outlining is a valuable study technique only when the incoming material is organized.

Summarizing

Unlike outlining, summarizing may be used with disorganized or poorly organized material. It, too, needs careful, even sequential, instruction. At first, the teacher may ask students to stop after reading each paragraph and write in their notebooks, in their own words, what the author seems to be saying. A formal lecture may be stopped after key sections for summaries to be written. Students, especially in secondary school and college, need regular practice in class writing one- or two-sentence summaries of each paragraph or four- or five-sentence summaries of each section. They also need opportunities to share their work with the group, with teachers pointing to successful summaries and to ways in which others may be improved.

Summarizing, like outlining, is a rather high-level recording technique compared with notetaking and underlining. Both assume the listener's or reader's ability to somehow "get into the mind" of the speaker or author. The student who jots down phrases, underscores, makes marginal comments, or lists key ideas is the "outsider" catching on paper those parts of the sender's message that he or she happens to pick up. When outlining, however, the student assumes that the sender has organized the message in some familiar pattern, and that enough recognizable signals (for example, transitional words and phrases such as *next, on the other hand, for example*) exist to allow a reformulation of the sender's plan or organization on the student's note paper. When summarizing, the student also makes several assumptions: (1) that the speaker or author has the necessary communications skills to really get his or her message "across"; (2) that the student has the experience to pick up the signals (lexical, syntactical, semantic) to "re-create" the original message; and (3) that the re-created, or reconstituted, message is comparable to the original. All of these considerations about outlining and summarizing need to be examined with high school and college classes. The final assumption about summarizing should be developed in any class in which summarizing is taught. Students must know that their summaries are *not* equivalent to the original spoken or written messages. Their summaries are approximations, highly useful for study purposes but, nevertheless, only one receiver's version of the original. (Summarizing and comprehension are examined in Chapter 9.)

In teaching summarizing at any level, students should be given opportunities to compare different versions produced in class, to discuss their merits and inadequacies, and to consider the summarizing process in general. One useful lesson at all levels from fourth grade to fourteenth is to select a significant passage from the textbook, allow time in class for each student to write a summary, and then compare these, asking such questions as: What was the author's main point? How do we know? In what ways may the author have failed to get across his or her point? In what ways may our own personal experiences have prevented us from getting the point? An important follow-up lesson to this is to have students (fourth grade or fourteenth) write a paragraph on a topic, either related to classwork or of a personal nature. Duplicate these, and have individuals in the class summarize the student writers' paragraphs in one or two sentences. Again, the group may ask the same questions, but now the "author" is present in the room to comment about the success or failure of the summarizers.

Students in high school and college should note the technical distinctions between summary and precis and the precis and synopsis. Teachers need to explain that a summary is defined by five characteristics: (1) no key ideas are omitted, (2) no new ideas are introduced, (3) no personal ideas of the summarizer are included, (4) the original author's point of view is maintained, and (5) the words used are the summarizer's, not the original writer's. A precis, on the other hand, has a sixth characteristic: it follows the order and proportion of the original (that is, if half the original material comes second in order of presentation, then half of the precis—roughly the same proportion—must come second in order). Both summary and precis may be distinguished from a synopsis, which is a brief and general summary, usually used with stories, novels, and poems, and written in broader strokes.

Students at all levels who are taught summarizing techniques should be led to see the five values of summary writing:

1. Summarizing is one of the best student methods for review.
2. It leads to improved ability to condense.
3. It forces a student to distinguish between main and supporting information.
4. It aids in recalling the main points of reading or listening.
5. It leads to the ability to organize and write more coherent and complete answers on written examinations.

RESEARCH IN KINDS OF NOTETAKING AND RESPONDING SKILLS

Most authorities agree that summarizing, outlining, underlining, and other kinds of notetaking are important to effective study. Individual students and teachers often favor one technique, a variant of it, or combinations of methods. Enough research has been completed in the area, however, to allow two generalizations: No single notetaking or responding technique appears to be more effective than another, but any single one is better than none at all.

In a review of five decades of notetaking and responding research, one investigator found no evidence that any one technique was consistently superior to another. Individual students may be more comfortable and successful with one approach, but no evidence points to the "consistent significant superiority of one technique over another." More significant, from the point of view of this book, is the finding that each technique discussed here was significantly successful for an experimental group which utilized it versus a control group which did not (Bizinkauskas 1970).

For practical day-to-day improvement of study skills, a teacher may infer that students should be taught how to use all four methods and given regular practice in their use. Each student may eventually come to favor one over another, but the goal of the teacher is that students do use *some* technique. As two psychologists have noted, "It makes little difference how important material is identified so long as it is identified. This may be done by notetaking, by outlining, by underscoring, or in any other way desired by the reader" (Garrison and Gray 1955).

THE HOMEWORK PROBLEM

Discussion of notetaking and other responding skills leads to one of the most talked about and least researched areas in the study skills program: homework. Homework—defined here as the study students do when they are not under the direct supervision of their teachers (that is, study done at home, in the library, or in study hall)—has been talked about, written about, and argued about for decades.

A survey of the *Readers' Guide to Periodical Literature* and the *Education Index* indicates that almost 500 articles on the subject have been published since the turn of the century! In addition, newspapers and magazines regularly print articles, letters, and editorials on homework. Yet, despite the evident concern (and the millions of student hours spent in preparing homework assignments), little actual research has been done in the area. As one authority noted after examining eight decades of research findings, "One of the few generalizations that can be made is that opinions and practices about homework differ widely" (Hedges 1971, p. 479).

A basic premise of this book is that study skills can be learned. An underlying assumption is that students can become self-directed enough to manage study tasks on their own—in the classroom, in the library, and at home. Therefore, homework is an important dimension of an effective study skills program. Before incorporating regular home assignments into a program, however, teachers need to think through their own answers to four important questions:

1. What are the arguments against homework?
2. What are the arguments in favor of it?
3. Can research findings help shape my thinking?
4. Shall I give homework assignments or not?

What's Wrong with Homework?

Those who argue against homework note that students, particularly younger ones, are fatigued after a long school day and need rest, relaxation, and play. They worry that students will be deprived of opportunities to grow in nonacademic areas, neglecting, for example, their interests in sports, music, hobbies, camping, collecting, and other important dimensions of life. Critics of conventional homework practices also believe that parents sometimes either do much of the homework themselves (thus undermining all efforts to promote self-reliance and study skill disciplines) or approach lessons in ways that are contrary to the teacher's (thus confusing students and increasing misunderstanding of the content to be studied). Critics also point to the frequent distractions found in the typical home (ringing telephones, phonograph music, television, and ordinary household noises) and the lack of resources (good dictionaries, modern encyclopedias, and other reference materials).

Why Should Students Do Homework?

Arguments in favor of homework generally fall under three headings: (1) better home-school relations, (2) improved study skills, and (3) extended time for coverage of subject matter. Teachers, parents, and administrators who support regular homework for students point out that it is a device for keeping the home and school in touch: parents are able to see what the curriculum is as it is reflected in the assignments students bring home, they may note particular teachers' approaches to the subject matter, and they can keep regular watch on student progress—or lack of progress. In addition, advocates generally note that it is somehow good for character in that it forces the student to learn to budget time, follow written and oral directions, make better use of out-of-school time, and develop habits of discipline and self-reliance. Supporters also note that the information and ideas encompassed in each subject-matter field have increased so greatly in recent years that there is not time enough in the school day for teachers to cover all material in depth.

What Does Research Reveal?

Few controlled studies have been completed in this area. In one examination of almost 300 articles reported in a thirty-year period, fewer than 6 percent were reports of experimental studies (Goldstein 1960). In general, findings have been equivocal or contradictory: "Many of the researchers can be criticized from the standpoint of design, unclear description of procedures, inadequate measuring instruments and failure to explain different results for subgroups within the sampling" (Strang 1967, p. 28).

Survey results are not encouraging. One reported that (1) current homework practices did not harmonize with research-related to sound principles of teaching and learning; (2) differences among individual students were ignored; (3) most teachers do not correct, grade, and return homework assignments; and (4) homework seldom involved student research or problem solving (Bond and Smith, 1966).

What Should Teachers Do About Homework?

Previous chapters on listening, reading, vocabulary, and thinking have regularly pointed to recommendations which rest on solid research findings. When confronted by "the homework problem," teachers find few directions in reviews of research and, perhaps, some befuddlement in arguments for and against the practice. What should individual teachers do? Answers must be based upon

1. Perceptions and knowledge of their students' backgrounds, needs, interests, and readiness levels
2. The philosophy and practices of the school and the school system
3. Convictions about the efficacy of study skills instruction to carry over into the nonclass activities of students.

In other words, there is no single or "official" answer to the question. This book is posited upon the belief that students, under the guidance of skillful teachers, can learn to study and become self-directed in study tasks. The answer *suggested* here is: Assign homework but show students how to do it.

The carefully prepared *study guide* may be the best single instrument for improving homework (and for solving "the homework problem"). Before examining study guides in the concluding part of this chapter, here are four general suggestions about homework practices, based on observation of classrooms where teachers make homework work.

Discuss Homework with Students

Students may be encouraged in group discussions to spell out their own feelings about homework and discover common problems associated with study outside the classroom. Such discussion may be stimulated by questions such as: What is the best home assignment you have ever had? What kinds of assignments do you dislike? Where do you do homework? When? What kinds of problems do you encounter? Secondary school students may examine the arguments for or against homework in general; college students need to see that, for them, "homework" is a major part of college life and needs to be reexamined from a more adult point of view. Time spent in class discussion at the beginning of the school year is time well spent if teachers allow frustrations and problems to surface and frankly express their own reservations about common practices and their justifications for including home assignments in their lessons or courses.

Show Students Ways to Overcome Distractions

Class discussion may lead to examinations of the two major causes of distraction: *emotional* (In what ways do your feelings interfere with study? Which emotions regularly get in your way? Can you overcome emotional distractions? Should you? How can you handle them and still study?) and *physical* (Can your brain work well if you are fatigued? Ill? Undernourished? What part does sleep play in study? Can a person be mentally fatigued?). Students may list common distractions apart from the emotional and physical (noise, movement, poor habits) and then note ways to overcome such common distractions (such as establishing a regular study time, choosing a quiet work area, planning ahead, periodically checking study plans). Elementary and middle-school students need opportunities to examine problems and solutions together in class; many may see for the first time that they can control at least parts of their lives (the academic) by physical arrangements (studying alone in a favorite place for a brief time each day). High school and college students also need to be reminded that as individuals they, too, can influence their own success by their decisions about time and place of study.

Link Notetaking Skills with Home Assignments

One approach to study outside the classroom is through discussions of the difficulties students find in concentration. Teachers need to explain that everyone's attention span varies at different times during the day or hour; that, for almost all people, it is short, and that one can only pay attention to one thing at a time. Many students, particularly those who have been academically unsuccessful, do not realize that attention is not an aspect of intelligence; some believe that because they cannot concentrate, they are somehow less able. Teachers need to discuss problems of attention, perhaps note problems of attention, perhaps note problems they themselves have encountered in not being able to concentrate, and demonstrate these problems in a variety of ways. One way is to leave students, place a watch so that it can just be heard, listen carefully to notice how the ticking seems to increase in intensity and can fade and increase again, observe how difficult it is to attend to the ticking because of outside distractions, and realize how transitory concentration is even when forced as in these experimental conditions.

At this point, teachers may link previous instruction in notetaking techniques to the discussion of concentration by noting that concentration is maximized by pen-and-paper responses to assignments. Students at all levels need to realize that simple listing on paper of important points in reading forces the student reader to concentrate on the material more than if he or she read casually. Underscoring and marginal commenting help concentration and, as has been noted earlier in this chapter, outlining and reading to summarize force the student reader to pay greater attention to assignments. This is an appropriate time to review the SQ3R method or one of its variations (see Chapter 3). Students should come to realize that problems in concentration are common to all, and that notetaking, in one form or another, helps them to focus attention on the work before them.

It may be that the best justification for homework is that it allows teachers and students to further develop notetaking skills. Instruction in outlining, summarizing, and other recording study skills may extend outward from the classroom to the study hall, the library, and the home. Students may be given more frequent opportunities to read-with-pen-in-hand, noting an author's main points, organizational plan, biases, and approach to the material as they read their textbook assignments outside the classroom. Instead of saying, "Read Chapter 9," a teacher may say, "As you read Chapter 9 . . . "

1. "Note what you believe are the five most important points the author wants to get across," or
2. "List the five points and under each, in outline form, note two or three supporting examples or details," or
3. "After noting the five main points, write a summary of the chapter as it might appear in a telegram or a magazine digest article," or
4. "Write a one-sentence summary that includes the author's five main points," or
5. "Be prepared to tell the class tomorrow (from notes) why these five points are important to a person studying this topic," or
6. "Turn the five points into five questions which may be given to the class as a quiz," or
7. "Be prepared to explain (using your written notes) ways in which the author might have done a better job in writing the chapter," or
8. "List five important questions about the chapter that the author did not raise," or
9. "Use the author's five main points as the basis of a short paragraph relating the topic to your personal life," or
10. Any combination of the above.

Correct and Return Homework to Students

A consistent criticism of homework programs is that teachers too often fail to systematically correct, grade, and return assignments to students (Bond and Smith 1966). When teachers choose to "play the homework game" (as one student phrases it), they have an obligation to respond to the work that their students do outside of class. If they assigned questions to be answered, they should take time to read the answers, or at least "go over" them in class. If they tried to stimulate research or creative thinking, they must allow students time to share their discoveries and ideas with the group. When a policy of homework-for-the-sake-of-homework prevails in a class or a school, it is time for teachers, administrators, and parents to reexamine their conceptions of not only the study skills program, but their philosophy of education.

USING STUDY GUIDES TO IMPROVE NOTETAKING AND HOMEWORK

Study guides come in all shapes, sizes, and degrees of complexity. They serve to guide students through lectures, assigned readings, laboratory work, mathematics problems, and other learning tasks. Sometimes they challenge students and promote effective study habits; sometimes not. They have been little researched but frequently discussed and recommended in the professional literature. How may they be used to improve students' notetaking skills? Homework and school assignments? General study skills development? The following offers suggestions for using study guides.

Begin with a Simple Guide

Some of the study guides described in books and articles on improving school learning are provocative, comprehensive, and often more detailed than the textbook assignments they are intended to lead students through! They may serve as models or goals. For teachers who want guides to immediately improve homework and study skills, they may prove cumbersome, even nonproductive. At the beginning of the course or school year, a guide should be direct and to-the-point.

The simplest guide may be a duplicated set of directions, telling students how to respond to the assignment. Instead of instructing students to "Read Chapter 9," the teacher prepares specific directions, such as:

Page 100:   The main idea for the chapter is in the second paragraph. Find it and rephrase it as a question in your notebook.

101–102:   Skim this material quickly. You can return to it later. (*Recapitulate* means "repeat in concise form." How does the Latin root for *head* get in here?)

102:   Why doesn't it change? The author implies the question, but doesn't answer it. Write your answer.

103:   The author gives evidence here to support the main idea. Don't forget to copy it in your notebook.

104:   Slow down and read this very carefully. This is the heart of the chapter!

105:   Before you read this, go back and check the main idea. Is the author getting off the subject? Why?

106:   The italicized statement must be important. Copy it.

107:   Stop here and write a two-sentence summary of the chapter so far.

Such a guide may contain as much or as little help as the teacher wants to provide. It tells the students, page by page or paragraph by paragraph, what to focus on, what to skip over quickly, what to remember, what to ignore. It serves as a *map* to lead the class from point to point in the class or home assignment. It may include questions, suggestions for further thought or creative endeavors, specific directions for notetaking, and ideas for research and individual projects.

Such a Teacher-Over-My-Shoulder Guide is *not* intended only for unsophisticated students. High school and college teachers have used variations of it successfully; students at all grade levels have profited from them. It is wonderfully flexible and, most important, highly personal. A teacher may relate an assignment to a previous class discussion, reteach key vocabulary items, ask questions geared to a specific group within the class, and focus questions and comments for individual students (for example, "Tom, isn't this what you and Bob asked about last week?"). Clearly, such a guide provides more effectively for study skills development than "Read Chapter 9 for tonight." The wonder is that more teachers do not take the additional planning time to improve notetaking, homework, and learning through the use of such a guide! (For a description of an excellent variant of Teacher-Over-My-Shoulder, see the Selective Reading Guide-O-Rama, Cunningham and Shablak 1975.)

Ask Many Kinds of Questions

As has been frequently noted, some teachers restrict their questions on study guides (and in class) to the factual level (those of the Who-Did-What-When-Where-To Whom-How variety). Such questions have an important place on guides; they may provide a jumping-off place to greater comprehension and learning. But, as many authorities point out, they constitute a base level: other kinds of questions must be asked.

One popular theory on levels of questions notes literal, interpretive, and applied comprehension levels (Herber 1978). Another also distinguishes three: forming, interpreting, and applying concepts (Taba 1965). The influential *Taxonomy of Educational Objecives* notes: Level 1—to know; Level 2—to comprehend; and Level 3—to apply, to analyze, to synthesize, and to evaluate (Bloom et al. 1956). Some study guides group questions so that students are forced to move from one level to the next. In following the guide (even one of the Teacher-Over-My-Shoulder variety), they first answer factual or literal level questions, then questions that encourage them to interpret, and, finally, questions that make them evaluate, synthesize, analyze, and apply. Sometimes, such guides are coded to individualize instruction so that "immature" students respond to first-level type questions, while "average and brighter" students respond to second- and/or third-level type questions (see, for example, Tutolo 1977). Sometimes, such guides arrange questions in reverse order, having students start with highest level questions and go backward to Level 1-type questions (that is, from Herber's applied to literal comprehension levels) (Donlan 1978). There is no clear-cut research evidence to suggest that any one way of arranging questions in a study guide is superior. There is considerable consensus among authorities, however, that many kinds of questions need to be included.

Even the simplest guide should include questions at the factual level (Who did what? When? Where?), the interpretive level (Why?), and the highest or applied level (In what ways did this affect future actions? Is this true, according to the standards set up by the author? What do you infer from this?).

The difference between guides that remain at the factual level and those that promote higher levels of thinking may be seen by contrasting the following homework guides, both prepared for a fifth-grade social studies class.

☐ Read pages 79 to 108. Answer in complete sentences the ten questions on page 109. (The ten are all of the Who-What-Where-When variety.)

☐ Look at the photographs of Mexico (pages 79–108). Come to class tomorrow prepared to answer questions: Why do you think most Mexicans live in the highlands? (page 82) Why have few people settled in the tropical forest? (page 89) How do you think this land has been used? Why do you think only a few Mexican people live in the rock-covered mountains? (See photograph on page 99.) What problems do these people have to deal with? Of all these three types of land, which is best suited for settlement? Why? Write out your answers to these questions in your notebooks so that you can better participate in tomorrow's discussion.

Include Practice in Notetaking Skills

It is not enough to teach various notetaking skills in class se sions. tudents need daily practice in using the skills in a variety of s tuat ons. A study guide may include opportunities for students to apply these skills as they complete assignments in school or at home. It may note:

☐ As you read pages 90 to 120 at home, list in your notebook the five key ideas the author wants you to focus upon. (Does he or she help you locate these ideas by using italics, boldface type, or some other device? Can you rephrase these key ideas as possible test questions?)

☐ Chapter 8 seems to be based on an outline. Read it first for the ideas, then go back and see if you can see the skeleton underlying it. There are five main headings. List these in your notebook and fill in as much of the basic outline as possible.

☐ Read up to page 95 and write a three-sentence summary. Next, read through page 105 and write another three-sentence summary. In your notebook, combine *both* summaries into a single sentence.

☐ In Chapter 10, the author uses several transitional words to indicate a chronological arrangement (such as *first*, *later*, and *finally*). Some of these are obvious; some are subtle. In your notebook, list all that you can identify.

☐ Of all the notetaking systems we have discussed this year, which do you think is most appropriate to use on Chapter 15? Be prepared to justify your choice in class tomorrow.

Review Homework Guides in Class

A comprehensive study guide may provide students with an overview, plus assignments, for one or several weeks' study. Indeed, a *unit study guide* often includes general and specific objectives, core and optional related learning activities, all questions and assignments, plus a bibliography. A unit guide, because of the extent and depth of coverage, may require an introduction. The brief guides discussed here, however, are primarily intended to ease students' entry into a single class or homework assignment. Teachers need to remember that, no matter how well written guides may be, they do not always introduce themselves. Class time (at the end of a period for homework guides) needs to be spent telling students how to use the guide.

The simplest guides (lists of questions to be answered or directions of the Teacher-Over-My-Shoulder variety) need to be distributed and, perhaps, read aloud to make sure that everyone understands the teacher's language. Vocabulary and syntactical problems need to be cleared up before students take a homework guide home because the teacher cannot really remain over the student's shoulder. If a guide is problem-centered, the teacher may need to develop the background to the problem and insure that the problem is understood in all its dimensions by everyone in the group. If the guide is written on the chalkboard, time must be set aside for the group to copy it. If the guide is duplicated, typographical and/or reproduction errors need to be accounted for.

One of the most effective ways to introduce a short study guide for class or homework assignments is suggested by the Guided Reading Procedure (Manzo 1975). Students are instructed to read through the assignment before the guide is distributed. Then, with books closed, they tell what they remember as the teacher records their responses on the board. Responses frequently trigger fresh responses, and much of the content of the assignment is placed on the board. In his description of the Guided Reading Procedure, Manzo (1975, p. 290) notes the "spiralling effect which often draws in even the most silent students." GPR is a valuable teaching technique in itself; it is especially useful in introducing an assignment because after the recall-respond-record session, students then take their study guide, reread the assignment with the guide's assistance, and come back together as a group (the next day, if the assignment is homework), and compare their first round of recorded recollections with their study notes. The approach is stimulating and remarkably effective.

Develop Own Guides

Beginning teachers sometimes ask, "Why can't really effective study guides be published?" The answer, of course, is that one of their primary sources of effectiveness is their uniqueness. An effective guide is created by an individual teacher for an individual class comprised of many separate, distinct, and unique people. It serves as a bridge between a group of individual students and study material which is, by traditional design, impersonal, objective, generalized, and often unrelated to the lives of the people in the group. It is the teacher's responsibility (and great challenge) to make the objective subjective, the generalized specific, the unrelated related, and the impersonal personal.

Effective guides, therefore, frequently include directions, questions, and comments such as these (from a fifth-grade social studies guide):

1. Read the four paragraphs on page 90 about the Battle of Bunker Hill. The first says General Gage was "unpleasantly surprised" when he saw the trenches and cannons the patriots had on the hill. In your notebook, write answers to these three questions:
   a. Why was he surprised?
   b. Why shouldn't he have been surprised?
   c. If *you* had been the general, would you have been surprised? Why or why not?
2. Why was the hill so important? Be prepared to tell the class the answer you write in your study notes. (Bill and David should be able to answer this one!)
3. Have you ever seen a cannon? Where? When? What did it look like? How many men would be needed to pull one up a hill at night? Be prepared to share your answers.
4. Paragraph 3 says that the third time the British marched up the hill, "few shots were fired at them." In your notebook, write the sentence that tells why few shots were fired.

5. Have you ever seen Bunker Hill? Do you know anyone who has? Can you find a picture of it? How high is it compared to hills in our own area? Write your answers in your notes, and be prepared to share them.

6. Paragraph 4 says the Americans lost the battle. How could they have won it? What went wrong for them? If you had been the American general, what would *you* have done differently? Again, write your answers to these three questions. (Lisa has researched this subject more than others. She can lead the discussion.)

7. What does it feel like to lose? Can you lose and win at the same time? How? Compare the feelings of the American soldiers with your own at some time in your life. Don't write these down. Think about them. We will share these ideas together.

The teacher prepared this guide for a class she knows well. Another teacher in another class would use different questions, different phrases and terms, a different focus. An effective guide is, in all senses of the word, a highly *personal* teaching tool.

Select Guides that Encourage Divergent Thinking

Mass education is often criticized for its emphasis on "right" answers. It is said that students are encouraged to seek out correct answers, accepted concepts and theories, and establishment points of view. An effective study guide, especially one posited upon the belief that effective study skills are intrinsically related to effecting thinking skills, needs to include directions, comments, and questions that encourage divergent, as opposed to convergent, thinking. In addition to helping students study the content of a subject, a guide needs to help them scrutinize and evaluate it and *use* it to extend their horizons and explore further. It should provide practice in important critical reading-thinking skills, such as distinguishing fact from opinion, recognizing bias, and evaluating sources. It should allow opportunities for inference-making, inference-testing, predicting, and anticipating outcomes. It should give practice in problem solving, associational thinking, and creative thinking (see Chapter 8).

The fifth-grade social studies guide previously quoted also included the following questions:

1. General Gage is quoted in the first paragraph as shouting, "Drive those rebels off the hill!" How do we *know* he said that? In your notebook, give at least two answers to the question.

2. Paragraph 2 says, "Three thousand British soldiers marched up the hill." How do we know that? (Could there have been 300?

Who counted so exactly? Should the author have said *approximately* 3000 soldiers? Why?) Be prepared to discuss your answers.
3. None of the American or British soldiers are alive today. In your notebook, write three ways in which we could know what happened more than two hundred years ago.

Questions such as these are too often missing from textbooks and commercially-prepared materials. Study guides—if they are intended to do more than promote factual learning—must include questions and comments that challenge an author's authority, raise questions in students' minds about sources of information, and stimulate thought. Guides also need to include opportunities for students to ask questions and react to the text. Open-ended questions and space for personal reaction belong in all study guides.

STUDY GUIDES AND HOMEWORK

Study guides come in all shapes, sizes, and degrees of complexity. As the previous discussion indicated, skillful teachers may exploit them in a number of ways: to act as a teacher-over-the-student's-shoulder, to ask a variety of questions, to give practice in notetaking skills, to make such textbooks relevant and personal, and to promote creative and divergent thinking.

One of the best single justifications for preparing and using guides is that *they structure homework*. Instead of the vague, "Read Chapter 9 for tonight," teachers present students with a clear-cut set of directions for what to do with Chapter 9.

A homework study guide may:

1. Define the purpose for the reading and study.
2. Explain difficult words, terms, and concepts.
3. Provide definite questions to answer (at all levels of comprehension: literal, interpretive, and applied).
4. Specify notetaking skills ("List the ten main points," "Outline the first 3 pages," or "Summarize the main idea on page 42").
5. Relate the material to previous learnings and the lives of students.
6. Personalize by speaking directly to individuals and, thus, provide for individual differences.
7. Stimulate creative and divergent thinking through specific questions, activities, and research projects.
8. Provide the student (and parents) with a *document* defining all dimensions of the learning task.

Definitive, controlled research on the power of study guides to positively influence learning has yet to be reported. Studies on the positive relationship between homework and study guides are incomplete. Yet the observations and insights of successful teachers through the years indicate the value of well-prepared study guides to "pull together" and systematize classroom and home study. As one professor of education observed after visiting literally thousands of American schools: "The single feature that distinguished classes where learning was clearly taking place from those where it was not was a printed guide that showed students exactly what to do as they studied, in class and at home." Impressionistic evidence may have no place in reviews of research, but, when research evidence is lacking, teachers may be guided to at least some extent by such an observation.

Idea Box
Notetaking, Homework, and Study Guides

An important first step to notetaking and outlining is to list on the chalkboard all the major points of the lesson and note, as the lesson proceeds, the points under discussion. Students begin to see that there may be a plan behind lectures and classroom presentations.

Simple how-to-do-it presentations present opportunities for notetaking. Have individual students explain to the class how to repair a flat tire, how to make fudge, how to use a book's index. Tell the other students to jot down the specific steps presented. Explain transitional words or phrases, such as *first, second, next, finally.* After the presentations, students should compare the steps they listed and recall the transitions used by the speaker.

One way to begin notetaking and outlining with classes is to distribute duplicated sheets at the beginning of the lesson with the three or four major points clearly stated but with enough space so that students may fill in the examples, details, or evidence presented to support each point. Time should be set aside toward the end of the period so that students may compare their responses. While they are discussing their papers, write on the chalkboard the supporting material which you believe most important. Students may then check their responses to one another's and to yours.

Some teachers occasionally collect—without warning—student notes and return them after careful reading with suggestions for improvement. These notes are kept in student notebooks or folders so that student growth in notetaking skills can be monitored.

To illustrate effective summary writing, have students check on course topics in a good encyclopedia. Here they will see topics, such as "money," "the stock market," or "algebra" boiled down by professional writers into paragraphs and pages. They can also check for literature and discover Homer's *Iliad*, for example, rewritten in a few paragraphs. Encourage students to compare summaries in different encyclopedias: What has been omitted? Which features did both authors consider important? Which summary did you prefer? Why?

Students may write synopses of the novels they read outside of class. They are forced when doing this to make decisions about who are the main and subordinate characters, about the main plot line and any sub-plots, and about the time and place events took place. Their synopses may be neatly written or typed on cards and filed in a central location for class use, or posted on a bulletin board for other students to read. This exercise in summarizing may serve as a stimulus for out-of-class reading by other students.

English teachers may use precis-writing in teaching theme. Students may condense a short story or even a poem into one line, thus forcing them to focus on the exact theme of the work and to exclude relatively minor details of plot, setting, and character.

Once students have grasped the basic skeletal form of an outline, they need practice in filling in simple teacher-prepared (and later student-prepared) outlines. They need to know that the basic outline form helps them select and judge between the important and less important, and also that the form has been standardized through the years to look like this:

  I. Main topic
    A. Subtopic
 II. Main topic
    A. Subtopic
    B. Subtopic
      1.
      2.
        a.
        b.
          1.
          2.

After students recognize outline form, they need practice at using it for their own presentations, both orally and in writing. Ask volunteers to give short talks before the group (first give the others a duplicated outline or write one on the board). Written papers should be accompanied later by a copy of the outline the student writer used to guide his or her preparation of the paper.

When students have learned basic standardized outline forms, encourage them to invent new systems, using color coding, arrows pointing from main topics to subordinate topics, or even circular arrangements. Ask them to explain to the class their reasons for preferring their own personal systems to the standard one, and to present examples for bulletin board display. Advanced students may prepare an outline on overhead transparencies, using more sophisticated techniques such as the overlay, arrows, or colors or varying print sizes to force attention to main points.

High school and college students may seek examples of material that cannot be outlined or summarized. They may start with examples of narrative fiction, poems, and personal essays by famous writers and then go on to discover examples in newspapers and magazines. Help them understand that, although summarizing and outlining are valuable study techniques, all written material does not lend itself to these study methods.

Encourage students to create their own coding systems for responding to reading. They may use colors, stars, boxes, triangles, circles, hearts and flowers, danger signs, and question marks. Suggest that they plan the system, draw up an explanatory chart, and use it on one page of a textbook to show how it works. They may duplicate their systems for class presentation or simply tell about it.

Encourage interested students to use their tape recorders as tools in note-taking. Explain that learning styles differ—some students learn by their ears and some by visualizing. Have them prepare tape recorded notes of a chapter or selection and share their "notes" or their experiences with the group afterwards.

College students may test out—by actual observation—the case against passive underlining presented by one college teacher: "We drive home the argument by describing a student in the college lounge, slouched in an over-stuffed chair. Amid interesting conversations, attractive traffic, and entertaining rock, we find him doing a reading assignment, in one hand the book, in the other a palette of markers. There he sits, transforming the crowded page into what at first glance appears to be a work of abstract art (strong horizontals)" (Policastro 1975, p. 373). Is this a true picture? Do college students study this way? What are the dangers inherent in the underlining method of textbook notation? Ask students to share their observations and comments.

To help students maximize the value of their homework, have them keep Homework Logs in their notebooks with (1) specific assignments written out completely, (2) dates assigned, (3) dates due, (4) dates completed, and (5) personal reactions to the nature and scope of the assignments ("It took much more time than expected," "Impossible to complete in the time set aside," or "May be used later for research paper"). The group should be given opportunities to share their responses to assignments with teachers and with one another.

Encourage students at all levels to share their Coping Techniques. They may post on the chalkboard, especially in elementary or middle school classes, or discuss together ideas they have discovered for best managing problems of time and place for doing homework and personal tricks for overcoming common distractions (such as taking the telephone off the hook or completing assigned reading at odd hours in the early morning).

To encourage accurate notetaking, organize (at most grade levels) a Notetaking Contest. Award one point for each main idea identified and another for each supporting detail or example. Allow time for students to read the selection or chapter while taking notes. (Another point may be added for legible writing and good appearance of the notes.) A "jury" of judges, using an answer key of main ideas and supporting examples, may select the award-winning notes.

Most libraries have books on how to study in their collections. Have students examine these books to discover what advice the authors give on doing homework. Students may give oral reports, prepare lists of ideas for distribution, or make wall posters.

Suggest that volunteers conduct surveys to discover other people's study habits. They may interview students in other grades, teachers, friends, or members of their families. Their collected "Tips on How to Study" may be posted or duplicated.

Suggest that volunteers, working individually or in small groups, develop study guides for material the class will study next week. They should read through the material, prepare questions and comments, suggest activities, note possibly difficult terms and concepts, and prepare summaries. These may be duplicated and distributed to the class for actual use.

Have high school students prepare study guide questions at different levels. Explain the differences between factual and interpretive, and interpretive and applied levels of comprehension. High school and college students can prepare lists and code them according to question levels. These, too, may be duplicated and distributed for study.

References

Bizinkauskas, Peter A. "An Evaluation of the Effectiveness of Tape-Recorder Note-taking Versus Written Note-taking Versus Rereading As A Study Technique." Ph.D. dissertation, Boston University, 1970.

Bloom, Benjamin, et al. *Taxonomy of Educational Objectives, Handbook 1: Cognitive Domain.* New York: David McKay Co., Inc., 1956.

Bond, George W., and George J. Smith. "Homework in the Elementary School." *The National Elementary Principal* 45 (1966): 46–50.

Courtney, Brother Leonard. "Organization Produced." In *Developing Study Skills in Secondary Schools.* Edited by Harold L. Herber. Newark, Del.: International Reading Association, 1965, pp. 77–96.

Cunningham, Dick, and Scott L. Shablak. "Selective Reading Guide-O-Rama: The Content Teacher's Best Friend." *Journal of Reading* 18 (February 1975): 380–382.

Donlan, Dan. "How to Play 29 Questions." *Journal of Reading* 21 (March 1978): 535–541.

Garrison, Karl C., and J. Stanley Gray. *Educational Psychology.* New York: Appleton-Century-Crofts, Inc., 1955, p. 418.

Goldstein, Auram. "Does Homework Help? A Review of Research." *The Elementary School Journal* 60 (1960): 212–224.

Hedges, William D. "Homework." In *The Encyclopedia of Education,* Vol. 4. Edited by Lee C. Deighton. New York: The Macmillan Company and The Free Press, 1971, pp. 477–482.

Herber, Harold L. *Teaching Reading in Content Areas.* Englewood Cliffs, N.J.: Prentice-Hall, Inc., 1978.

Manzo, Anthony V. "Guided Reading Procedure." *Journal of Reading* 18 (January 1975): 287–291.

Palmatier, Robert A. "Acquisition and Utility of Three Note-taking Procedures." Ph.D. dissertation, Syracuse, New York: Syracuse University, 1968.

Palmatier, Robert A. "A Note-taking System for Learning." *Journal of Reading* 17 (October 1973): 36–39.

Palmatier, Robert A. "Note-taking Habits of College Students." *Journal of Reading* 18 (December 1974): 215–218.

Policastro, Michael. "Notetaking: The Key to College Success." *Journal of Reading* 18 (February 1975): 372–375.

Strang, Ruth M. *Guided Study and Homework: What Research Says to the Teacher.* Washington, D.C.: National Education Association, 1967.

Taba, Hilda. "The Teaching of Thinking." *Elementary English* 42 (1965): 534–542.

Tutolo, Daniel J. "The Study Guide—Types, Purpose and Value." *Journal of Reading* 20 (March 1977): 503–507.

8

USING RESEARCH SKILLS: THE LIBRARY AND THE RESEARCH PAPER

Intrinsic to any successful study skills program is systematic, organized instruction in the use of the library and the development of the library research paper. Such instruction has three overlapping concerns: (1) introducing the library to *all* students (not just the "college-bound"); (2) teaching basic library skills needed to learn, both in school and after graduation; and (3) providing guided opportunities for personal search and discovery.

It is ironic that at a time in history when the humblest school or neighborhood library offers more ideas, information, and possible insights—and in greater range and depth—than students can encounter in a lifetime of formal schooling or exposure to popular media, many are unable to use the card catalogue, locate a current journal, find books to assist them in solving personal, family, or vocational problems, or discover the intellectual and emotional pleasures of questing through the shelves.

Suggestions follow for introducing young people to their libraries, teaching basic library study skills, developing "library appreciation," and setting up opportunities for personal research. The first part of this chapter discusses ways to introduce students to the library, teach needed library skills, and encourage individual search and discovery. Approaches to the writing and evaluation of library research papers and a list of basic library research skills are then presented. The appendix to the chapter discusses a Student Guide Book for Research Reports (which may be modified for various grade levels). An Idea Box concludes the chapter.

INTRODUCING STUDENTS TO THE LIBRARY

All students need to be introduced to the workings of the typical library. Then they need to be shown how to use basic library skills and given regular practice in their use. They also need to be encouraged by concerned adults (their teachers and librarians) to experience the pleasures of extending their horizons through the world of print.

Many children come into school programs with a high degree of library awareness. Parents or other interested adults have taken them to libraries in their early years, encouraged them to participate in story hours, poetry readings, puppet shows, films, and other library-sponsored activities, and, most important of all, allowed them to browse and check out books for themselves. These fortunate students are familiar with the physical setting and are comfortable with the routines; they have often developed high positive feelings about libraries and their own roles as library users. Many other students, however, have never been in a library building, talked to a librarian, browsed, or taken books from the shelves. All teachers need to encourage those students who are already aware of what libraries have to offer to continue their explorations and use, and they must also introduce the others to the rich possibilities of school and public libraries. What can teachers do to introduce or reintroduce students to their libraries?

Take Students to the Library

This suggestion may appear naive to some teachers, but observation indicates that many students have never been into a school or public library. Teachers need to arrange informal tours with classes, indicating directional signs, posted rules and regulations, physical arrangements, floor plans, the locations of the circulation (or loan) desk, the reference desk, special collections, microfilms, magazines or periodicals, and copying machines. Students need to walk around the rooms, look at other people using the facilities, and later talk about their observations. Several excellent guides to student use of libraries stress the importance of tours and other orientations. They also provide suggestions for teacher-guided visits or tours by staff members (see, for example, Shapiro 1978; Katz 1979; Whipple 1975; and Brogan and Buck 1969, written for college-level students).

Invite a Librarian to Speak to the Class

Nonusers of libraries are often intimidated by the librarian. One way to overcome student fears is to invite the school or public librarian into the classroom to discuss the uses and purposes of libraries, to speak informally of a librarian's training and responsibilities, and to answer questions about procedures and practices. Students should have opportunities in class to discuss the types of questions usually asked of librarians (directional questions, ready reference questions, research questions), the need to spell out the scope and purpose of questions (How much do I want on the subject? Do I need elementary or advanced material? Do I need current information? Must the information be in a special form?), and the value of writing questions in advance (see Katz 1979, pp. 8-12). Teachers can discuss these concerns in class before the library visit, but the presence and responses of an actual librarian during the discussion helps ease student discomforts.

Talk About Libraries

Students should have opportunities in class to discuss the history of libraries in America, the place of libraries in the development of civilization, famous libraries, famous people who educated themselves in libraries, and the possibilities of self-education for them after they have completed high school or college (for information, see Breswick 1967; Branscomb 1940; Gould 1965). Elementary school students may conduct panel discussions or debates around Shapiro's statement, "Learning your way around libraries—any kind of library—makes you your own teacher" (Shapiro 1978, p. 2); high school students, her comment that "education is not totally school-based" (p. 171); and college students, the suggestion made in the 1950s by a group of college librarians, disillusioned with the lecture-textbook-reserve reading pattern of college instruction, that "the library is the school" and that large lectures and traditional classroom instruction be curtailed in favor of independent study by students in the library (Shores 1966).

However the individual teacher handles the matter, it remains of paramount importance that all students are physically introduced to their library, told about the purpose and functions of libraries, and meet actual librarians face-to-face.

Encourage Library Research Projects

The best single way to introduce students to the possibilities of the library, as many teachers have discovered, is to set up *personal* (even private) library search projects. In the years that students spend in school they will need to use reference books, the periodical indexes, and the card catalog; the skills they acquire in basic library use will affect their academic success. However, many teachers have long noted that the most effective approach for getting students into the library (and for keeping them returning in later life) is to start with nonacademic, nonschool-like, nonscholarly projects. Such teachers encourage students to spell out specific questions *they* personally want answered. All introductory instruction in the use of the library can then be based around "ways to answer your question." Shapiro (1978) gives general questions of this nature:

1. What kind of person am I?
2. What kind of person do I want to be?
3. How can I become economically independent?
4. What should I know about social security? Health insurance? Income taxes? Voting?
5. How do I develop whatever creative ability I have?
6. What kind of future is in store for me in the year 2000?

Shapiro devotes almost eighty pages to showing students how they can develop specific library skills needed in seeking out information about their personal questions.

Most teachers, however, can set up situations on their own in an introductory unit on library use which allow students to practice basic skills as they pursue their own quests. Recently, students from an urban high school jotted down these questions on cards distributed at the beginning of the course:

1. Do I have to do jury duty? (The student had just turned eighteen and had been summoned to jury duty, a responsibility he felt interfered with his summer job.)
2. Is a ten-year-old automobile with only 20,000 miles of use necessarily a good buy?
3. Is "spot-reducing" a way to take excess poundage off a particular body area?
4. Can acne be cured by vitamins?
5. Does writing a resume really help a person get a job?
6. Is it true that going to college does not always mean you get a higher salary later on?

Other questions focused on drug abuse, pregnancy, religion, and parental conflicts. Students did not share their questions with the group, only with the teacher. In class sessions and library visits, they learned to use reference books, periodical indexes, and the card catalog. In practice sessions in the library, they sought answers to *their* questions, always with their teacher acting as a resource person. At the end of a week, each student reported privately to the teacher on the results of the individual search and discovery projects. Only after the teacher was satisfied that certain basic library skills were mastered in the personal research projects did the class as a whole meet to share more academic projects. At the end of a period of a dozen library activity sessions, when all students had completed two or three individual response projects, the class "transferred" the skills developed in their personal quests to the content of the high school course. Such an approach to library study skills assumes a teacher who cares about individualization and is sympathetic to students' personal questions, as well as an easily available school or local public library. The approach may be modified by individual teachers to provide a more meaningful and personal introduction to library study skills than found in even the best manuals and traditional formal instruction.

TEACHING BASIC LIBRARY SKILLS

A professor at a large university tells of encountering one of his own graduate students before the card catalog in the university library. Somewhat timidly, the student asked, "What are those cards you're going through? I've seen people using them but never had the nerve before to ask." He explained, wondering to himself how a student could graduate from high school and college unable to manage what is probably the best single information source in any school or college. His experience raises several questions for teachers developing a study skills program: What library skills should students master? Which are truly basic? Which cut across all subject areas? How can they most effectively be taught?

A systematic way of approaching basic library study skills is suggested here. After students have been introduced to the library, the librarian, and the concept of the library as a learning resource, they need to learn how to locate general information through reference books, specific and current information through the periodical indexes, and ideas and information in greater depth through books obtained by means of the card catalog. These three approaches, basic to intelligent library use at all levels, are examined under the three headings, reference books, periodical indexes, and the card catalog.

Reference Books

Explain that such information as names, dates, and general background on a topic is best obtained through use of reference books such as encyclopedias, dictionaries, and almanacs.

Show students several *encyclopedias* in the library, and tell them something of the history and development of encyclopedias (by looking up and reading aloud, for example, the entry "Encyclopedia" in a good encyclopedia!). Also, show, by examples, how volumes are arranged by alphabet and how the index works. Naturally, such instruction is best accomplished not by classroom lectures but by actual demonstration *in the library*. Explain that encyclopedias give background for a topic to be studied, an overview, dates, history, and biography, and that they are the best tool for learning rapidly and in a general way about a variety of topics such as constitutional conventions, rabies, Albert Schweitzer, Kamikaze pilots, and so on.

Show that *dictionaries* provide definitions of words, spellings, pronunciations, and etymologies. Explain that dictionaries differ—some are ideal for quick use while writing, while others give extensive word histories and are more appropriate for certain kinds of research projects. Make it clear to students that there is no such entity as "The Dictionary." Libraries contain dozens of dictionaries, some up-to-date, some prescriptive, some descriptive; all are human-made tools subject to vagaries and inconsistencies, and none constitutes absolute authority. Students may contrast differing definitions in several dictionaries, note publication dates, and study the quality and comprehensiveness of definitions to see that when they quote a dictionary it is important for them and their readers to note the exact name of the dictionary with its publisher and date.

Show students several *biographical sources.* Note that many are available in the average library (for example, *Who's Who in America, Who's Who of American Women, Who's Who in Finance and Industry*), and that the best way of tracking down a name is through the *Biographical Dictionaries Master Index* (Detroit: Gale, 1976 to date) which is truly a "master index" to fifty-three biographical dictionaries, covering over 800,000 names. Students should be encouraged, during this introduction, to check information about people who interest them in fields such as sports, music, politics, and so on. (How old is Mohammad Ali? When and where were each of the Beatles born? Where did the president go to school? College?)

To help those students who are seeking odd types of facts (such as the average age of people in California, the number of Japanese automobiles imported in 1980, or the percentage of rock records compared to country-and-western records sold in a given year), show them how *almanacs* work. Explain that after checking the index of the encyclopedia, they should check a major almanac, such as *The World Almanac* (New York: Newspaper Enterprise Association, 1868 to date) or other yearbooks, directories, atlases, and gazeteers. Such sources provide summaries, charts, and statistics on almost all current and not-so-current topics.

Periodical Indexes

For information and ideas more current than those found in books, students need to use the periodical indexes. Explain that magazines and other periodicals are more up-to-date, more apt to present different aspects of a controversy, longer and more informative than reference book articles but shorter than books, and often easier to read. (Students should be encouraged to "test out" these four characteristics in their own library explorations.) Tell students the difference between popular and semi-popular magazines, and between these and scholarly and technical journals. Show them specific examples, taken from the shelves, of each type and ask them to suggest titles of magazines they already know and read. (This general introduction to periodicals is an excellent opportunity to broaden student knowledge of the wide range of magazines published each week and month; for many students this may be the only opportunity they have to receive adult guidance in magazine selection and reading.)

Next, explain that it is not necessary to go through the library stacks to locate an article on a specific topic: *Readers' Guide to Periodical Literature* (New York: Wilson, 1900 to date), *Access* (Syracuse, New York: Gaylord Brothers, 1975 to date) or *Popular Periodic Index* (Camden, New Jersey: Robert Bottooff, 1973 to date), among others, provide indexes to current articles. (For more specialized indexes, see, for example, Katz 1979, pp. 38–51.) Students should then be given some practice in the library (with the teacher or librarian present) in locating specific information, using, for example, the *Readers' Guide.* (How would I find arguments *against* trade with the Republic of China? *For* trade with Cuba? Where could I find a current definition, by a musician, of "rock"?) Remind students that when they use one of the indexes they should jot down (1) the name of the magazine, (2) the exact date published, (3) the exact title of the article, and (4) the page numbers where the article appeared.

The Card Catalog

For more substantial background on a topic, students need to go directly to books. To locate the best books for them in their search, they need to know how to use the card catalog. This involves competence in several specific skills. Four suggestions for teachers for helping students develop this competence are given.

Explain three cards.   Show the students the card catalog and explain that the trays or drawers contain 3 × 5 cards arranged in alphabetic order, three for each book in that library's collection: one with the author's name on top (last name first), one with the book's title on top, and one with the subject above. Note that each of the three cards has a *call number* which helps readers find that exact book on the shelves.

Discuss other information on cards.   Show the students in class or in the library, that other important information is given on the cards; such as subtitles, names of translators, illustrators, or coauthors; the place and date of publication; the name and date of publication; the name of the publisher; the number of pages in the book; and the *tracings*, or subject headings, under which the book is listed in the catalog so that they can trace other, similar books.

Explain the call number system.   Students should know that there are two widely-used systems in the United States: the Dewey Decimal Classification, used in smaller libraries; and the Library of Congress Classification System, used in large public and university libraries. To give students some idea of how and why a classification system is used, tell them how Melvil Dewey, more than one hundred years ago, tried to make the library user's task easier by, first, assigning a fixed number in the hundreds to different kinds of books, and then a number in tens (hence the ''decimal'' system) for subdivisions within the different larger categories. The Dewey System is simple enough so that teachers can duplicate it for the class with a decimal breakdown for at least one of the major groupings:

000   General works (books about books, magazines, newspapers, lists of books)
100   Philosophy and psychology (human behavior, but not psychiatry)
200   Religion (history of religion, mythology)
300   Social sciences (economics, occupations)
400   Language (linguistics, grammar, dictionaries)
500   Pure sciences (physics, chemistry, botany)
600   Useful arts and applied sciences (engineering, medicine, including psychiatry, farming)
700   Arts and recreation (music, sports)
800   Literature (plays, poetry, speeches)
900   History (also includes travel books, geography, biography)

For the 600 grouping, Useful Arts and Applied Science, Dewey used these subdivisions:

610   Medicine
620   Engineering
630   Agriculture
640   Home economics
650   Business
660   Chemical technology
670   Manufactures
680   Mechanical trades
690   Building construction

Point out that the Library of Congress System has the advantage of a broader base because it is based on the twenty-six letters of the alphabet and, in many ways, it is more flexible and capable of greater expansion:

A   General works
B   Philosophy and religion
C   History and auxiliary sciences (such as coin collecting and geneology)
D   Universal and old world history
E-F American history
G   Geography and anthropology (including folklore and sports)
H   Social sciences (such as economics, sociology)
J   Political science
K   Law
L   Education
M   Music
N   Fine arts
P   Language and literature
Q   Science (including mathematics)
R   Medicine
S   Agriculture (including hunting and fishing)
T   Technology (including engineering and manufacturing)
U   Military science
V   Naval science
Z   Bibliography and library science

Explain that in the Dewey System fiction is arranged by the author's last name, but in the Library of Congress System books by and about the author are grouped together under "P."

Point out that library users do *not* have to memorize these numbers because they can follow directional signs in most libraries to locate the books they want.

Give students practice in use of the card catalog.   Much important information may be provided in class through discussion and duplicated explanations, but developing true competence in management of the card catalog requires demonstration and practice. Students need to be shown exactly how to look up a book's call number and find the book on the shelves. Then they need actual practice, under the guidance of a teacher or librarian, in locating several books before they are "on their own."

The anecdote about the graduate student, which began this section, is unfortunately a true one. In general, students do not always know how to use the card catalog. Elementary teachers assume that the necessary skills will be taught later by secondary school teachers; secondary school and college teachers assume that the skills have been taught earlier in the grades. These assumptions lead to the development (by default) of countless students, at all levels, who cannot locate a book in a library.

PREPARING THE RESEARCH PAPER

Learning to use the library is more than simple groundwork for writing the research paper. It is, for most serious students and their teachers, a basic foundation for study in all school subjects and, perhaps more important, a key to learning and the pleasures of learning throughout life. However, for many students in many schools, the culmination of introductory work in library skills is writing a research paper. Therefore, any examination of study skills programs needs to look at research paper writing as a learning activity, its justification, and ways to help students research and write it.

In some secondary schools the research paper seems to be the end point of all instruction: throughout the school year, teachers teach library skills, outlining, notetaking, footnoting, and bibliography-making, preparing classes for the actual production of the paper. In other schools, the process is subordinated to other learning activities if not deleted entirely from the curriculum as overly time-consuming, unrealistic, and too far removed from the lives and concerns of young people. Teachers in both kinds of schools advance support for their beliefs and practices. Their positions may be summarized by noting:

1. Research paper writing can be a meaningful way of pulling together skills taught in lessons on the use of the library.
2. It can be highly personal, relevant to student concerns—even exciting.
3. It can unfortunately become an end in itself, dull, nonproductive, even detrimental to the goals of a study skills program in that it may promote negative attitudes toward books, the library, school, and learning itself.

Each teacher needs to think through his or her own rationale for spending class time on writing research papers, and then decide as an individual on the basis of personal enthusiasm for the process and the ability and readiness of students. From the point of view of this book, the researching and writing of the "library paper" is viewed as important: students, even in elementary school, need opportunities to search out information and ideas, and evaluate and use them. Their learning of many basic study skills is highlighted and made meaningful in the context of research paper preparation. The following are suggestions for research paper writing which foster success while avoiding common pitfalls.

Discuss the Purposes of Library Research

Teachers need to note, even with fourth graders, the importance in thinking and communication of supporting inferences and generalizations, distinguishing fact from opinion, recognizing bias, and generally being critical readers and thinkers (see Chapter 5). They need to discuss in all classes the values of research as an important human "way of knowing" and, with senior high school and college classes, the epistemological considerations involved in all writing and thinking. Such instruction may begin with examining unsupported statements in newspaper letters-to-the-editor (such as "The drinking age should be raised to 22" or "Every school needs a smoking lounge") and continue through examining statements on the meaning of life, truth, and beauty. Students need to realize that an hour or two in the library can help them clarify and organize their thinking so that it becomes defensible, more logical, and easier to live with. One way to present the value of library research is to have students write three sentences from their own current thinking (possibly, "Alcohol stimulates the brain" or "American athletes are overpaid") and discuss in class, without revealing writers' identities, evidence needed to better understand the terms used, where more information and ideas may be obtained on the topics, and whether the statements can ultimately be proved or disproved.

Another approach to research paper writing is to discuss well-known (or favorite) books or articles which resulted from extensive library research, leading students to see that investigators gather ideas and information, organize them, and make inferences not based on ignorance or wishful thinking but on facts, evidence, and expert opinion. Preliminary discussions of the *purposes* of library research may be more important in a large educational context than the mastery of specific techniques for preparing the research paper.

Help Students Choose Topics

The first problem for students at all grade levels is selecting a research paper topic they can manage within the limits set by the course. They must select one that (1) they are personally curious about, (2) they are qualified by age and experience to handle, and (3) they can deal with in the time limitations set by the course and teacher. Two other considerations need to be examined by the class as a whole before students make final choices: Are library resources available in this subject? Is the question open to investigation? Students need to realize that some topics of great interest to them are not manageable in school or college library research because prior research has not yet been done or, in some cases, cannot be done. They need to distinguish, too, between questions that can be answered by research findings (Do TV commercials help increase sales of a product? Why do TV commercials help sell a product?) and those that cannot (Is commercial television destroying the American way of life?), and between questions that can be answered by research information and those that involve value judgments and preferences (What is the best current TV show?) and, consequently, can be answered only by quoting survey results or other people's opinions. Most important—they need to distinguish between "questions" and "topics."

One exercise is to list possible topics on the chalkboard (Superman, show-offs, beauty contests, repairing flats, Watergate, slavery, General U. S. Grant, growing tulips, man's ancestors, great athletes), and ask the class such questions as:

1. Which may be researched without using the library?
2. Which are you curious about? Why?
3. Are any too technical for you to handle?
4. Which cannot be dealt with in a short paper?
5. Do some lead to questions? Which?
6. Are the questions answerable? Why? Why not?

Have the group list in their notebooks or on the board as many possible topics as they can. Then group these under headings such as Library Research and Nonlibrary Research, Too Broad and Too Narrow, or Curious About and Not Curious About. Next, have students try to develop questions from each item ("Show-offs," for example, may lead to "What is a show-off?" or "Why do people become show-offs?"), and then decide whether the questions may be answered by library research.

No matter how a teacher approaches topic selection, time spent in discussing and evaluating topics is important to students' success in developing the research paper.

Help Students Narrow Down Topics

Teachers need to give guided practice in cutting down broad areas into specific topics or questions that can be managed in a reasonable time. One basic exercise is to have the class rearrange items in a group from broadest to narrowest:

1. the entertainment industry   2. front-wheel drive
   popular reading material   invention of the automobile
   Superman   transportation
   comics   improvements in car design
3. Nixon as president   4. the war in Europe
   life of Richard M. Nixon   the invasion of Normandy
   Watergate   D Day

| questions about the | Eisenhower's appointment as |
| Watergate tapes | Commander |

Another approach to narrowing the subject is to have students simply go to the library shelves and select three or four books on a general topic of interest to them (the Second World War, for example). Tell them to check the Tables of Contents in these books for the authors' breakdowns into sections ("The Western Hemisphere," "The War in Asia"), into parts ("Sources of the War in Europe," "Europe under the Nazis"), and into chapters ("The Fall of France," "Barbarossa"). Show them how they may benefit by observing ways in which professional authors block off a large subject area, divide it into sections and parts, and, finally, focus on narrower topics for their chapters.

Much of the student's actual work in the library will be independently done, usually with minimal teacher or librarian guidance. Selection and narrowing down of topic, however, should not be left to students—even in college. They need much help and supervision at these early stages.

Show Students Ways of Approaching Topics

While the selection process is still going on, some teachers spend time on a review of possible approaches to a topic, noting that student researchers may adopt and stay with one of them, work with one temporarily until "the pieces begin to fall into place," or combine approaches. Eight standard approaches are often suggested (Morse 1975, pp. 19-20):

Bibliographical approach. Students may simply assemble a list of books, articles, and other resource material; examine each item; and write a brief annotation. This is a truly basic approach, but one used by many professional researchers and authors.

Biographical approach. If one name is associated with the topic, the researcher may start with it, check biographical dictionaries, *Who's Who*, or standard biographies. This approach sometimes delimits the researcher's viewpoint and is appropriate only with certain topics, but it is a legitimate "jumping off place."

Chronological approach. Sometimes a topic (such as Cable Television, The Conflict in the Middle East, or Watergate) lends itself to chronological investigation. Remind students that they have to start somewhere, and a simple time line can be a helpful guide to research.

Geographical approach. Some topics (slavery, man's earliest ancestors, even great athletes) can be approached by geography. Students tentatively block out areas on the map and start their search by focusing on areas, locations, or countries.

Linguistic approach.   Often key words in the topic or tentative title need definition. Remind students that they can start with a dictionary and move outward to articles and books that help define and set verbal limits on the topic. A student writing about The Entertainment Industry or Library Research needs to define *entertainment, industry,* and what he or she means by *library* and *research.*

Practical approach.   Some topics lead to what rhetoricians call the Process Analysis, or "How to Do It," paper. Repairing Flats, or even The Invasion of Normandy can be written from a practical, point-to-point angle. Students need help in sequencing, identifying steps along the way, and using appropriate transitional words and phrases (such as *next, after that, finally*).

Statistical approach.   The Entertainment Industry or Popular Reading Material may be treated "statistically" in the sense that writers collect, present, analyze, and interpret data. The student who decides upon this approach needs guidance in the use of almanacs, yearbooks, directories, gazeteers, and similar sources of numbers, charts, and statistical summaries.

Theoretical approach.   Some topics demand theoretical analyses, inference-making, casual analyses, and predictions. The Causes of Watergate or even Drag Racing may be treated theoretically; topics such as The Future of the Automobile or Life in the Year 2000 demand theoretical sophistication of student researchers.

Teachers need to emphasize that a choice of one of these approaches is not necessarily binding. A researcher adopts one to "get off the ground" and, as he or she works, modifies it or combines it with other approaches.

Review Basic Library Skills

Once students have selected topics, teachers need to review (or teach) the basic library approaches discussed earlier in this chapter. Teachers may start with general reference books (such as an encyclopedia or dictionary), move to the periodical index to discover relevant magazine articles, and arrive at the card catalog to locate specific book-length treatments of their topics. Researching for the library paper clearly provides excellent opportunities to go over all the study skills involved in library use in a relatively meaningful context. The student who previously accepted instruction in use of the periodical index as vaguely academic may now find he or she *needs* to locate certain magazine articles to discover who first ran the four-minute mile or which rock groups first sold a million records.

Help Students Evaluate Material

The library research process allows opportunities to review what students have learned about critical reading. One high school teacher distributes the following ten sets of questions for students to keep on hand as they develop their library research projects:

1. Does the author have the background to write about the topic? Does he or she seem to have the experience and scholarship necessary to discuss the issues?
2. Does the author display any biases? Do you detect overly strong opinions, emotional language, or prejudice?
3. Does the author cite sources? Are these given in full?
4. Have all sides of issues been presented? Does the author seem to be "covering up" certain matters?
5. Does the author cite *primary sources* (actual documents) or other authors' references to them?
6. Does the author stand to profit from persuading readers to believe his or her point of view?
7. Why has the author written this particular work? What reasons are given? What reasons might you infer?
8. Is the work a contribution to scholarship or a popularization? Do you think it will be kept on the library shelves ten or twenty years from now?
9. Does it have adequate references, notes, index, and bibliography?
10. What are the work's strongest and weakest features?

The value in presenting and discussing such questions in class is twofold: students are reminded of certain key critical reading skills and attitudes, and they are cautioned—by implication—about their own responsibilities to readers (that is, they, too, must strive for accuracy, fairness, and careful writing).

Guide Students in the Preparation of Research Papers

Suggest that all students follow a working outline as they research, write down information and ideas, begin to assemble material for writing, and prepare first drafts. Such an outline may include:

☐ Tentative title.

☐ Purpose of the paper. This is best stated as a declarative sentence: "The purpose of this study is to describe events leading up to Pearl Harbor"; "The purpose is to list recent improvements in automobile design"; "The purpose is to show the best way of changing a tire." Teachers need to work individually with students at this stage because, to a great extent, the success of the research and writing depends upon the quality of this purpose statement. They need to discuss the key words (for example, *describe, show, list*), and realize that the choice of verb shapes the entire outline to follow.

☐ Justification. Students should write at least a short paragraph presenting their own reasons for taking on this research task. The justification may never appear in the final paper, but its writing may force students to think through their motivations.

☐ Plan of procedure. This is a *tentative* list of the steps needed to arrive at an answer to the question posed, directly or by implication, in the purpose statement. It guides the student researchers while they work in the library, and it provides the teacher with a tool for overseeing the operation.

☐ Findings and/or conclusions. The last phase of the outline cannot be written in advance, but students can make hypothetical statements predicting what their findings may be.

☐ Working bibliography. This last item on the working outline is developed while students are still shaping their purpose statement. Teachers need to emphasize that the bibliographies are developed concurrently with the researching and writing. Students probably should keep 3 × 5 cards for each book or article they go to, indicating on each the author, title, publisher, and date and place of publication.

Explain the Differences between Primary and Secondary Sources

Some college students are still unsure of the distinctions. Teachers need to explain that (1) a *primary* source includes the actual words of a (famous) person, a historical document, a literary work, and so on; (2) a *secondary* source includes the words of another author talking about the original events or person; and (3) primary sources are better to use and quote because the secondary source is, by its nature, an intermediary (or screen) standing between the present writer-researcher and his or her readers and the original person or event.

This may be demonstrated by presenting, side-by-side, a letter written by a minuteman who participated at the Battle of Concord and Lexington and a historian who tells *about* the battle later on. The distinction may be dramatized in class by encouraging a volunteer to describe an event he or she actually witnessed or participated in and another student to describe the same event basing his or her description on the words of the first speaker. Students will see that distortions and subtle biases change the second student's account (the "secondary source") from the first student's telling (the "primary source").

Caution Students about Plagiarism

Often students, even at the college level, do not understand the basic unfairness—and dangers—of plagiarism. Elementary school students sometimes copy paragraphs from encyclopedias and other books, unaware that they need to use quotation marks. Teachers at all levels need to spend class time regularly distinguishing among direct quotes (which need quotation marks), indirect quotes (which do not need quotation marks but require reference notes) and paraphrases (which may or may not need reference notes). They need to discuss, too, the ethical and legal implications of plagiarism while emphasizing the value of using other authors' material (which is, indeed, one of the purposes of research paper writing) and drawing conclusions and inferences from it.

Teach a Reference System

Unsophisticated students (and sometimes their teachers) discuss "how to footnote" or "how to 'do' a bibliography" as if there were only one way. There are many reference systems used today in schools, colleges, journals, and publishing houses. Some teachers and editors prefer the MLA (Modern Language Association), the APA (American Psychological Association), the "Chicago" (see, for example, Turabian 1963), or another. Elementary school students may be introduced to the concept of the bibliography (List the titles of all the books you looked at and arrange them alphabetically at the end page by their author's last names), and perhaps the notion of a footnote. Secondary school and college students should be given a guide (a published handbook or a duplicated sheet from their teacher) with information on forms, procedures, abbreviations, and other technical matters. If teachers encourage the use of footnoting and bibliography-making (and it seems unavoidable in high school and college), they must choose one system and insist that all students abide by it.

EVALUATING THE RESEARCH PAPER

More will be presented in Chapter 10 on report writing. This section on library research papers jumps ahead to suggest a Research Evaluation Report Form. When teachers have read students' first drafts, made suggestions for possible improvements, and indicated that they may prepare final copies, many teachers find an evaluation form valuable—for the student writers and for themselves. The following form is useful for students at both the writing and editing stages:

RESEARCH EVALUATION REPORT

	Unacceptable	*Poor*	*Fair*	*Average*	*Good*	*Excellent*
A. Form						
1. General appearance						
2. Title page						
3. Footnotes						
4. Bibliography						
B. Content						
1. Title						
2. Thesis statement						
3. Supporting evidence						
4. Logical development						
5. Summary statement						
6. Plan of organization						
C. Style						
1. Word choice						
2. Sentence structure						
3. Paragraph structure						
4. Transitions						
5. Spelling						
6. Punctuation						
D. Research						
1. Quantity						
2. Quality						
3. Evaluation of sources						
4. Use of quotations						
5. Use of paraphrasing						
6. Interpretations						

Teachers of upper elementary and middle school students may adopt this type of evaluation form in a number of ways to suit the needs of their own classes. A version designed for seventh graders is presented here.

	Poor	Fair	Good	Excellent
A. Language				
1. Spelling				
2. Word choice				
3. Sentences (Complete? Run-ons?)				
4. Punctuation				
5. Paragraphs				
B. Form				
1. Footnotes (at least two)				
2. Bibliography (at least eight books used and listed)				
3. Appearance (neatness, margins, penmanship)				
C. Subject				
1. Title (Does it fit the purpose?)				
2. Organization (Do the parts fit together?)				
3. Clarity (Can the reader understand the writer?)				
D. Research				
1. Quantity (Did the writer use enough reference materials?)				
2. Quality (Did the writer go to the best sources?)				
3. Quotations (Did the writer use quotation marks and footnotes if needed?)				
4. Paraphrasing (Did the writer give full				

	Poor	Fair	Good	Excellent
credit when using his or her own words for the author's ideas?)				
5. Critical reading (Does the writer accept uncritically everything he or she read?)				

STUDY SKILLS IN LIBRARY RESEARCH

1. Locating important areas in one's library
2. Using encyclopedias, dictionaries, almanacs, and other reference books
3. Using periodical indexes
4. Using the card catalog
5. Distinguishing between the Dewey Decimal System and the Library of Congress System
6. Using the appropriate call number system
7. Asking appropriate questions of librarians
8. Selecting and narrowing down a topic
9. Evaluating material
10. Outlining a research paper
11. Distinguishing between primary and secondary sources
12. Recognizing plagiarism
13. Using consistently an appropriate reference system
14. Preparing a library research paper
15. Evaluating one's own research paper.

A Suggested Student Guide for Research Reports

Several excellent student guides may be found in the professional literature and in individual schools and classrooms. The following guide was developed by Dr. Kenneth A. Lexier for students in the Peter Thatcher Middle School in Attleboro, Massachusetts. It may be modified for other grade levels.

STUDENT'S GUIDE BOOK FOR RESEARCH REPORTS

Your Name_____
Subject_____
Teacher(s)_____
Date Due_____

YOU ARE TOPS!
Step Six
Step Five
Step Four
Step Three
Step Two
Step One

Color in Each Step As You Go!

Congratulations! You have been assigned a research report. Do you know what a research report is? You probably know what a book report is, don't you? Well, a research report is *not like* a book report.

In the book report you wrote about what happened in a book. You wrote about the plot and the people in the book. What you did was write about what you already knew.

In a research report you are an investigator. In a research report you want to find out things you don't know. Research is the search for truth.

Many of you have written book reports. Few of you have written research reports. This packet will help you write *A Great Report*. Follow it step-by-step. This is the way that most college students write research reports. When you are done you will know how to do something that few adults can do—that is, write a good research report.

Remember! Follow each step closely. There are many people in this school who will help you. Seek out help from many sources.

Good Luck!

STEP ONE:
DEVELOPING RESEARCH QUESTIONS
OR HYPOTHESES

This is the most important step. This step asks you to do two things. They are:

1. Narrow your topic.
2. Make research questions or hypotheses.

Narrow Your Topic

If you decide, for example, that you want to research air pollution, then you have a topic. But air pollution is a very broad topic. You could investigate air pollution from cars, from factories. You could investigate the health hazards of air pollution. You could investigate the laws made to clean the air. You could investigate the chemicals and particles that cause air to be polluted. Do you see what the problem is?

A good research report will investigate a very clearly defined area. You must narrow your topic. This is an important thing to do. On the lines below write what your narrowed topic is to be. Give it a lot of thought. Maybe you should consult with your teacher.

_____

_____

Make Research Questions or Hypotheses

This is the most important thing. Now that you have a narrow topic, you want to write questions on what you want to investigate. Or you could make statements (hypotheses) about your topic which your research will find true or false. For example, if your topic was air pollution from cars some research questions could be:

1. What are the major pollutants from cars?
2. How does a car change gasoline into air pollution?
3. Why do some cars create more pollutants than others?
4. What has been done to new cars to reduce air pollution?

5. How do pollution devices on cars reduce air pollution?
6. What is the government doing about air pollution from automobiles?

If you were doing a research report on air pollution from cars those questions would be good ones to answer. Can you think of more?

If you want to get fancy you can make hypotheses instead of questions. Hypotheses are statements about things which you believe are true. You do research to find out if the hypotheses are true or false.

Here are some examples of hypotheses about air pollution from cars.

1. Bigger cars create more pollutants than smaller cars.
2. The automobile industry does nothing about air pollution unless the government makes them.
3. The new air pollution devices do reduce pollution.
4. Pollution from cars causes lung diseases.

Do you understand what a hypothesis is? It is a guess that you prove right or wrong. You have to be honest in your research!

On the lines below write some research questions or hypotheses. If you need help, ask your teacher.

_____

_____

_____

_____

_____

When you are done with step one, color it in on the ladder. You are on your way. Good job!!

STEP TWO:
FINDING SOURCES FOR THE RESEARCH

Now that the questions or hypotheses have been made, you have to do the research. There are three things to do. They are:

1. Think about people, places, and things that can help you.
2. Check out the source to see if it will help you.

3. Write down information about the source so that you can use it
   when you write the paper.

This step is only about finding the sources that will help you answer
your questions or prove your hypotheses. You are not going to write your
paper now. That will come in Step Five.

Think about People, Places, and Things that Can Help You

There are a lot of things around you that can help you. There is more than
encyclopedias and books that can help you. The list below contains some
suggestions for people, places, and things that may be able to help you.
Check them off as you check them out.

Almanacs, Atlas	Science Fiction	Chamber of
Encyclopedias	Adventures	Commerce
Dictionaries	Graphs, Charts	State Agencies
Textbooks	*National Geographic*	Librarians
Biography	Autobiographies	Public Library
Magazines	Museums	Historical
Reader's Guide	Relatives	Societies
to *Periodicals*	Bibliographies	Businesses
Newspaper	Science-Refer.	Friends
Card Catalog	Movies/Film Strip	Parents
Tapes	City Hall	Records

Check Out the Source to See if It Will Help You

A source is good for you only if it helps you answer the questions or prove
or disprove your hypotheses. A source should not go on your list if it does
not really help you. When you do make up the list, make sure that everything on it helps you answer your questions or prove your hypotheses.

For example, a car mechanic may know a lot about fixing cars but he
or she may not know about air pollution. An article in an encyclopedia
may be about air pollution from cars but it may not answer any of your
questions.

Other important things to think about are:

1. Is the information mainly fact or mainly opinion? Facts are things
   that can be proven; opinions are just what people think. Stick to
   information that is factual.

2. Is the person an expert on the subject? Does the person seem to be giving you facts or opinions? What has the person done that makes him or her an expert?

Remember! When you are looking for sources, choose those that will help you.

Write Down Information about Your Source

In Step Three we will make a bibliography. A bibliography is an official list of the sources you are going to use. For now, just write down the following information:

Author, Title, Copyright Date, Pages   Books
                                             Encyclopedias
                                           Filmstrip
                                         Newspaper

Name of person, when interviewed

Keep a rough list on the back of this page.

STEP THREE:
MAKING A BIBLIOGRAPHY

Now we know what we are going to report about, we have put together a variety of materials from many sources, and we have thought about the materials so we know which ones are really the best. Step Three is about making a list of our resources. Why do it?

For a *great report* you want to put at the end of your report what is called a bibliography. This is a listing of your materials that you used. This is so the reader can use the same resources if he or she needs to. In a way, you are doing a favor for the reader. Also, when you make an outline in Step Four, you can think about what materials will go with what part of the outline. So let's do it now; and remember, these are all steps you take before you write the paper.

When you make your list we will divide it into sections. The sections will be:

Reference Materials   *Books*

Encyclopedias   Textbooks
Dictionaries   Fiction

Reference Materials	*Books*
Atlas	Nonfiction
Almanacs	Paperbacks
Magazines	*Miscellaneous*
Time	Newspapers
Newsweek	Films, Records, etc.
Sports Illustrated	Interviews
etc.	Any other material

Your list will be divided into those four sections, with those underlined words as title for the section. How do we list a reference source? For the first section do the following:

The Name of the Reference Material, the volume number, the date it was printed, the pages.

For example:

Students Encyclopedia, 16, 1973, pp. 143–157.

List all of the reference sources in this section.
    The next section is for magazines; use the following format:

Name of the magazine, volume or number, date, pages.

For example:

Time, 108, September 20, 1976, p. 19.

List all magazines, of any kind, under the heading *Magazine.*

    The third section is for books that you use. For this section use the following format:

Author's last name, first name. *Title.* Date of publication, pages.

For example:

Poe, Edgar Allan. *Great Tales of Horror.* 1972, pp. 13–18.

If you are using a textbook and there is more than one author, just use the first name that appears. Put all books and paperbacks in this section.
    The final section is marked Miscellaneous, which means anything else you used that was not in one of the first three sections should go in there. The newspaper is often a very good resource. If you used the newspaper, then follow this format for listing it:

Name of paper, date of paper, pages.

For example:

The Sun Chronicle, June 1, 1976, pp. 5-6.

Now go ahead and list your sources in these four sections. Follow the format for each section. Be careful to do it right. You do want to make a *great report*.

To help you when you write your report, fill in this page. Under each of your questions or hypotheses list the sources that will help you with it.

Question One or Hypothesis One

_____

_____

_____

Question Two

_____

_____

_____

Question Three

_____

_____

_____

Question Four

_____

_____

_____

STEP FOUR:
OUTLINING THE RESEARCH REPORT

You may be wondering why we have done all of this work and we still haven't written the report. All of these steps, including Step Four, are called prewriting and researching. The most important steps are the things you do before you write the report.

What have we done so far?

1. You have made questions or hypotheses.
2. You have located information that will help you with your question or hypotheses.
3. You have made an official bibliography.

This has been a lot of work. And you have done well.

Before the report of your research is written, a plan must be made for the organization of the report. This plan is called an outline. An outline will tell you in what order you will write the report.

There is a certain order for research reports. The order is:

    I.   Background
    II.   Purpose and Procedures
   III.   Research Findings
   IV.   Summary and Conclusions

The following paragraphs will tell you about each section.

I. Background

In this section you can help the reader by giving him or her information about your topic. This is not information that you give when you answer the questions. This is information that will help the reader understand your report. For example, in the report on air pollution from cars, my background could tell the reader:

    A.   The Invention of the Automobile
    B.   The Use of the Automobiles Today
    C.   The Problem of Air Pollution

This information would help the reader understand the rest of the report. This is why it goes first.

II. Purpose and Procedures

This section is simple. All you do is tell the reader what the research questions or hypotheses are. Also, you tell the reader how you got the information. This means you tell the reader if you used a certain library or special sources (people, places, things).

III. Research Findings

This section is also very simple. All you do is present the research you found. In other words, you answer the questions in the order you put them in the Purpose. Or you present information that will prove or disprove your hypotheses.

IV. Summary and Conclusions

In this section you sum up the major findings of your research. You also add your own thoughts on the topic. If you write hypotheses, then you must tell whether or not the hypotheses were true and *why*. This is the only section where you may add your own opinions.

An outline for a research report on air pollution from the automobile could look like this:

  I. Background
     A. The History of the Automobile
     B. The Problems with Our Air
 II. Purpose and Procedures
     A. Purpose—Research Questions (or Hypotheses)
        1. How Does the Automobile Produce Polluted Air?
        2. What Is the Government Doing to Curb Automobile Pollution?
        3. Why Do the New Cars Pollute Less?
     B. Procedures
        1. Library Research
        2. Interviews
III. Research Findings
     A. How the Automobile Produces Polluted Air
     B. What the Government Is Doing to Curb Automobile Pollution
     C. Why the New Cars Pollute Less
 IV. Summary and Conclusions
     A. Summary
     B. Conclusions

Using your own questions or hypotheses, try to make an outline. Follow the outline like it above and you won't go wrong. Ask for help if you need it. If you can make an outline like the one above, you have made a research outline. Go to it. Put your outline on the back of this paper.

STEP FIVE:
WRITING THE RESEARCH REPORT

You have done so much work already and still the report is not written. If you have done everything well up to this point, and you probably have, then the writing of the report will be easier than the other steps.

Let's see how easy it will be. You have in your hot hands the following:

1. You have your research questions or hypotheses.
2. You have a bibliography which tells you all the sources you are going to use.
3. You have an outline which tells you how your paper is ordered.

The next step is putting together a *rough draft* of the paper. To do this, you should:

1. Have your outline and bibliography.
2. Starting from the top of the outline, take notes in sentence or paragraph form.
3. Use the bibliography to guide you to the sources you found in Step Two.

When you put together a rough draft, you will be finding the answers to your questions or proof for your hypotheses. Just fill out the outline.

Write a few paragraphs on Background, a paragraph or two each for Purpose and Procedures, a few paragraphs for each of your questions, and a few paragraphs for Summary and Conclusions. Make sure the paragraphs have a topic sentence, details, and are well put together.

Notetaking

Some of you may be used to copying stuff right from the book. This is for babies. What you have been doing is called *quoting*.

Quoting should be done very rarely. Only quote when there is something written that says it so perfectly that writing it in your own words would destroy it. This should happen very rarely.

There are two other ways to take notes. One way is called *summarizing*. When you summarize, you write the main ideas and important details in your own words. Very often a few paragraphs from a book can be summarized into one paragraph. This is a good way to take notes. Summarizing means writing just the important information and leaving out the rest.

Paraphrasing is another way to take notes. When you paraphrase, you rewrite everything in your own words. The length of the paraphrase is the same as the thing you are paraphrasing. The important point is that you write everything in your own language. It is all right to use some of the same words but you can't copy word by word.

Your teacher can give you more help on these two skills. Ask for help if you need it.

Now use your outline and bibliography to make a rough draft. Read Step Six before you hand in your report. You control the quality of your report. Remember that!

STEP SIX:
THE FINISHING TOUCHES

You are to be congratulated. You have followed the same plan that many adults and college students wish they knew. The rough draft you have will soon be ready for the teacher. Below are listed some important things to think about.

☐ Does the teacher want a title page? Has the teacher given you a format for the title page?

☐ Does the teacher want a table of contents? Be sure that the bibliography is in the table of contents. Start sections (I., II., III., IV.) on new pages.

☐ Are your pages numbered? Don't number the table of contents, the title page, or the first page. Start the second page with the number - 2 -.

☐ Did you leave margins at the top, bottom, and sides? Are your tables and charts neat and eye-catching?

☐ Are there any smears, smudges, or erasures? Make the paper really neat. A sloppy paper will turn the teacher off.

☐ Check for spellings. If you are the slightest bit unsure of a spelling, use the dictionary. Check your punctuation also.

□ Do you feel good about this research report? Are you proud of it? Do you believe it is your best effort? This is what really counts.

Idea Box
Library Research

Suggest that students prepare a map of the school or local library, showing the location of the main rooms, circulation desk, magazine area, children's section, and other places of importance to them. Outstanding examples may be posted, and one or two may be duplicated for each student's personal use.

Have students write a short article (or prepare and give a short talk) on "How to Use the Card Catalog," "Locating Magazine Articles," or "How to Use the Encyclopedia Index." Written articles may be posted, and one or two may be duplicated for student notebooks.

As a first step into research, have each student select a topic, then check the library for at least five books that deal with the topic, noting the pertinent page numbers. Show students how to prepare a bibliography of pertinent books on their topics, with advice on alphabetizing, noting publisher, date, title, and author, all in correct bibliographical order.

Suggest that individual students put themselves in the place of a planner or architect preparing a new school library. They may write (or tell) how they would arrange the rooms, shelves, and conveniences. If interested, they may make sketches of their library's exterior and interior. They should be prepared to explain ways in which their creations depart from the ordinary conventions of library design.

Have students make posters for display in the library or the classroom showing how to use the card catalog, the periodical index, or important reference books. Outstanding posters may be singled out for presentation to the local public library or the school's library.

Have students select two different encyclopedias (or two editions of the same encyclopedia) and contrast articles on the same subject. Guide them with questions such as: Which encyclopedia gives more information? Which seems easier to read? Why? Which contains material not given in the other? How do you account for the differences?

Suggest that individual students (or groups) write definitions of the following library terms, to be posted or duplicated:

microfilm	stack
microfiche	periodical
cross reference	vertical file
carrel	classification system
branch	call number

Suggest that students create a personal library classification system to re-place the Dewey or Library of Congress System. Ask for a sensible justification of the new system.

Have upper-grade students note a topic that is *not* covered well in their course but probably should be covered (the Vietnam War or inflation in a history course, television drama in an English course, home mortgages in mathematics, or modern dance in music). Suggest they spend time in their library preparing a bibliography of books and articles upon which a course of study may be based. These may be later used as the basis for individual research projects.

Have upper-grade students think of a book they would like to read but which has not yet been written (amplifying an acoustic guitar, repairing catalytic converters, collecting World War I German soldiers' helmets). Have them prepare a bibliography of twenty items which may constitute the basis for the book's first chapter. Interested students may develop the first chapters or individual research or writing projects later.

Send individuals to the library to discover under what subject headings they would find books containing information on topics such as:

yoyos	life after death
growing tomatoes	ESP
repairing refrigerators	famous magicians
selling real estate	cold remedies
scrimshaw	notary public

Suggest that interested students tape record interviews with librarians. Make sure they prepare an interview guide first (with questions such as, "What first interested you in the field? Where did you receive your professional training? What part of your work is most satisfying?''). These may later be played (with the librarian's permission) or transcribed and discussed by the interviewer for the group.

Have students select five words from their own current vocabularies and check the ways in which these words are defined in, say, three different dictionaries. They should report back to the class on their findings: Which dictionaries seem to do a better job? Which fail to include current words? Which of the three is consistently the best? The worst? What inferences might a student make about dictionaries in general? Why, then, is it careless to refer to "The Dictionary"?

Note that dictionaries are reviewed just as novels are. Have interested students check the periodical indexes for "book reviews" of dictionaries and report back to the group on what reviewers say are the strengths and weaknesses of widely-distributed dictionaries.

Have students tell where they would go to find answers to questions such as the following (a "Scavenger Hunt" may be organized!):

1. Who invented the zipper?
2. Why are some words spelled differently although they sound the same?
3. What was the name of the plane that dropped the atomic bomb on Hiroshima?
4. What is an acoustic guitar?
5. When was the piano invented?
6. How does television work?
7. What was the weather in Washington, D.C., the day John F. Kennedy was inaugurated?
8. Where was basketball first played?
9. What is a "blurb"?
10. When and where was Fidel Castro born?

Have students report on famous libraries throughout the world (Bibliothèque Nationale, the Harvard University Library, Leningrad Public Library, the Library of Congress, the New York Public Library, the British Museum): Which has the largest collection of books? Of documents? Which are the oldest? Newest? Make sure students report also on the sources of their information.

Suggest that students prepare a book list *about* libraries. Students should locate five or ten books on aspects of libraries and present an annotated list for class distribution.

Interested students may prepare a Library Guide for the class. This may be a handbook on how to use the library, written expressly for the group, with references to their own library or libraries. It should contain specific information on physical lay-out, location of important points, advice on finding and checking out books, etc. It should be duplicated, if possible, so that every student has a copy.

High school and college students particularly may profit from a student-prepared glossary of library terms and abbreviations. Terms, such as *carrel, bibliography, appendix, micro-fiche,* should be alphabetized, defined, and used in context. Abbreviations often used, but seldom learned, include:

ab.	(abridge)
anon.	(anonymous)
bul., bull.	(bulletin)
c	(copyright)
ca.	(*circa* or about)
cr.	(confer or compare)
ed.	(editor)
e.g.	(*exempli gratia,* or for example)
et al.	(*et alli* or and others)
et seq.	(*et sequens* or and the following)
f. and ff.	(pages following)
ibid.	(*ibidem* or in the same place)
i.e.	(*id est* or that is)
infra	(below)
loc. cit.	(*loco citato* or in the place cited)
m.s.	(manuscript)
n.b.	(note below)
n.d.	(no date)
n.p.	(no place)
op. cit.	(*opere citato* or in the work cited)
p., pp.	(page(s))
passim	("here and there")
pseud.	(pseudonym)
q.v.	(*quod vide* or which see)
rev.	(revised)

seq.	(*sequens* or the following page)
tr.	(translator)
v., vid.	(*vide* or see)
viz.	(*videlicet* or "that is to say")
v., vol.	(volume)

Have students develop their own mastery test of library competence. Individually or in groups, they may isolate the skills they believe are most important (for example, using the *Readers' Guide to Periodical Literature* or the index to an encyclopedia). They then can create actual test situations—in the library or on a paper-and-pencil examination—to discover students' ability to use each skill. A sample written test item might be: The quickest way to find your favorite entertainer's birthday is to check: (a) an encyclopedia, (b) a dictionary, (c) *Who's Who in America*, (d) the *Readers' Guide.*

A well-developed test may later be useful to the teacher for pre-teaching or diagnosis!

References

Branscomb, Harrie. *Teaching With Books: A Study of College Libraries*. Chicago: American Library Association, 1940.

Breswick, Norman W. "The 'Library College': The 'True University'?" *Library Association Record* 69, no. 6: 198–202.

Brogan, Gerald E., and Jeanne T. Buck. *Using Libraries Effectively*. Belmont, Calif.: Dickenson Publishing Co., 1969.

Gould, Samuel B. *The Library: Core of Conscience and Community*. College of Genesco: State University of New York, 1965.

Katz, William. *Your Library: A Reference Guide*. New York: Holt, Rinehart and Winston, 1979.

Morse, Grant W. *Concise Guide to Library Research*, 2nd rev. ed. New York: Fleet Academic Editions, Inc., 1975.

Shapiro, Lillian L. *Teaching Yourself in Libraries: A Guide to the High School Media Center and Other Libraries*. New York: The H. W. Wilson Co., 1978.

Shores, Louis, ed. *The Library-College: Contributions for American Higher Education*. Philadelphia, Pa.: Dresel Press, 1966.

Turabian, Kate L. *Student's Guide for Writing College Papers*. Chicago: University of Chicago Press, 1963.

Whipple, Alan L. *Research and the Library: A Student Guide to Basic Techniques*. Wellesley Hills, Mass.: Independent School Press, 1975.

9

STUDY SKILLS IN COMPREHENSION

Study skills may be grouped arbitrarily into general areas: receptive, reflective, expressive; or under headings such as gathering new material, recording, organizing, understanding, remembering, and using (see Chapter 1). Previous chapters (on lecturing, reading, notetaking, etc.) have been chiefly concerned with the receptive area, with those study skills associated with gathering new information and ideas, subjecting them to critical evaluation, and recording them.

Chapter 9 focuses on the reflective area, upon such concerns as comprehending, synthesizing, relating, organizing, and "getting meaning"—in other words, upon study skills needed to "make sense" of new material. In it, some of the most perplexing and least understood topics in psychology and teaching-learning are discussed. (Note how elusive the very language is: terms such as *comprehension*, "getting meaning", and "making sense" are themselves slippery and difficult to pin down.) Because of the tentativeness of much of the research and theorizing (and the chameleon-like character of the language used to describe it), the chapter cannot pretend to provide definitive answers to key questions. Its purpose is twofold: (1) to suggest a model for "understanding comprehension," and (2) to present teaching ideas on one topic associated with comprehension that has been successfully explored in the classroom —teaching organizational patterns.

MAKING SENSE OF AN ASSIGNMENT

How do students "make sense" of a typical school assignment? To ask the question is to open the door into decades—even centuries—of philosophic inquiring and psychological theorizing into the fields of logic, semantics, semiotics, pragmatics.

It is instructive to examine what may happen in a student's mind as he or she deals with the following passages (to "read and study") from a middle-school social studies textbook:

Some Puritans did not believe that everyone had to follow the rules of the Massachusetts Bay Colony. One was a minister named Roger Williams. He did not like the way the rulers treated people who did not agree with them. He did not like the way Indians were treated. He insisted that people should be allowed to differ with the colony's rulers about religious matters. He also said that the colonists should pay the Indians for the land they took from them.

The Puritan leaders decided to punish Roger Williams, but he slipped away from them. He wandered southward through the cold winter. In the forests near Narragansett Bay, he was found by a tribe of local Indians who took him to their village. There they fed him and made him comfortable. He stayed with them through the winter.

In the spring, he asked to buy land from the tribe. They sold him a large area at the mouth of a river leading into Narragansett Bay. There he built a simple settlement which he called Providence. Other colonists came from the Massachusetts Bay Colony and lived with him. Jews, Catholics, and Quakers from other settlements came to Providence because Roger Williams did not insist that they join his church.

Later Roger Williams sailed back to England and received a charter from the king for a new colony. He called the new colony Rhode Island. Unlike the Massachusetts Bay Colony, Rhode Island welcomed settlers of all religions. Each new settler was allowed to worship in his own way. No one had to pay taxes to support a church. Even settlers who had no religion were allowed to settle in Rhode Island. Today Rhode Island is the smallest state. It has the honor of being the first place in America where people of all religions were allowed to settle.

How do students make sense of that? Few theorists have the audacity to say they know exactly what goes on in a student's mind when confronted with the assignment "Read and study these four paragraphs." However, many teachers and investigators agree that certain stages on the way to understanding are identifiable. Unfortunately, the order in which the stages occur and what happens within them are not always clear.

The Three Stages of Understanding

Stage 1—perception, decoding, and acceptance.   Students must first perceive the coded elements (letters, sounds, numbers) in the message (in the case of a school assignment: a printed text; a spoken lecture; or a formula, arithmetic task, or mathematical problem "spelled out" in numbers, letters, or other symbols). Once perceived, the message must be decoded. This clearly implies that the receiver (student) and the sender (teacher or textbook author) share the same language or symbol system. Most school assignments are in written/printed language so this means that students must distinguish the graphemes, or letters, on the page, relate these to other known graphemes and (but not necessarily) to the sounds they represent, and fit these into known morphological and syntactical patterns (words and sentences). Perception and decoding have been discussed in great depth and at a great length in the professional literature, particularly in books on the teaching of reading (see, for example, Durkin 1978; Farr and Roser 1979; Gibson and Levin 1975; Harris and Sipay 1979; or others). In these discussions, *acceptance* is often assumed.

Once students have perceived and decoded the message (the assignment), they must accept the information and ideas; that is, subject it to standards already established in their minds. If the author of the textbook passage previously presented said that Roger Williams *bicycled* southward to Narragansett Bay, most students would reject that specific information on the basis of general knowledge most have about the history of transportation. If the author had written that the Massachusetts Puritans threatened him with "death in the electric chair," most would reject the statement on the basis of what they know about technological development. If enough "bad" information (false, contradictory, alien to their own world view) is included, students reject the entire message (assignment) even though they have perceived and decoded it. The acceptance aspect of Stage 1 is clearly related to critical thinking and critical listening-reading).

Stage 2—organization. The material comes to the students in bits and pieces. "Understanding" is contingent upon recognition of some known plan of organization; that is, the discrete bits of information must be patterned in some way, previously known to the student, for him or her to grasp it. As Pearce (1971) states, "We impose our categories on what we see in order to see."

The four paragraphs taken from a textbook are arranged in a vague chronological pattern (first, Williams disagreed with the rulers, then he left, next he met the Indians, and so forth). If the phrases and sentences of the passage were jumbled out of sequence (in this case, a time sequence), students would be unable to "comprehend" them. The effect of incoming information and ideas that are randomly juxtaposed is to puzzle the receiver, and to limit or prevent comprehension.

In this suggested comprehension model, organization plays a key role. Perception, decoding, and acceptance are influenced powerfully by the organizational patterns shared by the sender of the message and its receiver. (Even when there is no sender, as in the case of one's viewing of a landscape, observing a crowd scene, or sensing a problem in the physical world, the receiver's (observer's) perceptions, decodings, and acceptance are affected by the organizational patterns already established in his or her mind.) If both share a clear-cut set of organizational patterns, eventual comprehension is maximized; if both half-share vague patterns, comprehension is possible but chancy. In the first case, the author and student, for example, both look at the world the same way (in the Roger Williams assignment, both tend to see the information and ideas in a time frame, one of the most basic patterns of organization); in the second, the author may see his or her material in a cause-and-effect frame, a pattern with which the student may be unfamiliar. (It is said, by the way, that one of the reasons great painters, poets, and scientists are "great" is that they do not perceive the world through previously-established patterns; they look afresh and see new, different ways of organizing reality—which they later teach to the rest of us.)

The number of organizational patterns available to authors, teachers, and students (and other thinkers) in the tradition of Western civilization is finite. Some of the most widely-used patterns are discussed later in this chapter. The importance of organization not only as an influence on perception, decoding, and acceptance, but upon comprehension has become a topic of concern to scholars in the fields of *schema theory* and *discourse analysis* (see, for example, Catterson, 1979). Evidently, the extent to which the receiver (student, reader, listener) shares an overall organizational system with the sender (author, teacher, lecturer) influences the degree of comprehension. Just as they must share the same language or symbol system, they must—at least to some extent—share the same organizational pattern system.

Stage 3—comprehension. The professional literature contains many excellent definitions of comprehension (Smith 1971; Gibson and Levin 1975; Pennock 1979; and other references for Chapter 9). The definition shaped by the model suggested here grows out of one proposed by Gibson and Levin (1975, p. 400): "We comprehend the meaning of a word, the meaning of a sentence, or the meaning of a passage of discourse when we apprehend the intention of the writer and succeed in relating his message to the larger context of our own system of knowledge." This implies that students must somehow reconstruct in their minds the message (with all its information, ideas, and subtleties) that was originally in the author's mind! Common sense would say, "It can't be done." And, "common sense" would, of course, be right. The student (Bob, age eleven) can never reconstruct in his cognitive structures the exact message of the author (Professor Jones, age forty-two)—no matter how skillful Bob is at decoding, scrutinizing critically, and recognizing patterns of organization. As semanticists have noted for many decades, 100 percent comprehension by the receiver of the sender's message can never take place (see, for example, Ogden and Richards 1930; Hayakawa 1978). The message may be *approximated*—and then only if the sender and receiver (in this case, the textbook author and the student) share a rather large backlog of common experiences (such as definitions of words, ways of arranging words in sentences, patterns of arranging ideas in discourse, observations of the world outside them both, and so on).

Confronted with the assignment on Roger Williams, Bob may "comprehend" it only if he shares with Professor Jones (1) definitions of words like *Puritan, colony, settlement, Quaker, honor,* and so forth; (2) information about the Massachusetts Bay Colony (which he may or may not have acquired by reading earlier sections of the book); (3) understanding concepts "religious bigotry," "tolerance," "intolerance," "freedom of religion," and so on; and (4) similar patterns for organizing ideas and information. These four points, identified here because they refer to teachable areas, represent only the tip of a metaphorical iceberg. To truly comprehend Professor Jones's message, Bob must share—and he cannot—the enormous backlog of the professor's personal experiences, his years of historical research, study, and scholarship, plus his personal life history. Clearly, perfect comprehension is impossible: messages may only be approximated in the receiver's mind.

How, then, may comprehension be improved for Bob? Somehow, the areas of overlap between his and Professor Jones's minds must be maximized. The more words, information, ideas, and organizational patterns they share before they encounter one another, the greater will be Bob's approximation of the professor's message.

Fortunately, these four areas (vocabulary, informational background, concept development, and organizational patterns) may be influenced and significantly improved by teaching. If he is a good textbook author, Professor Jones will construct his messages with Bob's experiential limitations in mind. Bob's teacher plays a pivotal role in the comprehension stage. As intermediary between the sender and receiver, the teacher can link the two as closely as possible, teaching definitions, developing and expanding concepts, providing background information, teaching organizational patterns, eliminating potential sources of confusion, and, generally, enriching Bob's experiences so that they begin to approximate the professor's.

In summary, four points need to be made about the suggested stages: First, the "stages" are stages only in the sense that they can be sequenced here for discussion. Like the "steps" in problem solving (see Chapter 5), they may overlap, occur in different order, or happen all at once.

Second, teachers can intervene in the comprehension process. They can assist students in perception and decoding (by instruction in appropriate listening and reading skills, for example) and in the accepting aspect of Stage 1 (by lessons in critical thinking through critical listening and critical reading). They can teach vocabulary, assist in concept development, build experiential backgrounds, and teach organizational patterns. They can also help students test out their approximated messages (as will be seen).

Third, comprehension is always approximate. The reader can never truly know the author's original message. Coding systems, even in mathematics, are never comprehensive enough to allow for all possible subtleties. Spoken and written language never permit the complete encoding of the sender's message (especially when the sender does not thoroughly know it himself or herself). Students at all grade levels should be helped to realize this important point: comprehension *is* a "guessing game." Much of the excitement of study and learning is stifled for students by simplistic views of comprehension. (A *noun* is not necessarily "the name of a person, place, or thing"; 2 + 2 do not always equal 4; Roger Williams may have gone to Rhode Island to find warmer weather!)

Fourth, the model allows for definitions of "slippery" words. Discussions of the so-called reflective area of study skills are too frequently obscured by words that almost defy definition. For example, books on reading often refer to "reading for meaning" without defining *meaning* or suggesting that their authors have no definition for the word. The three obvious definitions (meaning as an index or symptom of some occurrence; meaning as intent or purpose of a deliberate action; and meaning as whatever is referred to, signified, or expressed by words or other symbols) are available to readers of books on reading, but they do not really help the reader understand "reading for meaning." *Meaning*, as defined in the context of the suggested model, is the (approximated) restructuring in the reader's mind of what he or she *guesses* is the author's message. *Understanding*, rather than being synonymous with *perceiving*, *comprehending*, or *knowing* (popular dictionary definitions) may also be defined in relative terms: a student "understands" a passage, a problem, or a poem to the extent that he or she restructures, approximately, the original message, event, or observation, in his or her own mind. (For descriptions of several other theories of comprehension, see Lapp and Flood 1978, pp. 283–337.)

Teaching Implications

As noted, teachers can intervene to improve comprehension (by teaching vocabulary, concepts, organizational patterns, and generally, maximizing the areas of overlap between an author's and students' experiential backgrounds). There are at least four other specific approaches to improved comprehension that grow out of the model suggested here:

First, one can make use of summaries to help focus student attention upon the difference between the original message in the author's mind and the reconstructed message in the reader's mind. One way to make the difference apparent is to have students write summaries of the reading passage in the assignment and then compare theirs with a summary prepared by the teacher (the intermediary between student and textbook author and the one more likely to share the experiential background of the author). Another is to present the class with three summaries of the passage written by the teacher. One of these may be as correct as the teacher can make it, the second, almost correct, and the third, distinctly incorrect. In discussion, group members may examine their reasons for assessing one summary as more accurate than another. One effective way of comparing original with reconstructed messages is to have each student write a three- or four-paragraph essay on a topic related to the lesson, and then a four-sentence summary of the essay. The essays may be duplicated for the entire group (without the authors' summaries) for each student to summarize in order to later compare the student-reader's summaries with the student-author's summaries. (For further discussion of summarizing, see Chapter 7.)

Second, one can employ the technique of cloze procedure, which helps students "make sense" of an assignment. Frequently used by reading teachers as an evaluative device, cloze procedure provides an effective instrument for improving comprehension (Robinson 1978, pp. 106–109). This procedure involves giving students an entire section of a reading assignment (or a teacher's summary of it) with the first and last lines intact but every fifth word deleted. In the blanks where these words were, students write in possible replacements that occur to them (synonyms, related words, obvious syntactical or rhetorical connectives, etc). The "Guessing Game" aspect of comprehension is clearly highlighted.

After students have completed the exercise, they may discuss many of the characteristics of the comprehension model suggested here: In what ways does the natural order or pattern of the sentence help you guess a missing word? (syntactical clues) How does the order or pattern of a paragraph help you? (rhetorical or organizational clues) In what ways does your experience in this field help you to guess correctly? (experiential clues) In what ways does your lack of experience in the field prevent you from guessing correctly? (experiential clues) How does sentence context lead you to the right word? (context clues in vocabulary) How can you ever know if you have guessed right? What does this indicate to you about "getting meaning"?

Third, one can focus on organizational patterns, which lead to effective comprehension questions. Discourse analysis theorists suggest that readers will make correct responses to reading material if they approach the material from its overall "writing pattern"; that is, its form of discourse or rhetorical organization (Catterson 1979, p. 3). This theory notes that an author tends to follow certain organization patterns when writing, so readers should scan the material to see if they can recognize the patterns to help them better comprehend the message in the author's mind. (This chapter elaborates this point of view later.)

Questions that help students focus on patterns of organization while preparing assignments may include:

☐ What important event happens first? Next? What is the sequence of main events? Arrange the events on a time line and be prepared to explain *why* you placed items in the order you did. (chronological pattern)

☐ What two items are compared? What features of each does the author note? In what ways are they alike? Different? What else could the author have included in the comparison? (comparison-and-contrast pattern)

☐ Which event preceded X? In what ways did it "cause" X to happen? In what ways was it clearly *not* the cause of X? What other events may have caused it? (cause-and-effect pattern)

☐ What is the author's main point? What evidence is offered to support it? What other evidence would you like to see here? Are you convinced that the evidence "proves" the point? (generalization-plus-evidence pattern)

One can utilize study guides to highlight comprehension. Study guides structure student responses to school assignments and may range widely (as seen in Chapter 7) to include extensive vocabulary study, writing exercises, notetaking, activities to promote divergent and critical thinking, and so on. *Brief* guides for each assignment may be designed specifically to develop comprehension. A guide for the middle-school social studies assignment presented at the beginning of this chapter might look like this:

Why Roger Williams Left Boston!

1. Read these 4 paragraphs.
2. Write (here) any words you don't know. Guess at their meanings or look them up. Also, write the definitions here.
3. Write any sentence(s) you don't understand for discussion tomorrow.
4. Is there anything here you understand but don't really believe? Write it down.

5. Which organizational plan does the author use? Write one: time sequence, main idea and details, cause and effect, or comparison and contrast. Be prepared to tell why you selected it.
6. List, in correct order, the things Roger Williams did.
7. "Boil down" these four paragraphs into four sentences.
8. Now boil them down to one sentence!
9. If the author were coming to class tomorrow, what would you ask him? Write down at least one question.
10. Pretend you are a newspaper editor. Write a headline for this "story."

Organizational Patterns

One of the most effective approaches to the improvement of study is teaching students to recognize and use patterns of organization. Most material presented in book or lecture form is organized by the writer or speaker according to one or more rather well-established patterns. The writer or speaker consciously or unconsciously selects a plan of organization and arranges the ideas, concepts, information, or insights to be shared according to the plan. Indeed, it may be that a writer's or speaker's effectiveness depends to a large extent upon the selection and use of a plan or pattern of organization. Book chapters, articles, essays, and lectures that fail to do the job are often those that are chaotic, unplanned, or so poorly organized that readers and listeners are unable to get the point. To make students aware of basic structures of organization is to give them not only an effective approach to "getting meaning" in print and lecture, but to provide them with tools they too can use in writing and preparing presentations of their own.

What Are the Patterns?

Through the years, various authorities in reading and study skills have noted different listings of organizational patterns. In her analysis of paragraph structure in social studies, science, and language textbooks, Niles (1965, p. 60) found four major patterns: enumeration (simple listing), time order, cause-effect, and comparison-contrast. After examining material in subject matter areas, Robinson (1978) found certain patterns more common to certain subjects: in science, for example, enumeration, classification, generalization, problem solution, comparison and contrast, and sequence; in mathematics, concept development, principle development, and problem solution; in social studies, topic development, enumeration, generalization, sequence, comparison or contrast, effect-cause, and question-answer. Herber (1978) noted four patterns common to most content materials: cause and effect, comparison and contrast, time order, and simple listing.

Standard rhetoric books, frequently used in high school and college freshman English courses, list many of these same patterns as approaches to writing the expository theme paper. In them, terminology changes but the basic structures and patterns remain similar. The time pattern, for example, is discussed as *process analysis*; the cause and effect pattern, as *causal analysis*, and the generalization-plus-examples, as *exemplification* (see, for example, Brooks and Warren 1958). The titles of these textbooks indicate their point of view: *The Logic and Rhetoric of Exposition, A Rhetoric Case Book*, or *Modern Rhetoric*. Clearly, investigators and practitioners in several fields of study seem to agree that the human mind patterns information and ideas in recognized ways. (See also Chapter 10.)

(These are all *internal* plans or patterns of organization, resulting from the ways authors perceive and pull together the information and ideas to be communicated. Herber (1978) makes an important distinction between internal organization and *external* organization. The external plan or pattern is the visual arrangement of the material on the printed page (the format and physical features), selected by the author, editor, or textbook designer; it may be influenced by internal organization but, because sometimes it is not, it must become a concern to teachers trying to bridge the gap between the message in the author's mind and the student's comprehension of the message.)

Where Do Patterns Originate?

Considerable consensus exists today about the patterns. As noted earlier in this chapter, schema and discourse analysis theorists even suggest that overall comprehension may be improved significantly when readers recognize patterns authors use (Catterson 1979). However, teachers may well ask: Where did these patterns come from? Did someone at some time in history invent them? Are they somehow built into the human brain? Could they limit perceptions and creativity?

Before examining ways to teach students to recognize and use organizational patterns, two important points need to be made. The first is that no one really knows where the patterns came from or whether they are native to human thought. Classical rhetoreticians noted many of the same patterns Robinson and modern investigators find in contemporary textbooks, but it is impossible to say with assurance that these patterns are native to all human thought or (more likely) simply habits of thinking developed in the traditions of Western civilization. It may very well be that Greek rhetoreticians 2500 years ago stumbled on them, noted their value, and described them. Other philosophers, logicians, and rhetoreticians through the ages perpetuated them and kept them alive in our particular tradition so that today writers, speakers, readers, and listeners (thinkers!) tend to favor established patterns. The validity of the patterns is, of course, of concern to the modern day study skills teacher, but an important aspect of any discussion of patterns of thought in Western civilization is summed up by the college composition teacher who said, "We've got them; everybody uses them; teachers may as well teach them."

The second point may have implications outside of the study skills class, and may affect the entire educational process: thinking in patterns—no matter how well-established the patterns are in Western thought—may limit the thinker's capacity to perceive reality in *other* ways. As noted earlier, "great" thinkers (poets, artists, scientists) are great (that is, original, productive, seminal) because they often do not see the world according to predetermined modes. A Yeats, Picasso, or Einstein looks "afresh" at the world and reports back to the rest of humanity the patterns he or she perceived in structures that are of necessity new and "original." Overteaching of the useful patterns (listed by Niles, Robinson, Herber, and the authors of freshman composition textbooks) needs to be compensated for in the total schooling process by many opportunities for divergent thinking and activities that promote and encourage creativity. Yes, "we've got them; everybody uses them; we may as well teach them"; but even study skills teachers must be constantly on guard against what Ohmann (1976) called "administered thought."

Teaching Organizational Patterns

Six basic organizational plans are discussed here with suggestions for teaching each. Other plans and patterns exist, but this handful should open the way for students to see and hear more in their reading and classroom work than many of them are presently aware of.

Generalization supported by examples. The first, and in many ways most valuable, pattern is one taught in both reading skills books and in writing courses, but it is rarely related for students. Reading skills books refer to the same pattern when they teach recognizing main ideas or recognizing main idea sentences and noting supporting details and examples. Writing teachers at all levels talk about using topic sentences and supporting topic sentences with appropriate examples and details. The underlying pattern is the same. It seems ubiquitous in our culture and it has its roots well back in the rhetoric books of Greek and medieval theorists. Evidently, this pattern is basic to the way people think in our traditions. The evidence from research in reading and teaching composition is that it is teachable and testable. It may be the pattern most widely taught in schools—insofar as these patterns are taught at all.

The pattern, seemingly so simple yet still so valuable, is that the writer (or the speaker) presents a statement of a general nature, presumably one important in the context of the larger discourse. Once presented, the statement is then "supported" by the writer or speaker with two or three pieces of evidence, factual statements, anecdotes, quotations, etc. In actuality, the generalization may be (and often is) an inference or a statement of opinion; in a basic teaching situation, the term *generalization* may be most useful.

In introducing this first pattern to younger students, the teacher simply writes a statement on the chalkboard, such as "Sally is selfish," and points out that, as it stands, the statement is like the tip of an iceberg. It reveals what the writer believes but it does not give any evidence to cause readers to share the same belief. The teacher then asks students to suggest evidence, such as: "Although she had two extra sandwiches in her lunchbox and I forgot my lunch, she still wouldn't share with me," or "I forgot my money for a dance ticket and she had extra money in her pocket, but she would not loan me a dollar." The introductory lesson may be supplemented by: (1) small group discussions in which students suggest evidence to support a list of ten prepared generalizations (Tom is strong. The dog is affectionate. The leader is ambitious.); (2) individual writing exercises in which students write out statements to support the same or similar generalizations; and (3) home or class assignments in which students are asked to find samples of the same pattern in school texts, newspapers, or teacher-prepared exercise sheets. (An important follow-up lesson is for students to give students the supporting evidence *without the generalization.* Students are then encouraged to suggest generalizations to serve as topic or main idea sentences.)

The examples noted here seem more appropriate to middle-school and junior high school students, but some reflection will indicate that the basic thinking processes involved are to be found at every level of schooling. Indeed, college freshmen composition books are a rich source of ideas for teaching the same pattern (usually found in chapters on "the method of exemplification"). More mature students may be shown that the main idea or topic sentence may be a generalization (Democratic presidents have been supported by organized labor), an inference or, as some teachers have called it, an "educated guess" (Poetry is verbal music), or a statement of opinion (Astrology should be considered a science). The generalizations-inferences-opinions chosen as main idea or topic sentences can range the entire gamut of maturity, experience, and grade levels and they can fit the interests of all students (from "Japanese cars are technically superior to American cars" to "Existentialism is reflected in the films of our time"). The statements chosen for development by example can also be chosen from all subject-matter areas. This pattern is clearly useful in reading and writing about science, the social sciences, literature, or any aspect of student life.

Enumeration.   This pattern is related to generalization supported by examples. The enumeration is usually a listing, but not always, centered upon some main point or topic. Students find this pattern in textbooks, sometimes in lectures, and often in articles. The writer or speaker needs to present a list of items and, rather than scatter them randomly through a chapter or talk, groups them in a paragraph or related series of paragraphs. Because this seems to involve a less sophisticated mental process than generalization supported by examples, it is easier to teach. Some teachers choose to introduce the whole concept of patterns of organization by teaching enumeration.

A basic strategy is to present jumbled lists on the board or on dittoed sheets. For younger students these may be jumbled lists of items associated with lunch time activities, school sports, math lessons, recess, English class, and so forth. The first task might be to simply group these items so that "they make sense"; that is, all items related to sports under the appropriate heading, to math, under "Math Lessons," etc. Then students may be given a structure, such as the main idea sentence: "Our school day is *full* of different things," followed by five paragraph headings: "At lunch time, you can find _____" or "English class is the place for _____." Such an introduction to basic organizing of ideas may be supplemented again with (1) small group work in which students organize preprepared jumbled lists and try to find appropriate paragraph headings, (2) individually create their own jumbled lists for other individuals to unscramble, or (3) locate examples in textbook chapters and magazine articles of the pattern of enumeration.

Although the suggestions given here are for the younger students, the same lessons may be taught at higher levels. High school and even college students need to be shown over and over again that writers and speakers often use enumeration. More sophisticated students should be challenged to investigate the reasons underlying the use of enumeration: Why did the writer enumerate? Could he or she have used another plan of organization? Is enumeration inappropriate for this presentation? Does enumeration tend to bore readers and listeners? Why? How can a writer or speaker make enumeration more interesting?

Time pattern.   This third plan of organization is clearly related to enumeration and generalization-plus-example. In this, the material presented has some inherent chronological order. Events or items on a list are related as to type, as in enumeration, but they also have an additional relationship because one seems to come before the other in time; that is, item A evidently comes before item B, etc. The mental processes underlying the time pattern are probably easier to understand, teach, demonstrate; consequently, many teachers—who teach plans of organization at all—begin with time patterns.

One effective beginning strategy, culled from discussions of process analysis in the classical rhetoric books, is to teach the brief "how-to-do-it" paper. Here the challenge to students is to write in a paragraph or two explaining the steps needed to complete some task, such as how to make pizza, how to change an automobile tire, how to put on a coat, and so on. Students must break up the total process into a sequence of discrete steps and then place these into chronological order. Teachers then have students read out their papers in a "laboratory" setting, actually making fudge or pizza, changing tires, putting on coats, etc. Whether the classroom activities are "dramatic" (as in changing a tire in the school parking lot) or "academic" (as in how to write a term paper), students are forced to think in time order.

After students have experienced for themselves the need for segmenting and sequencing steps in a process, they should have practice in recognizing these same steps in reading and listening. At a relatively elementary level, students can (1) organize previously jumbled paragraphs into correct time order, either individually or in small groups; (2) prepare disorganized how-to-do-it papers and descriptions of historical events for other individuals or groups to reorganize in correct sequence; and (3) locate in chapters and articles good examples of time order as used by professional writers.

The importance of time patterns is easily explained in relationship to other school studies. Most stories and plays read in the literature class, most chapters in history books, and most lab reports are based upon some kind of underlying temporal sequence. Students may be shown these in books and may be asked to locate examples from materials studied throughout the school. More sophisticated students may be challenged to find deliberate "violations" of normal sequencing (such as flashbacks in novels and films, and authors' use of temporal changes in historical writing to highlight or explain particular events). Although recognizing and using time patterns may be more easily grasped than other basic plans of organization, it nevertheless needs regular review and practice at all educational levels.

Climax pattern. This next pattern is, in some ways, a variant of the time and enumeration patterns. The items are arranged in some special way: from least to most important, from poorest to best, from back to front, from smallest to largest, etc. For some reason—dramatic or pedagogical—the writer or speaker, while presenting the material in some sequence or order, plays with the plan in order to achieve a certain effect.

A good approach to teaching the climax pattern is through writing. Many school curriculum guides suggest that students be taught descriptive writing; not all, however, note that writers generally have a plan when they write description. They may order items from right to left, from front to back, from least to most important, and so on. Students may be introduced to climax patterning through simple lessons in descriptive writing in which they are asked to describe, say, their classrooms, automobiles, or, even, bookshelves. First, they enumerate; then order their lists according to some principle, such as time, importance, or size; finally, they write their descriptive paragraph using the principle selected. Other students may then read these to discover the organizing principle. Follow-up activities may include: (1) group descriptive paragraphs, (2) individual writing, and (3) reading lessons in which students try to discover the principle used in teacher-selected paragraphs.

Classwork in using (writing) and recognizing (reading) climax patterns may be extended, of course, to other areas of the total school curriculum. The traditional literature lesson in noting parts of plot (i.e., introduction, rising action, climax, falling action, and conclusion) is based upon one or more variations of the climax pattern. Even the mathematics lesson in which certain steps lead to the "discovery" of a necessary conclusion is, in its way, an example of the climax pattern. The climax pattern is not as simple for students as enumeration or the time pattern. It should probably be taught early (perhaps as part of simple descriptive writing) and retaught through the college years (as part of literature study and work in drama and film).

Comparison and contrast pattern. This pattern has many profound epistemological implications, for comparing and contrasting are basic ways of knowing. We know what we know because we constantly compare and contrast it to similar and dissimilar items in the world around us. We can only "know," for example, if we are tall or smart by comparing and contrasting ourselves with all the other people we come in contact with; we only "know" Faulkner is—or is not—a major novelist by constantly comparing and contrasting his work with the work of other novelists. How much a teacher chooses to explore the philosophic background for this pattern is, of course, a matter of his or her understanding and the sophistication of the students. One matter is fairly certain, however—the comparison and contrast pattern is deeply ingrained in the speech and writing of our culture. It may be found in the classic rhetoric books and in the language and thinking that surrounds our students. It is also one of the easiest to understand, remember, and use.

The basic teaching strategy suggested here is the writing lesson. Students are shown (through selected examples) that writers often point out the similarities or dissimilarities between people, ideas, or objects and that, almost always, they have two ways of doing this: by telling all about one and then the other, or by going back and forth from one to the other, point by point. Students are then asked to write one paragraph in which they compare and contrast two items (Toyotas and Pintos, life and death, The Rolling Stones and The Beach Boys, English and math, love and hate—the possibilities are unlimited). Before writing, they should be asked which pattern-within-the-pattern they plan to follow: writing about one and then the other, or going back and forth, item by item. When students seem reasonably aware of the processes involved, they should be given much practice in locating such patterns in their own school and out-of-school reading.

This instruction can begin with younger students, using clear-cut, easily-discernible examples. With older students, the instruction in the pattern can become something of an adventure in discovery as they select topics (people, ideas, objects) they know little about and compare and contrast with topics they think they know about. What appears to be a basic plan of organization and important study-reading-writing technique can become, in the hands of a skilled teacher, a tool of exciting intellectual exploration and/or individual self-discovery.

Cause and effect pattern. This pattern (or its corollary, the effect-cause pattern) is somewhat similar to the enumeration and time patterns, except that it notes (probable) causes or reasons for the item in a series. An event is given, followed by (or preceded by) the explanation for it. Although this pattern is found frequently in literature, the best examples may be located in science and social studies materials.

An introduction may be made through a writing lesson or in class discussion. Events are suggested (school happenings, incidents in the neighborhood or community, historical events) and students are asked to list possible reasons to explain them. With younger students, the events selected ought to be explainable in simple terms (the school dance was cancelled because not enough tickets were sold, or a favorite television program was not shown because of a presidential address); with more sophisticated students, the subleties of cause and effect may be discussed by asking such questions as: How can we be sure D really caused E? Are A, B, and C causes of D? If so, are A, B, C, and D all equally important causes of E? Just because D preceded E in time, does that make D the cause of E?

Students probably should have more class discussion of the cause and effect pattern than with the other five patterns. They may need to think through alternative possibilities and the merits of options in class with teacher guidance before they begin to write and find examples in print. As in teaching the other patterns, supplementary activities would include writing short papers which demonstrate cause and effect (or effect and cause) and locating in selected reading materials examples of the pattern. Newspapers, social studies textbooks, science and math books, as well as samples of student writing all provide rich sources for classroom exploration.

Guidelines for Teaching Organizational Patterns

Experience in teaching organizational patterns for the improvement of study skills leads to at least five general guidelines.

Reading and writing should be related throughout instruction. Although schools have regularly taught reading and writing, it is only in recent years that teachers have begun to see the need to connect the two in systematic, organized ways. For example, reading teachers have taught recognizing main ideas and recognizing supporting examples and details as specific and discrete reading skills; English teachers in the writing class (ironically, sometimes the same individuals) have taught the topic sentence and the method of exemplification. Yet, in students' minds—and, most important—in students' behaviors, the two sets of lessons have often gone unrelated. Actually, the mental processes underlying the reading and writing lessons are the same, but the classroom instructional activities have been compartmentalized (or departmentalized). In the descriptions of the six teaching organizational patterns, the introductions were in a writing context; probably an effective program in study skills would provide for constant parallel, complementary, even simultaneous teaching so that students may eventually come to realize that comparable higher mental processes underlie all writing, reading, thinking—and studying.

The speaking-listening dimensions of instruction in organizational patterns should not be ignored. If certain basic higher mental processes underlie reading and writing, they probably also underlie speaking and listening. The reading-writing relationship is currently much discussed in the professional literature and at professional conferences; unfortunately, speaking and listening seem out-of-vogue in many circles. Yet, students in a public speaking class (very out-of-vogue) can be taught to use the six patterns and, certainly, in any class can be taught to recognize a speaker's plan of organization. Listeners can also be taught to recognize a speaker's clues to his or her plan. (Is this simple enumeration? Is it a time pattern? Is item B the *cause* of item C or not?) If students had frequent opportunities to talk out their writing before picking up a ballpoint pen and to listen for speakers' patterns as well as read for writers' patterns, perhaps study skills and general thinking ability might improve along with reading and writing.

Teach transitional elements.   Each of the patterns previously described has peculiar to it certain transitional elements or devices. When a writer or speaker uses the time pattern (or process analysis model), for example, he or she tends naturally to use transitions such as *first, second, next, finally.* When using the cause and effect pattern, he or she says or writes *because, therefore,* and *one explanation is.* Transitions such as *on the other hand, in contrast, yet,* and *in comparison* are used in the comparison and contrast pattern; *for example* in the generalization-plus-example pattern, and *next* in the enumeration model. Students should be encouraged to make up their own lists of commonly-used transition, put these on the classroom bulletin boards, duplicate them for other students, and regularly watch for and use these useful clues to a writer's or speaker's plan of organization.

Visualize the patterns.   Various pictorial representations of the six models exist in the literature; individual teachers can create others and, even more important, encourage their students to make up "pictures" of the patterns. A graphic representation of the generalization-plus-examples model, for example, can be a bar across the top of the page with the generalization and visible support of it in the form of blocks, each containing the "evidence" sentence. The time pattern is often pictorialized in the form of time lines in history class, in reading and writing lessons, and in teaching narrative fiction and drama in English class, but some teachers have stimulated students to develop rather exciting and original variants with models, colors, collages, mobiles, etc. The comparison and contrast model lends itself to many ingenious visual representations: charts, cartoons, skeleton outlines, and so forth. Improving study skills (and reading and writing through the teaching of organizational plans) may lead to more effective reading, writing, thinking, speaking, listening—and drawing.

Give constant practice in "testing out" the patterns.   Once the six basic patterns have been taught and practiced, it is important to return frequently and attack the learnings from fresh angles. For example, a short list of titles (Yankees and Dodgers, Why Students Drop Out, The Development of Punk Rock, Setting Up a Bandstand, The Faces of Loneliness) can be distributed for students to decide which pattern is most appropriate for its development as a talk or essay; students may be given series of sentences to rewrite according to one of the six patterns and then explain why they chose the particular pattern; paragraphs with patterns of all six types, untitled, may be used for class discussion or for individual exercises to have students identify patterns used by authors. It may be presumptuous to suggest too bold a program, but experience suggests that all six plans of organization can be taught in a year (*every* year, from middle-school grades through college freshman year) in composition class, the reading program, speaking-listening lessons, and a study skills course; and that they should be retaught, tested out in new contexts, and hit from new angles regularly. The goals are: improved reading and writing, better listening and speaking, more effective study skills and thinking; the strategies include: direct teaching, reteaching, and practice in basic organizational patterns.

SUMMARY OF COMPREHENSION SKILLS

Previous chapters have concluded with suggested lists of study skills. Most of the listed skills may be rephrased by teachers into lesson objectives or behavioral objectives for testing purposes. Recognizing a speaker's purpose (Chapter 2), for example, may be rewritten as the behavioral objective: "From a group of 4 possible purposes, students will check the correct purpose of the lecture"; Using the card catalog (Chapter 8), as "Students will be able to locate titles of five books on a given topic in five minutes." Is it possible to articulate the topics and processes associated with comprehension as specific study skills? The answer must be both yes and no. It seems doubtful whether the best intentioned and most skillful curriculum experts can list, to the complete satisfaction of all other experts, study skills in comprehension (if *comprehension* is defined, as it is here, as "guessing the message in the sender's mind and trying to reconstruct it approximately in the receiver's"). On the other hand, it does seem possible to list specific skills involved with perception, decoding, critical thinking-listening-reading, and recognizing and using organizational patterns.

The following list is tentative and is intended as a starting point for teachers who want to isolate discrete skills involved in "making sense of an assignment":

☐ Recognizing the vocabulary words in the assignment

☐ Recognizing the organization and patterns of the sentences included

☐ Noting unfamiliar concepts

☐ Noting needed informational background

☐ Guessing at the speaker's or writer's purpose and intentions

☐ Noting the difference between the sender's and the receiver's experimental background.

References

Brooks, Cleanth, and Robert Penn Warren. *Modern Rhetoric*. New York: Harcourt, Brace and World, 1958.

Catterson, Jane. "Comprehension: The Argument for a Discourse Analysis Model." In *Reading Comprehension at Four Linguistic Levels*. Edited by Clifford Pennock. Newark, Del.: International Reading Association, 1979.

Durkin, Delores. *Teaching Them to Read*, 3rd ed. Boston: Allyn & Bacon, 1978.

Farr, Roger, and Nancy Roser. *Teaching a Child to Read*. New York: Harcourt, Brace, Jovanovich, 1979.

Gibson, Eleanor J., and Harry Levin. *The Psychology of Reading*. Cambridge, Mass.: The M.I.T. Press, 1975.

Harris, Albert J., and Edward R. Sipay. *How to Teach Reading: A Competency-Based Program*. New York: Longman, 1979.

Hayakawa, S. I. *Language in Thought and Action*, 4th ed. New York: Harcourt, Brace, Jovanovich, 1978.

Herber, Harold L. *Teaching Reading in Content Areas*. Englewood Cliffs, N.J.: Prentice-Hall, Inc., 1978.

Lapp, Diane, and James Flood. *Teaching Reading to Every Child*. New York: Macmillan Publishing Co., Inc., 1978.

Niles, Olive. "Organization Perceived." In *Developing Study Skills in Secondary Schools*. Edited by Harold L. Herber. Newark, Del.: International Reading Association, 1965.

Ogden, Charles K., and I. A. Richards. *The Meaning of Meaning*, 3rd ed. New York: Harcourt, Brace and World, 1930.

Ohmann, Richard. *English in America: A Radical View of the Profession*. New York: Oxford University Press, 1976.

Pearce, Joseph Chilton. *The Crack in the Cosmic Egg*. New York: Julian Press, Inc., 1971.

Pennock, Clifford, ed. *Reading Comprehension at Four Linguistic Levels*. Newark, Del.: International Reading Association, 1979.

Robinson, H. Alan. *Teaching Reading and Study Strategies: The Content Areas*. Boston: Allyn & Bacon, Inc., 1978.

Smith, Frank. *Understanding Reading: A Psycholinguistic Analysis of Reading and Learning to Read*. New York: Holt, Rinehart and Winston, 1971.

10

REPORTING

Study skills, as noted in Chapter 1, may be grouped under three often-overlapping headings: reception, reflection, and expression. Once students have taken in new information and ideas (for example, through listening, reading, and library research), recorded it somehow (perhaps using their notetaking skills), evaluated it (by using skills in critical listening-reading-thinking), and tried to "make sense of it" (by reconstructing as well as possible in their own minds what they guess are the messages in the senders' minds), they presumably do something with it! But what? They have moved from the receptive area skills, through the reflective, to the expressive. What do they do now? Need they do anything with the newly-acquired information, ideas, and messages? If they do, what help can teachers give them in developing skills in the expressive area?

Chapter 10 addresses these important questions. Study skills associated with the expressive area, particularly those in writing and speaking, have traditionally played prominent roles in the educational drama. Students at all grade levels are expected to demonstrate (or act out) their learnings by writing themes, essays, lab reports, and research papers; they are expected to demonstrate new learnings and insights by presenting oral reports, participating in panel discussions, and even preparing videotapes and slide sequences.

This chapter first discusses writing skills, especially skills in report writing. Report writing is distinguished from other kinds of writing activities found in schools, and models or formats for expository papers are presented, as well as suggestions for teaching proofreading, spelling, and punctuation skills. The chapter then focuses on ideas for improving various kinds of oral reporting, and examines possibilities for "reporting without words" (demonstrating new understanding through charts, maps, graphs, slide-tapes, pictures, and other media).

Must students *use* new ideas, information, and understandings? The question needs to be raised here and answered in the context of this book.

Some teachers would answer, "No; it is enough that learning takes place." Others may respond, "But how do we *know* learning has taken place unless we can see some clear-cut responses from students, such as papers, research reports, pictorial representations, *something?*" Underlying Chapter 10 is the assumption that expressive skills are important for at least two reasons: (1) the products (written, oral, or visual reports) provide teachers with feedback on the effectiveness of the study skills program; and (2) the processes involved in preparing reports are in themselves conducive to more effective learning. Both of these important points are treated at the end of the chapter.

WRITTEN REPORTING

There has been considerable public discussion in recent years of school writing programs. Some critics have noted a general failure on the part of schools to produce "good" writers. Many teachers have responded by noting that (1) "good" is poorly defined by critics, (2) yardsticks for measuring success are not readily available, (3) teachers generally have not been trained to teach writing, (4) teachers are not given time and facilities to develop writing skills, and (5) the term *writing* has not been clearly defined for the profession or the public. (For a good discussion of these problems, see Sauer 1961.)

What Is "Writing"?

One of the reasons instruction in written composition has presented problems to teachers, researchers, and curriculum designers is that few share a common definition: "Writing" means too many things to too many people. To some, it means *hand*writing, penmanship (and little, if anything, else); to others, it means storytelling, poem making, scripting, and other creative ways with words. Some teachers use the term exclusively for exposition; others for research paper writing. For some, it means personal writing (opinion essays, journals, reaction papers); for others, it is written exploration of ideas and feelings ("I don't know what I think and feel until I put it down on paper"). A glance at some school curriculum guides is disconcerting: under "Writing" appears haiku, letters (personal and business), free verse, proofreading, blocking out advertisements, and assorted grammatical terms. Many professional books lump together, in their chapters on writing, punctuation, exposition, argumentation, grammar, and so-called "creative" writing of stories and poems (as if students were not creative when they developed expository themes or research papers).

Part of the definitional problem grows out of the confusion of two different approaches to the teaching of composition in schools. Some teachers have traditionally emphasized the *structure* of written discourse: rhetorical analysis, modes of discourse (narration, description, exposition, and argumentation), the structure of the paragraph and essay, and similar concerns. They believe that students learn to write by being taught forms, organizational patterns, and the characteristics of good and poor writing. Other teachers have emphasized the *process* of writing and have preferred an unstructured, experiential, even inspirational approach. It is probable that *both* approaches are important for most students, although some profit more from structured, tightly organized, systematic rhetorical instruction and others from a freer, personal, less intimidating unstructured approach (West 1971, p. 364). The two coexisting—though often overlapping—ways of looking at the teaching of writing have not helped teachers in general to arrive at a shared definition. Advocates of rhetorical structure define writing in terms of argumentation essays, exposition, and research papers; advocates of process define it as personal writing, journal keeping, and "creative" writing.

Unfortunately, research has not clarified the definition problem. Although individual researchers increasingly investigate questions related to the area, most studies have centered on specific topics, such as transformational sentence combining, syntactical fluency, holistic scoring, etc., defining terms (such as "writing") only in relation to particular studies (see, for example, recent issues of the *Review of Research in the Teaching of English*, or reviews of research, such as Lundsteen 1976). After surveying more than 1,000 studies in written composition in 1963, a committee of the National Council of Teachers of English decided that "the field as a whole is laced with dreams, prejudices, and makeshift operations" (Braddock et al. 1963, p. 5). There is no evidence that the situation has changed since the NCTE review. What teachers do in the classroom is still based on preference, opinion, myth, and professional old wives' tales. Teachers still base classroom practices on a variety of approaches and operational definitions; researchers still base studies—often provocative and potentially valuable—on stipulative definitions of writing developed for individual studies.

Ideas for teaching writing abound. Older books are still available (for example, Sauer 1961; Hook 1965). Recent professional books are filled with stimulating approaches and activities (see, for example, Murray 1968; Moffett and Wagner 1976; Savage 1977; Simmons, Shafer, and West 1976). Each helps teachers define *writing*. However, individual authors sometimes favor a structured, rhetorical approach; sometimes a process-oriented approach; and sometimes both. Despite their individual excellences, none of the authors settle in on a definition of writing upon which study skills teachers may develop a program for teaching specific skills in writing.

What, then, is "writing"? For the purposes of this book, and for study skills teachers in general, it is *reporting on paper* the new information and ideas students have acquired (in listening, reading, and library research (Chapters 2–7)), recorded (Chapter 8), and tried to make sense of (Chapter 9). It is *not* personal writing, journal keeping, storytelling, or poem making; nor is it haiku, free verse, or "reaction papers." These are important concerns and probably vital to the development of the student as a human being, but they are not central to a study skills program. To succeed in school and college, students need to learn the skills required to report back to teachers and professors the information and understandings they have acquired in the classroom. This means they must learn to organize their ideas and present them in appropriate ways on paper. Writing as reporting, then, includes knowing and using organizational patterns, punctuating and spelling correctly, and using effective outlines and formats.

What Are the Most Useful Formats?

The most useful format, or model, for the expository report may be the *generalization supported by examples* (Chapter 9). Here the student writer-reporter makes a statement (usually, an inference, generalization, or opinion) and then tries to convince readers of its truth by supporting it with specific examples and details. It may be developed with fourth-grade students ("Roger Williams did not agree with the rules of the Massachusetts Bay Colony") and with college sophomores ("The president of this university makes a mockery of student government"). Fourth-grade writers may be shown that their generalization, or *topic sentence*, will impress their readers only if they can provide proof for it (in this case, Roger Williams did not like the way the rulers treated dissidents, nor the arbitrary manner in which they took Indian land without payment); sophomore writers may be shown that they have to "validate" their topic sentence by providing readers with specific examples of ways in which the president has undermined student government.

In reporting back to teachers and professors the results of their inquiries, reflections, and learnings, student writers have a responsibility to make generalizations and inferences and support them with evidence. Some teachers say that this "skill" is the single most important to be developed in a study skills program, no matter what the grade level. Together with the other organizational patterns described in Chapter 10 (enumeration, comparison and contrast, cause and effect, the climax, and time patterns) it constitutes the basis for other useful formats for expository reporting. These three patterns are, for many writers (and teachers of writing), the building blocks for developing successful themes and research papers. The models may be given to students at most grade levels.

The Five-Paragraph Expository Essay Plan

In the first paragraph, decide *exactly* what the main point of your message is. Write it down in a single sentence on a separate piece of paper to guide you. Decide *exactly* whom you are writing to (The teacher? The entire class? Younger readers? The superintendent of schools?). Write a first sentence that you think will catch the reader's attention. (Will it be different for a younger student than for the superintendent? In what ways?)

In the second paragraph, give one piece of evidence to support your main point. Will your reader know all the terms you use? If not, define them here. Reread this evidence. Does it really support your idea? If not, discard it and find better proof of your point.

In the third paragraph, give your readers another piece of evidence. Again, define your terms. Put yourself in the reader's place. Do you believe the evidence? If not, try to find more.

In the fourth paragraph, give your reader a third reason for believing your main point. If you cannot find a third reason, reconsider the main point. Is it worth making?

In the fifth paragraph, briefly restate your main point. Put yourself again in your reader's place. Do you follow the message so far? Are you convinced? What additional proof would you need? If you have reservations or doubts, indicate them; there is nothing wrong with being tentative and using words such as *may* or *seem*. Before you end, add a sentence to show why the main point is important. You *might* conclude with an anecdote or brief story that wraps up your message. Before rewriting for the reader, make sure the message is clear, the language is appropriate, and the spelling and punctuation are correct.

The Three-Paragraph Report Essay Plan

In the introductory paragraph, decide exactly who your reader is. Tell the reader exactly what you plan to report.

In the second paragraph, give the events in the order they happened. Don't be afraid to use signal words, such as *first, second, next,* and *finally*. Go through the events carefully and make sure the order is correct. Check to see if you have used words the reader knows. Put yourself in the reader's place and try to make sense of the order. Is it logical? Is it confusing?

In the concluding paragraph, tell how the order of events ended. What is the final step or conclusion? Double-check to make sure the events are clear and in order. Reread them as if you were a complete stranger to the subject. Try your first draft out on another person before you rewrite it.

The Five-Paragraph Argumentation Plan

In the introductory paragraph, before you write anything, decide exactly who your reader is likely to be and then state your position clearly on a separate sheet of paper.

In the first paragraph, describe the issue to your reader. Give any necessary background you think the reader might not have. State your position in relation to the issue.

In the second paragraph, give one clear-cut reason for your opinion and back it up with as much evidence as you can.

In the third paragraph, give another reason with evidence.

In the fourth paragraph, give a third reason supported with evidence.

In the concluding paragraph, restate your opinion and quickly summarize the reasons for supporting it. Write at least one sentence telling the reader why he or she should share your opinion.

Teachers who approach report writing through formats and organizational patterns usually note the value of teaching common transitional words and phrases. The following list may be duplicated for students' notebooks, posted, or placed on the board.

TRANSITIONAL WORDS AND EXPRESSIONS
OR
"SIGNALING YOUR INTENTIONS"

Type	*Where Usually Used*
Example Words for example for instance in other words as an illustration thus	In generalizations-plus-examples, argumentation, enumeration, exemplification, or where examples are to be used
Time Words first, second, third next meanwhile finally at last today, tomorrow, soon	In narration, chronological patterns, or wherever events or examples are given in a time sequence
Addition Words in addition also furthermore moreover another example	In enumeration, exemplification, argumentation, and description

Type	Where Usually Used
Result Words	In causal analysis or cause and
as a result	effect pattern
thus	
therefore	
accordingly	
so	
consequently	
Contrast Words	In description, comparison and
however	contrast patterns, sometimes in
but	enumeration, and wherever the
nevertheless	writer makes a comparison or
on the other hand	contrast
to the contrary	
in contrast	

Clearly, this approach to report writing falls into the structural, rather than the process, approach to the teaching of written composition. Critics may say that it is too structured, too tightly organized, and too "academic." School textbooks designed to teach writing this way have been disparaged (see, for example, Moffett 1968). Freshman English books for college students are criticized for forcing student writers to fit their ideas into preexisting forms, and, as Ohmann (1976, p. 162) notes, "This procedure (a useful one, undeniably) not only distances the composition from the student, it also domesticates it within social forms." However, as many teachers testify, given the time constraints of the school curriculum (and the limitations on their own energy capacities), a structural approach is better than none at all. Students at all levels can be taught to master widely-used organizational patterns and a handful of expository formats. They can learn to report back on their learning. And, as noted previously, "administered thought" may be compensated for by other opportunities for divergent thinking and creativity.

Help in Spelling

Spelling in English is more difficult than in other modern and classical languages because of the peculiar history of the English language. When Old English (the language of the Angles, Saxons, Jutes, and other Germanic peoples) merged after the Norman Conquest with the language of the conquerors (an essentially Latinate dialect used in northern France at the time), two different sound systems and two different spelling systems came together and—as every school child learns—clashed. Simple Anglo-

Saxon words, such as *hus*, often remained but took on a slightly different pronunciation and spelling (in this case, *house*). Once the tendency to tolerate two different sound-spelling systems in the same language became established, English went on to become the great borrowing language, taking new words from the Latin, Greek, Italian, German, American Indian, indeed, from the languages of all speakers with whom English travelers came in contact. The result today is a language with about forty-four different sounds, or phonemes, but only twenty-six letters of the alphabet to represent them. (This is in sharp contrast to modern Romance languages, Russian, Hawaiian, or Finnish, where sound-letter correspondences are high and consistent; Finnish, for example, has nineteen sounds and twenty letter symbols!)

Does this mean spelling cannot be taught? Although reformers from Benjamin Franklin through Bernard Shaw have suggested that the whole spelling system needed to be revised, there is probably enough consistency in sound-letter relationships to make spelling a teachable concern. Linguists (see, for example, Hall 1961) and other researchers (for example, Hanna et al. 1966) have been able to demonstrate that English spelling does follow certain patterns and, consequently, that there may be hope for poor spellers and their teachers. Recent linguistic theory suggests that current English spelling actually reflects certain elements in the deep structure of the language and is much more consistent and predictable than spelling reformers ever suspected (see, for example, Chomsky and Halle 1968).

Study skills teachers need to be aware of practices and research findings. (Reviews of research include Allred 1977; Geedy 1975; Fitzsimmons and Loomer 1977.) For them, the question is not, "Can spelling be taught?" but "In what ways may it be taught more effectively?" Several methodological approaches are suggested in the professional literature; some are based on research findings, some are not, but all are worth examination.

Employ Spelling Lists

The most common spelling lists have usually been based upon research on words most frequently used in adult and student writing. Compilers (Horn 1926; Thorndike and Lorge 1944; Rinsland 1945; Fitzgerald 1951) have graded the words according to frequency of use and difficulty. Many publishers have developed day-by-day programs to teach the words in a systematic way to students from grade one through grade eight or nine. Because of the discrepancies found from list to list, some teachers and researchers have tried to reorganize lists, not according to frequency or difficulty, but by patterns. They teach, for example, consonant-vowel-consonant words (dog, cat, big) in groups, and then go on to consonant-vowel-consonant-silent *e* words (make, mate, bite). Lists then move into consonant-vowel-vowel-consonant words (foam, mean, rain) and consonant-vowel words (by, lie, go). Words are never learned individually, but always in groups.

Many teachers point out that lists, whether organized by frequency-difficulty or common patterns, are artificial and irrelevant to the interests and practices of students. They recommend *personal* lists instead. They suggest that each student, at every grade level, keep a personal notebook of spelling words that cause trouble. The words are those that have been misspelled in the past or checked more than once in the dictionary. To the personal lists, teachers sometimes have students add "demons" common to other students at the grade level or common to adults (*receive, too, their–there*).

Teach Word Structure

Spelling lessons may be directly related to vocabulary study. As students learn and review common roots and affixes, they learn to spell. As Savage (1977, p. 273) points out, "Words are built from combinations of morphemes, or meaning units. Knowing the meanings of these word units and the process of combining them can help children over many spelling hurdles. The child with a sound knowledge of word parts—prefixes, suffixes, and roots—is likely to have fewer problems in spelling words in which these elements are involved." It is difficult to imagine a student misspelling *misspell* once he or she has learned the common meaning of the prefix *mis-*. Interesting lessons and strategies may be developed in using roots and affixes: word-building contests, homonym games, making word families, scrambling and unscrambling polysyllabic words, making and solving crossword puzzles, and creating new words from old roots and affixes (for teaching ideas, see Chapter 6).

Lessons and exercises in word structures lead to opportunities for reviewing (or teaching) basic dictionary skills. Teachers may remind students of the purpose and function of dictionaries, discuss the history of dictionaries, call attention to the phonetic alphabets used, note the etymological information, and give practice in noting and using both roots and affixes. Elementary school students may review syllabication, alphabetizing, and other basic skills; high school and college students may do independent or class research to discover, for example, spelling characteristics of Anglo-Saxon and Norman-French roots, the etymological difference between words that end in *-ent* and *-ant*, or the differences in origin among words that end in *-er* and *-or*.

Emphasize Spelling Rules

In the "good old days" (when all students knew how to spell) teachers taught spelling rules. Nineteenth century textbooks outlined definite rules for the arrangement of letters in English words; countless students learned the rules: some learned to spell—and some did not. English spelling does have areas of consistency and regularity; letters match sounds more often than not; patterns may be discerned. Unfortunately for students and their teachers, it is not possible to completely isolate the rules governing the areas of fit between sounds and letters. English orthography is a patterned system, but sometimes the patterns are imperfect.

Some teachers still emphasize rules and claim success. They encourage students to master generalizations (often remarkably complicated ones) and then master the *exceptions!* They insist that their students learn to spell. Other teachers are skeptical of such claims. How, they ask, can students spell, after mastering the popular "*i* before *e*" rule, the sentence: "Neither had the leisure to seize the weird financier"? (Savage 1977, p. 283). Other skeptics question the direct teaching of rules of any kind. Rule-teaching is time wasted, they note, since "the human brain does not function by learning lists or rules that are presented to it; the brain learns by looking at significant differences, establishing functional equivalencies and deciding how events go together" (Smith 1971, p. 182).

Why, then, do some teachers claim success with rule-teaching? The answer is suggested in the next approach.

Make Students Conscious of Spelling

Many teachers have noted that some students spell well because they are aware and care (others fail because they are unaware and do not care). Several analyses have examined the components of "spelling ability" and the skills associated with it (see, for recent examples, McGregor 1976; McPeake 1979). Researchers have raised questions about the relationships of spelling ability to sex, IQ, reading achievement, and factors involved in reading achievement such as visual and auditory discrimination, knowledge of phonics, and word attack skills. At this point in time, one of the few generalizations that may be made about spellers is that good ones tend to be more conscious of spelling than poor ones. This helps to explain why most approaches to the teaching of spelling (including the "rule" approach) work. Any classroom activities (memorizing lists, studying roots and affixes, or learning rules and their exceptions) help students become better spellers because they all tend to focus student attention on spelling. Truly, students who are not aware and do not care will not spell well. Students who have developed spelling consciousness (and some teachers would add, spelling *conscience*) tend to note the ways others spell words, to double-check their own spelling, to look up words in their dictionaries, to keep personal spelling lists, and to carefully proofread papers they produce in and out of class.

Implement a Plan of Attack

Through the years, many teachers have noted that some kind of systematic plan of attack increases student awareness of the ways words are spelled. A four-step plan used by many teachers works this way:

Step 1: Have students look carefully at a word that causes them trouble.

Step 2: Have them copy the word exactly, noting visual features and the way letters relate (or do not relate) to the letters.

Step 3: Have them cover the word, see it in their mind's eye, and rewrite it from memory.

Step 4: Have them uncover the original and check their reproduction. They do this over and over until they know the word's spelling.

Dr. Joyce McPeake of the Scituate (Massachusetts) Public Schools has tested out the following "attack system" (McPeake 1979).* She has had her sixth-grade students complete a duplicated sheet, such as the following, for *each* word they misspell:

1. I am going to spell the word _____, which I misspelled.

2. Below I will write the spelling word and circle the part or parts I misspelled:_____

3. A device to remember a misspelled part is helpful. My device I thought up is:_____

4. The spelling word_____means:_____

5. A good sentence using_____is:_____
   _____.

6. The spelling word_____has_____syllables.

7. As I write the spelling word below, I will softly say each syllable:
   _____

---

*Joyce McPeake, © 1979.

8. Now I will close my eyes and see the syllables of the spelling word_____in my mind.

9. Below I will write each syllable separately:_____
_____

10. I will write the spelling word from memory five times:_____
_____.

Proofreading

Many experienced composition teachers agree that most so-called "errors" on student papers are the result of carelessness, inattention, and lack of concern on the writer's part for the effect the paper may have on readers. Problems that clearly fall under the "error" heading are those related to spelling, punctuation, and mechanics. Problems of organization, diction, coherence, unity, emphasis, and those associated with the writer-reader relationship also are rooted—though less clearly—in the writer's attitude toward the writing task. An axiom tested in countless classrooms is *the more the writer cares about the reader's opinion, the fewer errors the paper will contain*. When student writers know their papers will be read in a perfunctory manner and discarded, they "forget" all they have ever learned about effective writing. On the other hand, when they know their papers will be read carefully by someone who cares, they tend to read, correct, reread, and critically evaluate their own work.

Two key questions, then, for composition teachers are: How can we insure that student work will be read by caring readers? and How can we make students care more about their own written work? Many successful writing teachers note that the two questions go together, and that, indeed, the second is answered with the first. Such teachers emphasize the reader. They—as teachers—make sure that they read every student paper with care and concern. They try to establish themselves in student minds as readers who are sympathetic and genuinely concerned about the writing task and the production resulting from it. They also try to *extend readership*, by maximizing the number of readers each paper will have. They do this by:

☐ posting final drafts in conspicuous places on classroom bulletin boards

☐ having students frequently copy final drafts on ditto-masters for duplication for the entire class

□ having successful papers reproduced and shared

□ encouraging students to read aloud and share papers with others

□ having students check one another's papers as they write

□ producing class magazines or anthologies of student writing

□ preserving all student papers in folders for a year-long classroom file.

These, and similar practices, are important because they highlight the reader and acknowledge the importance of student writing. Teachers who emphasize the reader dimension of the writing task recognize that writing is not simply a private activity, the results of which are "looked over" by an adult (and, by definition, *critical*) teacher-reader, but an important public activity, crucial to a study skills program and academic success. They also recognize the importance of student writing by "publishing," sharing, and preserving it.

Implicit in all publishing-sharing ventures is proofreading. Proofreading is sometimes a mechanical, perfunctory classroom activity. In many classrooms, however, it is a powerful strand linking together a variety of lessons in study skills. Two proofreading guides were presented in Chapter 8 for student use in preparing library research papers. Two guides are presented below, one for elementary and middle school students and one for high school and college-level students, plus a list of common writing problems that teachers may use in developing their own proofreading guides.

A Basic Proofreading Guide
On a separate sheet of paper (to be attached to your final copy) answer each of the following questions:

1. What was my purpose in writing this paper?
2. In what ways have I succeeded? Failed?
3. Are my sentences complete? (Read aloud each one. Does it *sound* right? Does it have a subject and a verb? Does it begin with a capital letter and end with a period, exclamation point, or question mark?)
4. Are my paragraphs indented? (Do the sentences really belong together? Should I consider splitting larger paragraphs?)
5. Can I explain every comma? (There must be a reason for using a comma. If I cannot find a reason, maybe I should omit the comma!)
6. Is each word spelled correctly? (Spelling counts! Readers don't always trust the message when it contains misspelled words. If there is a hint of suspicion, check the word in a dictionary or with someone else.)

7. Will readers be able to read my writing? (There's no point in going to all this trouble if the writing can't be read!)

8. Is my paper good-looking? (Neatness counts, too! Readers assume that you don't care about your message if you present it in a sloppy way. Check margins, spacing, titles, and other features; make sure your final product is attractive enough to catch the attention of a reader.)

An "Advanced" Proofreading Guide

Before preparing a final copy for the reader, check the following items:

1. What was my purpose? Have I done what I set out to do?

2. Who am I writing for? Is my language appropriate for that reader? Are the words right for the reader? The sentences?

3. Have I double-checked mechanics? Spelling? Punctuation? Have I eliminated run-on sentences? Fragments?

4. Have I followed an appropriate plan or pattern of organization? Is this cause-and-effect? Comparison-and-contrast? Process-analysis? If I am not following a well-known plan, will my reader follow me?

5. Have I used appropriate transitional devices? Do ideas move logically from point to point? Will readers understand the basic outline I followed?

6. What about levels of English? Is my language *too* formal? *Too* slangy? Inappropriate in any way?

7. Have I used jargon, foreign words, technical language, or private in-group language that my reader will not understand?

8. Do I have grammar problems? The most common are: (a) the incomplete sentence; (b) ellipses (where I assume the reader knows what I intend to say and so I leave out a phrase or clause); (c) run-ons; (d) misplaced modifiers, lack of agreement between subjects and predicates; and (e) pronouns without antecedents. Read each sentence aloud. Does it *sound* right? (Better yet, read it aloud to a friend and get a "second opinion.")

9. Is there any feature of the paper I might be ashamed of? The most ordinary, pedestrian paper reflects aspects of the writer's thinking and personality. Have I said anything I might rue at a later date?

10. Does the final copy look good? Younger students ask, "Does neatness count?" The answer, for even graduate students, is "Yes; always." If the paper was worth writing in the first place, it is important to submit a handsome, well-spaced, error-free, legible, final copy to your reader.

"Canned," or prepackaged guides for proofreading are better than none at all, but most composition teachers agree that it is better to have guides developed by the class. When students are actively involved in the preparation of a proofreading guide, they are more apt to heed it. Here are ten problem areas that students need to incorporate into class guides: writer purpose, intended audience, organizational plan, appropriateness of language, diction, spelling, punctuation, elimination of common grammatical errors, legibility, and appearance. Individual classes may add other areas of emphasis, some more than others. The main point behind the preparation and use of proofreading guides is, of course, to provide students with an *instrument for caring*; that is, a device to focus their attention on the reader's response to products of their writing endeavors. Any proofreading guide that will make them more aware of the effect of their writing on the reader is an effective guide.

Guidelines for Teaching Writing

Writing, even when defined as it is here as *reporting on paper*, is a complex, multidimensional task. A single, generalized plan for its teaching is surely difficult, if not impossible, to articulate. However, an *approach* to a lesson plan for writing is feasible and desirable. The guidelines presented here are based on successful experiences at all levels.

First, prepare students for the task. Prewriting activities include: (1) defining the specific writing job to be done, (2) helping student-writers specify their possible readers, (3) pointing out sources of information about the topic, (4) teaching or reteaching useful patterns of organization, (5) helping individuals to select the pattern most appropriate for their purpose, (6) listing transitional words and phrases in advance, and (7) providing plans or formats to guide writers as they develop their first drafts. Successful teachers of writing regularly note that time spent before students actually write is more important than time spent afterwards in "correcting." Small group discussions, brainstorming sessions, and general classroom talk on the topic, the task, and ways of implementing it, all set a mood for student-writers. This is the time for teachers to provide models of similar papers, to discuss alternative approaches, and to allow students to "think through" the problems involved. Prewriting activities may take an entire class period; certainly, they require a sizable portion of the time allowed for the lesson.

Second, provide time for in-class writing. All student-writers need on-the-spot guidance, *while* they write, not later. Elementary school and junior high school teachers frequently set up "writing workshops" or "writing laboratories." High school and college teachers should, too. As students prepare first drafts, teachers should move about the class, pointing out other ways of organizing paragraphs, noting awkward syntax, suggesting different words, correcting mechanical problems *as they occur*. Small groups of students with similar problems and concerns may be placed physically in one area for ease of access by the teacher. Individuals with special problems may receive more teacher time than others. The important feature of a workshop-laboratory environment is the ready availability of the teacher, acting not as an adult critic-judge, but as a concerned resource person.

Third, emphasize rewriting. Even the great Romantic poets rewrote. Student-writers need to learn that a first draft is a tentative attempt to organize their ideas for a specific reader or readers. Time for rewriting may be set aside during the school day, but it is usually included as part of the homework schedule. Before students rewrite, they should be given a copy of the proofreading guide they (or the teacher) have developed and shown how to use it. Whether rewriting is done at home, in the library, or in the classroom, students need to realize that common faults (spelling errors, fragments, incomplete sentences) are eliminated at this stage of the paper's development, not after the paper has been turned in to the teacher.

Fourth, make sure papers are read. The writer's intended readers may have been other students or people outside of the school setting, but, in a program designed to teach study skills in report writing, the teacher must read each paper. If the student-writer has used one of the preceding formats, the teacher-reader should go over the finished product side-by-side with the student's worksheet: Did the writer do what he or she set out to do? Is the main point of the message clear? Is it clear who the reader is supposed to be? Does the writer support generalizations with evidence? Are the words appropriate for the reader and the topic? And so on. Final drafts should be posted, duplicated, or read aloud. Report writing is not like poetry, journal keeping, or personal writing; it is public and needs to be shared widely.

ORAL REPORTING

Reporting on learning does not *have* to be in print. Indeed, many students are psychologically, emotionally, temperamentally, even physically unable to report the results of their classroom learning with pencil, pen, or typewriter. And often, even the most successful student-writers need a respite from writing tasks. If the process of reporting is intended to promote learning and provide the teacher with feedback on the effectiveness of instruction, then alternatives to report writing are feasible, even desirable. Fortunately, many oral reporting activities are available to teachers of all subjects and at all grade levels. Five are noted here.

Group Reports

As most teachers will testify—and generations of students agree—everyone does not like to stand up before an audience and talk. Some confident fourth graders would unhesitatingly stand before the assembled delegates of the United Nations and talk without preparation (and without knocking a knee) for an hour. Most students, however, are reluctant to stand before a class and speak from well-prepared notes. (In one survey of adult Americans, it was discovered that the single fear listed most often, by most people, was talking in front of a group (Wallechinsky, Wallace, and Wallace 1977).) Skillful teachers have learned through the years that one way to give students at all levels experience with oral reporting, while sitting down, is through group reports.

Students are given a list of topics associated with the course objectives and asked to indicate the one that especially interests them. Then the teacher carefully selects groups of four or five with similar interests and suggests that they develop a report together. Each group is assisted in the preparation of an outline and given specific references for research. In time set aside for writing workshops or laboratories, students collect and organize their material. They use plans, or formats, similar to those used for preparing a written report (for example, the Five-Paragraph Expository Essay Plan presented earlier in this chapter), and work out, together, what they believe will be an effective oral presentation. Instead of submitting written reports, students in each group present their findings to the class orally. If groups are arranged in the room so that students are sitting together, individuals may "say" their sections from seats within the group. No one has to stand up and be intimidated by the larger audience. For students who have not had opportunities to speak before a class, the first presentations at the beginning of the year or course may be made directly from written notes. For more experienced students (or students unable to write), presentations may be made from memory. Many of the skills associated with written report writing may be developed by such small group oral reports.

Group Research Reports

Related to the group report is the more elaborate group *research* report. Instead of presenting orally, rather than in writing, the Five-Paragraph Expository Essay or the Five-Paragraph Argumentation Paper, students in the group share with the class the results of a more formal piece of library investigation. Questions for research may grow out of class discussions, textbook or out-of-class reading, and/or the personal concerns of people in the group. Questions in some classes have ranged from "What personal qualities indicate a successful athlete?" to "Why are there still regional dialects in an age of mass radio and TV?" to "What are the detrimental effects of alcohol?" Group research reports allow teachers opportunities to review (or teach) basic library skills (see Chapter 8), and may be used to supplement and reinforce class work in writing the library research paper.

As in the case of the group oral report, teachers cluster students with similar interests. They then help them divide their search into manageable divisions so that each student investigates and reports on one facet of the topic. One seventh-grade English teacher skillfully picked up on a student complaint about grammar rules. She suggested that students concerned about the matter search out an answer to the question: "Where do grammar rules come from?" One student was charged with the task of assembling definitions of the term *grammar*. Another took on the job of checking the introductory sections of several dictionaries. A student with distinct library inclinations was assigned the job of checking several readable grammar books suggested by the teacher. A less bookish person decided to interview five English teachers in the school. The fifth student met with the others to summarize the findings. On "Report Day," each of the five reported his or her findings orally. Many of the values of the library research paper were attained, but in an oral language setting.

Group Reports on Various Viewpoints

Many topics, by their nature, include or imply several points of view (Legal Drinking Age, The Vietnam War, American Recognition of Red China, Inflation, Television, the list is endless). Oral reports may be structured to provide students in each group opportunities to examine and report dissimilar or conflicting viewpoints. One structure is the Five-Paragraph Argumentation Paper Plan presented earlier. One student prepares and "says" the introductory paragraph, in which the issue is defined, opposing points of view presented, and the group's position made clear. A second student "says" the second paragraph, in which one reason for supporting the group's position is given with supporting evidence. A third and fourth student provide, orally, two other reasons with evidence, and the fifth student restates the group's position and summarizes the arguments. Many teachers use the oral form of the argumentation paper as a substitute for the actual written report; others use it in conjunction with the written paper to help students understand the basic structure of a simple argumentation theme.

In instances where the group does not have a common position, the structure may be varied so that each student reports orally on a point of view he or she favors. One middle-school teacher suggested a group examine the topic "Television in American Life." The first student presented background material; the second and third presented arguments to demonstrate television's deleterious influence on contemporary life; the fourth and fifth students each summed up arguments to show its positive value to the society; and, at the end, the first student summed up the arguments on both sides.

Interviewing

In many classes, teachers use a variety of interviewing strategies to substitute for or reinforce report writing.

☐ One student interviews another who has researched a topic thoroughly. Interviewer and interviewee plan the questions in advance so that listeners will learn as much as possible about the "expert's" area of study.

☐ The student interviewer asks questions of another student who is posing as an important historical figure. The interviewee researches her or his figure carefully and tries to provide listeners with a point of view and additional information that they may not acquire from the textbook alone.

☐ The interviewer conducts street-corner interviews on current issues. Each of the interviewees plans in advance to present a different point of view so that the interviewer may reveal, through careful questions, basic differences among the viewpoints.

☐ Students actually interview people who have important things to say about the topic. Classes studying the Second World War, for example, may profit by listening to interviews with parents, teachers, custodians, and others who were in the Normandy Invasion or fought in the South Pacific. Often interviewees may come to class or agree to be tape recorded. Such a strategy brings "oral history" directly into the classroom.

☐ Students interview other students who have had significant experiences related to course topics. Often students in the class (or in other classes) have visited the United Nations, Bunker Hill, Alcatraz Island, etc., and can provide information and insights not found in books.

Individual Reports

One regularly hears of students who have completed twelve years of public education plus four years of college and have *never spoken aloud before a group.* An effective oral language component in a school curriculum should allow for opportunities for all students to have experience in preparing and presenting talks before groups. However, when such opportunities are minimal or not available, study skills teachers may want to include individual oral reports in the reporting program. Students may prepare reports as they would for a writing situation and present them, at first, from their seats and, later, standing before the class. Teachers who successfully use oral reporting as a substitute for or supplement to written reporting suggest six guidelines for helping students with individual oral reports:

1. Define the task. Especially in their first attempts, students need more than a vague topic—they need specific instructions which set firm parameters for their research and reporting. ("Tell exactly what you discovered about Roger Williams's life before he came to America. You will have only five minutes.")

2. Allow preparation time. Much of the research may be done in the library or from the textbook, but some time needs to be set aside within class periods. The teacher then has some assurance that students have, indeed, prepared.

3. Give guidance. Even more sophisticated students need assistance in relating the instruction they have received in writing reports to preparation for oral reporting. Teachers need to review the importance of defining purpose, selecting main points, choosing appropriate examples, and fitting the material to the audience. Some teachers tie this study directly with writing workshop activities; some use it separately to review, reteach, and supplement writing activities.

4. Give a structure. Previous lessons in organizational patterns may be reinforced as students prepare their talks. The teacher may review patterns and show students how to select the best for their purposes. ("Why is it better to use a time pattern to tell about an individual rather than a generalization-plus-examples format?")

5. Set up a nonthreatening climate. There is a place in a public speaking program for critiques (by the teacher or the group) of student presentations. In a content area classroom where the teacher's primary objective is to have students improve learning by organizing and reporting new information and ideas, the climate should be nonthreatening. Discussion should focus on the information and ideas, not on oratorical skills. Just as students are reluctant to report in writing when they know their papers are to be critically scrutinized by an unfriendly teacher-editor, so students will be reluctant to report on what they have learned when they think their voice and manner are to be "torn apart."

6. Remember the purpose. Individual oral reporting is *not* necessarily part of the speech program. The purpose is to provide opportunities for reporting and, to a lesser extent, to supplement and reinforce learnings in report writing. The focus in class needs to be on the course content and ways to learn more about it. Oral language activities have an important place in the overall curriculum: students need to learn discussion techniques, specific speaking-listening skills, public speaking, even

Robert's Rules of Order. The purpose of individual oral reports (as well as group reports, group research reports, interviewing, and reports on different viewpoints) is to help students sharpen skills in clarifying, organizing, and "making sense of" their new learnings by the processes involved in reporting. (For excellent discussion of the importance of oral language in the curriculum, see Moffett and Wagner 1976, pp. 2–45.)

REPORTING WITHOUT WORDS

Students do not always have to report in words. The two chief purposes of reporting are to help learners better understand the material by organizing and shaping it for others, and to provide teachers with immediate feedback on the success of lessons. Written and oral reporting clearly aid in achieving these purposes. However, alternate ways of reporting are encouraged in many classrooms. Five are described here.

Preparing Charts, Graphs, and Other Visual Representations

Science and mathematics teachers, especially, have made good use through the years of visual representations in their classes—often, to show or explain a concept, and sometimes to develop the concept in the student's mind by having the student actually prepare the visual representation. It is this latter use that needs to be explained more by all teachers concerned with study skills. What happens when a student tries to represent pictorially an idea, an event, a process, or a group of facts? The student, clearly, has to make decisions about the central thrust of the message (that is, the pictorial representation), what is relevant to it and what is not, how it is to be organized, to whom it is directed, etc. —all matters that concern the student preparing a written or oral report. Evidently, these essential rhetorical concerns are basically the same whether a student reports with words or pictures, verbally or visually. The student must critically check his or her perceptions, try to see relationships, note patterns of organization, discard irrelevant items, and focus on the main point or points. *Preparing* graphs, charts, figures, tables, and other pictorial representations is akin to *preparing* reports in words. The processes underlying visual and verbal reporting are more alike than different. It is only the final products which appear different.

The wonder is that more teachers do not make greater use of visuals preparation! Many important concepts, processes, events, and other aspects of social studies, business, health education, industrial arts, even literature, can be learned by preparing visuals. Yet, too often teachers in other content areas believe pictorial representations are the property of colleagues in science and mathematics.

Some examples of ways in which content-area teachers use the *preparation* of visuals as learning activities and reporting devices include:

☐ To help students understand why the human body must take in Vitamin C each day, one health education teacher has each member of the group make a *flow chart*, indicating how the vitamin is absorbed, circulated, temporarily stored, and excreted. In preparing the chart, students must collect information from several sources, organize it, place events in sequence, and present it (the teacher insists) in "a form that even a child can understand."

☐ To help students follow the events and characters in a complex novel, an English teacher encourages each to construct a *time chart*, noting the events as they occur in both chronological time and narrative time; and a *tree chart*, in which they fill in the antecedents of the main characters, their family members, friends, and other characters they encounter in the book. An otherwise passive reading experience for some becomes an active search for relationships, patterns, and structures.

☐ To make clear the qualities of various fibers, a home economics teacher has students make a *comparison chart*, in which they note the characteristics of each, its melting temperature, its affinity for different dyes, its tendency to mat and pill, and so forth. Everyone in the class reports the results of his or her research in individual charts which are posted and used in class.

☐ To help students organize and summarize information presented in the geography textbook, one teacher has students make a *general purpose table*, in which they list the important features of each South American nation (area, population, form of government, etc.), and then the data they have collected in appropriate columns.

Visual representations which may be developed in most subject-matter areas also include: pie graphs, bar graphs, process charts, organization charts, stream charts, profile graphs, pictographs, and others. (For descriptions of types, see Summers 1965.) Teaching students how to make their own graphs, charts, tables, and other forms of visual representations also provides opportunities to teach (or review) their interpretation. While students are actively engaged in the processes of preparing their "pictorial reports," teachers can teach techniques for reading them. Effective questions for improving reading and interpretation skills in this area include: What is the title (of the chart, graph, etc.)? What is its purpose? Why are you using it? What type is it? (Pie graph? Flow chart? Comparison chart?) Are there verbal explanations? Where? Do you understand them? What special symbols are used (if any)? What do the symbols mean? Are data arranged horizontally? Vertically? What units are used (if any)? Is a key given?

Making Models

Teachers of science, industrial arts, home economics, and related fields frequently use models to teach by and use model making as a learning activity. Students make models of windmills, water wheels, canal locks, even atoms and internal combustion engines. Teachers and students recognize the value of both model making and the study of working models.

How can teachers in other areas use model making? Surveys of actual classrooms reveal a variety of approaches:

☐ A high school teacher of English has his students make an actual model of the stage set of the play they are studying. They use plywood walls and floors and doll furniture to create settings to help them visualize the action of the play and the characters' movements in each scene.

☐ A junior high school social studies teacher has helped students make a paper-mache reconstruction of Lexington Green with miniature soldiers to represent British and Colonial troops. The actual model is based upon countless hours of student research in the library and is used by students to show the stages in the historic battle.

☐ One high school speech teacher encouraged students to make a cutaway model of the human throat and mouth (with moveable tongue and teeth) to demonstrate technical features of voice production. Students located the necessary information in various speech and biology books, then organized and summarized it in the model.

☐ An elementary school social studies teacher had one group build a working model of a cotton gin. Students reported on their learnings by showing the class how the machine atually worked, and then explained its importance to the development of agriculture in the prc-Civil War South.

Making Maps

Making maps is too often seen as a social studies activity. Actually, it is useful in many other content areas and at all grade levels. Students may be shown that maps present simplified overviews of features and events in space and are enormously useful as learning and reporting devices. Beginning with street and road maps, students can examine relief maps, po-

litical maps, historical maps, and weather maps. They can also be given
practice in using such basic map skills as telling direction, using map
scales, understanding latitude and longitude, noting symbol keys, com-
puting distances, locating specific places by means of grid systems, and
making inferences and drawing conclusions based on information presented on a map.

How can nonsocial studies teachers use map-making? One health
education teacher suggested that students could report on the spread of a
specific virus by plotting known occurrences on a map. For example, one
student reviewed reports on the so-called "Legionnaire's Disease," then
indicated on her map the first outbreak in Pennsylvania, later ones in
Toronto, and a still later one in Massachusetts. Her final report to the
class was an individual oral report structured around copies of the map
she distributed to the group. A high school English teacher had students
report on their research and learnings in American dialects through map-
making. One student indicated the loss of the r sound as one traveled
from upstate New York, through Pittsfield, Massachusetts, into the
coastal New England area (where, she noted, people "pahk their cahs in
Hahvahd Yahd"). Another student drew an isogloss on his New England
map to indicate where speakers stopped referring to flavored, carbonated
drinks as "tonic" and began to call it "soda" or "pop."

Clearly, maps of one kind or another may be used by students to
better understand certain concepts and relationships and to better report
on their learnings. Making maps serves as a viable alternative to verbal
reporting and as an always-useful adjunct to both oral and written reporting.

Dramatizing the Message

Dr. Marilyn McCaffery of Fitchburg (Massachusetts) State College regularly uses "acting out" as a device for helping students learn poetry. She
suggests that students understand a narrative poem better, remember it
longer, and enjoy learning more when they break up into groups, extem-
porize a working script, and present their play version of the poem to the
entire class. They understand better, she believes, because they are
forced to think through the events or story line of the poem, make decisions about the behavior and motivation of characters, and indicate details of the setting. Theme, mood, and other literary considerations are
no longer academic but intrinsic to the "production." They enjoy more
because of the social activity and personal involvement, and they remember longer because of the physical participation (McCaffery 1973). Certainly, "acting out" a poem, as she describes it, is a form of reporting.
Students in the groups are forced to perceive critically, decide upon main
points and purpose, see relationships, note the way the material is organized—in short, to do all the things they do in preparing a written or oral

report. As in the case of making charts, graphs, models, or maps, the difference is in the end product.

How can teachers encourage students to report through drama? Teachers in all subject areas and at all grade levels do it. Here are some more alternatives to traditional written and oral reporting:

☐ Instead of testing to discover if students have read an assigned novel or short story, one teacher allows students to select key scenes from the narrative, prepare brief scripts, rehearse, and "report back" on their understanding of the work by presenting short playlets.

☐ A history teacher regularly has groups act out important moments from American history (the Scopes trial, the impeachment of Andrew Jackson, White House deliberations preceding the Bay of Pigs decision, the Watergate break-in). He would agree with Dr. McCaffery: students understand the "moments" better, remember them longer, and enjoy studying them more.

☐ Another history teacher stages "Meet the Press' interviews. Students assume the roles of famous people in contemporary history and are interviewed by student reporters. He notes that these short dramatic representations stimulate more research on the part of students while providing them with opportunities to discover how well they understand the material.

☐ For students who are reluctant to stand before a large group (and for teachers who are reluctant to let them), there are several alternative approaches to acting out: shadow plays (done behind a white drop and spotlight), puppet shows (in an open-ended box), mime shows (in which actors act silently while a narrator reads off-stage), or radio dramas (done with a tape recorder). All allow opportunities for student research, reflection on the learning, and learning through reporting.

Preparing Pictorial and Photographic Essays

Through the years, many teachers have encouraged students to report on their learning through pictures. Some of the outcomes have been as bland and pedestrian as the assignments ("Show the ghost of Hamlet's father"); others have been as provocative and imaginative as the directions that stimulated them ("Select what you think is the high point of *Great Expectations*—or *A Day No Pigs Would Die*—and sketch the scene"). History teachers have had students draw famous scenes and people from history; science teachers have suggested drawings of great events in the history of science—from Pasteur inoculating a child against rabies to the first moon landing. Many teachers have successfully used individual cartoons and cartoon strips as devices for learning and reporting.

In recent years, many teachers have taken advantage of the widespread ownership of cameras by their students to move into photography as a way of reporting. Students now prepare photo sequences to illustrate contemporary novels and social studies textbooks. They construct often impressive photo essays on topics related to class study (actual examples include: The Technical Revolution, Urban Blight, or The Commercialization of American Highways). They prepare arresting slide-tapes on social problems (The Alcoholic in Downtown Cleveland), poems (Frost's *The Death of the Hired Man*), and local government (How Our School Committee Really Functions). They do photo exhibits, collages, and photo supplements to their textbooks. Students may be assisted in their endeavors by a variety of helpful, recent books. *Painting With the Sun*, for example, is a complete do-it-yourself photography manual for elementary school students (Suid 1970). *Media and Kids: Real-World Learning in the Schools* is a detailed guide for teachers for using photography, videotape, and motion pictures (Morrow and Suid 1977).

How can teachers help students report pictorially? The possibilities seem infinite. A few examples taken from actual classrooms are:

☐ In a class of reluctant, nonverbal high school juniors, a teacher assigned Saki's *The Open Window* for home reading. "Instead of writing a paragraph report tonight," she said, "why don't you prepare a collage to show you understood it." After explaining collage to her urban young men, the teacher noted that they had to decide what the story was about, who the characters were, where the story took place, and what happened. The next day, the room was filled with poster boards pasted over with pictures from magazines of a country setting, a teenaged boy and girl, a dog, and a frightened visitor. A few minutes' examination revealed to the teacher that the students had read the story, understood it, and indeed reported on it.

☐ For a report on the pros and cons of teenage drinking, one student prepared a photo essay in which he presented photographs of young men and women following dignified, useful pursuits (studying in the school library, working in stores, attending church services) contrasted with his own photographs of students buying beer in local stores, drinking on street corners, and standing in bars. His message, which was clear without verbal explanation, was that one could not generalize about teenage drinking: some young adults were mature and businesslike, others were on their way to alcoholism.

☐ For a pictorial report to substitute for a how-to-do-it paper in English class, one student drew a series of cartoons demonstrating the correct way to change an automobile tire. Each step was clearly defined and sequenced properly. As he noted, an illiterate person could change a flat tire following his drawings.

☐ To report on her research on horses in North America, a sixth-grade student drew a series of pictures of horses found in America since their introduction by Spanish explorers. Each picture was accompanied by a one-paragraph written description of the horse with information about its history and special characteritics. Because she used her drawings to enhance an oral report, her report may be said to be oral-written-pictorial!

THE IMPORTANCE OF REPORTING

Reporting takes time. Teachers need class time to explain the reporting systems, suggest formats and models, and describe assignments. Students need time, in and out of class, to prepare their reports and then *more* time to present them to the teacher or the group.

Is reporting worth it? Teachers (and parents and principals) sometimes ask, "Shouldn't valuable school time be better spent in learning study skills and course content? Aren't we wasting time having students write reports and present talks? Make charts, graphs, and models? Aren't photography, drawing, and collage-making frills?"

The justification for teaching reporting skills and allowing time for their development in class falls under two headings: (1) the processes involved in preparing reports are themselves conducive to more effective learning, and (2) the products (written, oral, or visual) provide teachers with feedback on the effectiveness of their programs. These points sometimes need to be explained to other teachers, to parents, and even to some school administrators.

Ideas and information received by students (through reading, listening, and library research) remain, as far as anyone can tell, dormant and largely meaningless in the mind *until used.* No matter how effectively the student practices the intake skills of reading, listening, and researching, the material taken in remains in a kind of limbo, or, as one teacher puts it, "stacked in the storage spaces of the mind." It becomes meaningful to the student only after it is assimilated, which involves conceptualizing, arranging, organizing, focusing, structuring, restructuring, and other mental operations. These operations seem best stimulated when the learner is forced to *use* the new material. Faced with a need to use his or her learning in a real situation, the student must make decisions about focus, centrality, purpose, organization, and structure.

One of the pivotal questions (perhaps *the* pivotal question) in teaching and learning, then, is: How can teachers set up situations to provoke the use of new ideas and information? One way, short of following students out into the "real" world for decades after graduation, is to set up *simulation games* (that is, replications of a real environment that call for students to take action and make decisions as if they were actually functioning in that environment). Unfortunately, simulation games may not be easily made for all aspects of all subjects in the school curriculum. Another way to provoke the use of new learnings is to have students *report on their learning*, to organize and focus it in such a way that they can communicate it to others. The very process of preparing a report (whether written, oral, or visual) forces students to "think through" their learning, to "take it off the storage shelves of the mind" and arrange it so that it will have some impact on other human beings.

In short, it is not enough for students to *know about* Vitamin C, American dialects, or *Great Expectations*. They need opportunities—in the classroom, under teacher guidance—to focus, organize, conceptualize, and structure their learnings. Reporting to others (in any form) is a viable and effective way of "thinking through" and assimilating new material. Given the constraints of the school day and school setting, it may be the best way.

Unfortunately, paper-and-pencil tests remain the primary feedback system in American education. Teachers teach and hope that their students learn. The chief device for checking their own effectiveness and the success of their students has always been the paper-and-pencil test or some variant of it. However, by their nature, such tests are limited to measuring only certain aspects of school learning. They can test for learning at the factual level, sometimes at the interpretive level, but rarely at the applied level. As long as teachers emphasize *facts* in science, history, or literature, they can rely on their own or published tests to provide them with feedback. When they move to the interpretive or applied levels, the tests become increasingly less dependable and their scores more suspect. If real learning is more than the recovering of material from "the storage spaces of the mind," teachers need a better feedback system. If learning involves conceptualizing, focusing, organizing, structuring, and similar mental operations, the paper-and-pencil tests found in schools—no matter how expensively designed, reproduced, and advertised—will simply not do the job.

Teachers who want to discover how well students assimilate more complex learnings should rely more on the actual reports students prepare for their classes. An oral or written report (a learning device in itself) can reveal more about a student's understanding of the material taught in class than the most expensive published test. A chart, graph, map, or model can give the teacher insights into the student's success in assimilating and restructuring new material that the most skillfully-designed multiple-choice test cannot give. A dramatization, collage, or photo essay may reveal more about a student's grasp of a topic than several standardized or teacher-made tests. Indeed, the effectiveness of lessons in expository writing may be measured only by the final product. Paper-and-pencil tests, "home-grown" or nationally-normed, have a place in the educational enterprise, but it may be a more limited one than many teachers, parents, and administrators have so far recognized.

SUMMARY OF SKILLS IN REPORTING

Previous chapters have ended with suggested lists of study skills in listening, reading, library research, vocabulary, and other areas of concern to study skills teachers. Are certain skills particular to reporting? Reporting, whether in writing, orally, or nonverbally, requires relative mastery of skills from the expressive area—although many of these overlap with receptive and reflective area skills. Those that are most significant to the reporting process include the following:

1. Recognizing the values of reporting (organizing and understanding material in one's own mind so that it may be communicated to others)
2. Distinguishing report writing from other kinds (such as poetry writing, journal-keeping, storytelling, etc.)
3. Recognizing and stating the purpose of the report
4. Identifying the intended reader(s)
5. Deciding the main point(s)
6. Selecting an appropriate organizational pattern (enumeration, cause-and-effect, comparison-and-contrast, time order) if one can be used
7. Selecting and using appropriate transitional words and phrases (or "signal words")
8. Dividing the report into sections or paragraphs
9. Selecting a topic sentence for each
10. Supporting the topic sentence with appropriate details and examples
11. Choosing words appropriate to the task and the intended readers
12. Selecting and using an appropriate style or level of language (informal, chatty, formal, scholarly, scientific)
13. Proofreading
14. Noting and correcting spelling errors
15. Using appropriate punctuation (especially to avoid run-on and fragmentary sentences)

16. Using standard English grammar (avoiding common errors such as pronouns without antecedents, misplaced modifiers, and lack of subject-verb agreement)
17. Writing or typing legibly
18. Transferring appropriate skills from written report preparation to oral reporting (see, especially, items 1 to 12)
19. Supplementing written and oral reports with graphs, charts, maps, models, and other kinds of nonverbal reporting
20. Using nonverbal reporting as a substitute for verbal reporting when appropriate
21. Seeking reader or audience reaction and criticism
22. Rewriting or repreparing when necessary.

Idea Box
Reporting

To help students distinguish report writing from other kinds, go through a magazine or newspaper with them in class, calling attention to the characteristics of news reports, stories, poems, interviews, editorials, etc. Lead them to see that a report writer has gathered information and ideas, organized them carefully, and presented them in a clear-cut form to readers. The writer's purpose is to *inform* rather than entertain or provoke thought.

Students may be made more aware of purpose by reading through several newspaper articles and deciding together the main purpose of each. Have them write one-sentence statements summarizing the purpose of each article, and allow time in class to compare and discuss the summary statements.

Share a simple proofreading guide with the class, and then suggest that students redesign it for their own use. Allow time to itemize the main points a guide should consider. Select a committee to develop the first-draft of a guide for class analysis. Have volunteers prepare a final copy for duplication so that all students will have copies for their notebooks throughout the year.

To increase spelling consciousness, suggest a City-Wide Search for Spelling Goofs. Note that advertisers, businessmen, government officials, and others make errors in *their* spelling. Set up a Central Control Office where volunteers (perhaps poor spellers themselves) keep a record of the findings of the class "investigators." Findings may be recorded, posted, and even sent to the local newspaper!

Conduct class research on Demons in Our Midst! Many experienced teachers have noted that certain errors seem peculiar to certain grades: seventh graders tend to be bothered by the same bunch of words; and college freshmen by another bunch. Spelling researchers have not been able to help because the words differ from school to school and region to region. Encourage the students to do a class research project on Spelling Demons in their class, grade, and school. One way to start is to have each person keep track of his or her errors for one month. Then the class, or a special Demons in Our Midst Committee, can examine the personal lists for common items. Compile these, duplicate them, then post or publish them. The class may decide to distribute the list throughout the school and encourage classes at other grade levels to do the same. Such a project does much to heighten spelling consciousness.

Another way to increase spelling consciousness is to have students build a Spelling Box. They construct, paint, and decorate it. Then each time a student misspells a word, he or she writes it on a card and deposits in the box. The contents become the source for weekly reviews, drills, and tests. Elementary teachers who use the Spelling Box approach often prefer it to commercially-developed spelling textbooks because it's more personal.

Remind students at all levels that everyone has special tricks for remembering how to spell different words. (One student never fails to get *piece* right, because he thinks of "a piece of *pie*.") Discuss mnemonic devices and encourage people to share theirs. These may be placed on cards and posted on the bulletin board or duplicated for class notebooks.

Proofreading guides must provide for punctuation, but what are the problems? Actually, there are only a few. Many teachers have discovered that the main problem areas are easily isolated, listed, and duplicated for student notebooks. Then some of these teachers *let the students take over!* They say, "Okay. These are the problems. What's the best way to learn to avoid them?" Students create exercises, games, wall charts, drills, and self-tests.

The following "8 Times to Cap" and "6 Times to Com" were given to one sixth-grade class. On their own, students developed a baseball-type game, a Punctuation Bee, a Twenty Questions-type game, several colorful bulletin board displays, and a set of easy-to-hard, sequenced exercises with self-scoring answer keys! The information given by the teacher was:

Capitalize

1. The first word in every sentence.
2. Names of months, days, and holidays.
3. Names of people and pets.
4. Names of particular streets, schools, and buildings.

5. The first and every word in a title except prepositions and articles.
6. Names of countries, states, cities, mountains, and rivers.
7. First words in greetings and closings of letters ("Dear John" and "Sincerely yours").
8. Words referring to the deity.

Use Commas

1. Between names of city and state.
2. Between day of month and year.
3. After greetings in personal letters ("Dear John,").
4. Before and after the exact words of a quotation.
5. Separating items in a series.
6. Separating from the rest of the sentence, clauses that begin with *when, since, after,* or *if.*

Many students do not know that professional writers write and rewrite and rewrite and rewrite and rewrite. To demonstrate this important truth to student-writers, share samples of "real writers'" work. Books on writing, such as Donald Murray's (1968) *A Writer Teaches Writing*, provide photographs of the first, second, and third drafts of famous writers' work to show how the most successful practitioners rewrite constantly. In many communities, professional writers are available. Newspaper men and women, novelists, poets, and technical writers may be invited to classes to show their work, sometimes in various stages, and talk about their experiences. Student-writers at all levels profit from knowing that good writing is not easy.

Writers need readers! The writing act is incomplete until a reader gets involved. Teachers know many ways of increasing readership (posting papers, publishing a classroom newspaper, clipping student papers together in a folder, and so on). Students frequently have ideas about publication. After discussing the importance of publication for writers, encourage students to suggest ways of "getting into print." A brainstorming session can lead to ideas teachers may not think of!

Letter writing can be report writing. Too many students graduate from school (*and* college) unable to follow the standard conventions of personal and business letter writing. Show students the most popular formats for each:

Personal Letter	Business Letter
5 Green St.	5 Green St.
Boston, MA 02130	Boston, MA 02130
December 9, 1982	December 9, 1982

Dear John,

C.W. Jones Company
98 Jones Ave.
Dallas, Texas

Dear Sir/Madame:
(or Gentlemen/women)

Sincerely,

John Smith

Sincerely,

John Smith

Explain the reasons for the conventional formats, discuss alternative positioning, and show possible alternative wordings.

Then use letter writing as report writing. Students can write *personal* letters from the points of view of characters in fiction, of historical personages, or of made-up people taking stands on various issues. They can also write business letters about real issues in the school or community or about controversial issues in social studies, industrial arts, science, health, or other school subjects. Letters (final corrected copies, not first drafts!) may be duplicated, displayed, or actually mailed. Students can report on their reading, research, and learning in this form as well as in the more academic expository essay.

Highlight persuasion! Many teachers have noted the best writing they get often comes from persuasion. When student-writers know exactly whom they are trying to convince and what they want those readers to do (or believe), their writing takes focus and "punch." Preview the chapter in the textbook, and note ten topics which lend themselves to position-taking. Then, instead of having students write traditional reports, suggest that they choose one of the topics and persuade a particular reader or readers of the legitimacy of their position. Writing in one high school history class improved markedly when students argued topics such as: Benedict Arnold Had a Case, Pearl Harbor Was Not a Surprise Attack, The

Germans Needed Someone Like Hitler, American Advertisers Have Made Us a Self-Indulgent People, Propaganda Can Be Good. Social studies, science, and literature lessons frequently provide excellent topics for persuasion papers.

Younger (and sometimes more mature) students need help in listening to oral reports, especially group reports. Allow time to set up Ground Rules for Discussion (for example, listeners should look at the speaker while he or she is talking; questions must be saved until after the presentation; only one person may speak at a time, etc.). This is the occasion, too, to remind students of the purpose of oral reports—they are not listening to evaluate the speaking skills of classmates but to learn more about the topic. Critical listening should focus on the ideas and information speakers present, not on the way it is presented.

Have students report on their reading by presenting "conversations." After they have read, for example, a section in an American history textbook that deals with the Bay of Pigs invasion, suggest that two students (instead of taking a test or writing a paper) prepare a conversation between John and Robert Kennedy (or two cabinet members) in which they discuss the pros and cons of the invasion of Cuba the night after the formal deliberations. After they have read the chapter on the Korean War, two students may present a conversation *that might have taken place* between President Truman and General MacArthur. After trying out "conversational reports," students may be encouraged to set up other similar report situations between famous historical figures or ordinary citizens talking *about* historical events.

Students should have opportunities to try different kinds of reporting. Suggest that they choose a topic related to the course and then prepare three reports: one in written form to be passed in to the teacher, one to be presented orally, and a third to be presented visually (as a slide-tape, photo essay, or cartoon sequence). In setting up reporting activities throughout the year or course, try to provide for alternative ways of reporting (for example, "Research and report on the reasons why we have different dialects of American English; the final report may be a typed, formal library research paper, a slide-tape, or a series of visuals, drawings, or photographs which highlight the main points of your report"). Students should also have an opportunity to discuss the advantages and disadvantages of different kinds of reporting.

"The best way to learn something is to teach it to someone else!" This old saw has enough truth in it to have kept it alive for many decades (maybe centuries). The wonder is that teachers themselves forget it. Why not allow students to teach course material to one another?

Divide the textbook chapter into six to eight sections. Assign one group the task of teaching the chapter to the entire class. Each group member must read the entire chapter, and then *study* his or her section so to become expert enough to teach it. Time must be allowed, in or out of class, for preparation. Students should be encouraged to research their special topics in the library and/or in other textbooks. On the day of teaching, each group member can come to the front of the room or teach from his or her seat. Each can contribute test questions to be combined at the end for a chapter test (which group members may correct). During the course or year, every member of the class may have several opportunities to "learn by teaching."

To demonstrate the importance of the intended reader on the writer's approach to a topic, have students report on the same subject, using the same material, but for two different audiences. Suggest two written (or oral) reports on Changing an Automobile Tire, one written for a younger student, one for a new classmate who "knows cars" but has a limited English vocabulary. Suggest two reports on Drug Addiction, one for a child and one for a college student (or one for *Rolling Stone* and one for *Boys' Life*). Try Chinese Cuisine in two versions, one for a dietician's magazine and one for a campus paper; or Cancer Research, first for a newsletter of the American Tobacco Growers Association, and then for the *AMA Journal*.

Give high school and college students the basic organizational patterns (enumeration, time sequence, comparison-contrast, cause-effect, climax, generalization-plus-evidence). Discuss them, show examples, and note the advantages and disadvantages of using them. Then have students search through magazines, anthologies, textbooks, and newspapers to locate good examples of the use of each. These may be read aloud, passed around in the group for quick reading, or duplicated. When students have become skillful at spotting the common patterns, suggest that they find articles which (1) combine patterns, (2) rely on a pattern not studied, and/or (3) seem to be based on no pattern at all. These "exceptions to the rule" should be shared and discussed.

A good exercise for helping students recognize common organizational patterns and their use is to have them list these in a column in their notebooks. Dictate (or write on the board) made-up titles for students to place under appropriate headings. Why We Have Inflation, for example, would go under Cause-and-Effect; Hitler and Stalin under Comparison-and-Contrast. Some titles that may be used include: Preparing Chinese Food, Replacing a Fuse, Japanese vs. American Cars, National vs. American League Baseball, The Contents of Milady's Purse, Producing a Play, Flower Arranging, The Growth of Little League Sports, Growing Cucumbers. After practice, students can bring in their own fictitious titles to try out on the group.

When students understand the purposes of organizational patterns in writing, have them make their own charts of Common Transitional Words and Phrases. Start them off by providing two or three examples under each heading (*first, next, finally,* for Time Patterns), and then have them make, individually or as a class, charts such as Signaling Your Intentions (seen earlier in this chapter). A master chart may be developed in color for display in the room during writing workshops.

Some college freshmen say that they improve their grades in composition courses by finding and using an "all purpose" format. Suggest to high school and college students that they search college rhetoric and composition books in the library and collect several such generalized formats. They may be duplicated and discussed in class. (What are the disadvantages of an "all purpose" format? The advantages? When may they be helpful? When not?)

References

Allred, Ruell A. *Spelling: The Application of Research Findings.* Washington, D.C.: National Educational Association, 1977.

Braddock, Richard, et al. *Research in Written Composition.* Champaign, Ill.: National Council of Teachers of English, 1963.

Chomsky, Noam, and Morris Halle. *The Sound Patterns of English.* New York: Harper and Row, 1968.

Fitzgerald, James A. *A Basic Life Spelling Vocabulary.* Milwaukee: Bruce Publishing Co., 1951.

Fitzsimmons, Robert J., and Bradley M. Loomer. *Spelling: Research and Practice.* Iowa City: University of Iowa Press, 1977.

Geedy, Patricia S. "What Research Tells Us About Spelling." *Elementary English* 52 (February 1975): 233–236.

Hall, Robert A., Jr. *Sound and Spelling in English.* Philadelphia: Clinton Books Co., 1961.

Hanna, Paul R.; Jeanne S. Hanna; Richard E. Hodges; and Erwin H. Rudorf, Jr. *Phoneme-Grapheme Correspondences as Cues to Spelling Improvement.* Washington, D.C.: U.S. Department of Health, Education and Welfare, 1966 (OE-32008).

Hook, J. N. *The Teaching of High School English.* New York: Ronald Press, 1965.

Horn, Ernest. *A Basic Writing Vocabulary.* Iowa City: University of Iowa Press, 1926.

Lundsteen, Sara W., ed. *Help for the Teacher of Written Composition: New Directions in Research.* Urbana, Ill.: ERIC Clearinghouse on Reading and Communications Skills, 1976.

McCaffery, Marilyn. "The Development and Evaluation of an Oral-Dramatic Approach for the Teaching of Poetry." Unpublished dissertation, Boston University, 1973.

McGregor, Sr. Marilyn. "Multiple Regression Analysis of Essential Variables Contributing to Spelling Achievement." Unpublished dissertation, Boston University, 1976.

McPeake, Joyce. "The Effects of Original Systematic Study Worksheets, Reading Level and Sex on the Spelling Achievements of Sixth Grade Students." Unpublished dissertation, Boston University, 1979.

Moffett, James. *Teaching the Universe of Discourse.* Boston: Houghton Mifflin Company, 1968.

Moffett, James, and Betty Jean Wagner. *Student-centered Language Arts and Reading, K–13: A Handbook for Teachers,* 2nd ed. Boston: Houghton Mifflin Company, 1976.

Morrow, James, and Murray Suid. *Media and Kids: Real-World Learning in the Schools.* Rochelle Park, N.J.: Hayden Book Company, Inc., 1977.

Murray, Donald. *A Writer Teaches Writing.* Boston: Houghton Mifflin Company, 1968.

Ohmann, Richard. *English in America: A Radical View of the Profession.* New York: Oxford University Press, 1976.

Rinsland, Henry D. *A Basic Vocabulary for Elementary School Children.* New York: Macmillan Co., 1945.

Sauer, Edwin. *English in the Secondary School.* New York: Holt, Rinehart and Winston, 1961.

Savage, John F. *Effective Communication: Language Arts Instruction in the Elementary School.* Chicago: Science Research Associates, Inc., 1977.

Simmons, John S.; Robert E. Shafer; and Gail B. West. *Decisions about the Teaching of English.* Boston: Allyn and Bacon, 1976.

Smith, Frank. *Understanding Reading: A Psycholinguistic Analysis of Reading and Learning to Read.* New York: Holt, Rinehart and Winston, 1971.

Suid, Murray. *Painting with the Sun.* Boston: Dynamic Learning Corporation, 1970.

Summers, Edward G. "Utilizing Visual Aids in Reading Materials for Effective Learning." In *Developing Study Skills in Secondary Schools.* Edited by Harold L. Herber. Newark, Del.: International Reading Association, 1965.

Thorndike, Edward L., and Irving Lorge. *The Teacher's Word Book of 30,000 Words.* New York: Teachers College, Columbia University, 1944.

Wallechinsky, David; Irving Wallace; and Amy Wallace. *The People's Almanac Presents the Book of Lists.* New York: Morrow, 1977.

West, William W. "Teaching of Composition." In *The Encyclopedia of Education.* New York: The Macmillan Company and the Free Press, 1971, vol. 2, pp. 363–370.

11

REMEMBERING, RELATING, AND TEST-TAKING

All instruction in study skills rests upon the phenomenon of memory. Indeed, all study, all learning, all schooling as we know it, implies retaining. Clearly, if nothing were left from previous experience, the process of education would be futile. Thinking and reasoning are contingent upon remembered information and ideas. The abilities needed to infer, predict, evaluate, and use material found in all content areas and at all grade levels rest upon the endurance and availability of memories.

But what is memory? How does it work? How can it be improved? In what ways can teachers best exploit psychological theory and research? How can a study skills teacher use research findings to help students study more effectively?

These and other important questions are the concern of this chapter. It explores what is known about memory; the kinds of remembering, retrieval processes, and the nature of forgetting. The chapter then looks at the ways of improving memory, mental imagery and recall, the organization of memory, drill, self-recitation, and the effects of overlearning. A variety of strategies for helping students take tests are suggested, and the chapter concludes with an Idea Box.

A THEORETICAL FRAMEWORK FOR MEMORY

Memory, like "thinking" (see Chapter 5), is an omnibus word. It has come to mean many things to various people, and it shifts meaning in different contexts. One way to approach definition and provide study skills teachers with a meaningful and useful "handle" on the term is to look at kinds of memory, at retrieval, and at forgetting.

Kinds of Memory

The type of memory most easily tested in the classroom is straight *recall*. Here, a student demonstrates that he or she has learned a certain behavior, mastered a skill, or stored away a fact by the act of doing the action, displaying the skill, or saying, writing, or responding to the fact. Has John learned the skills and appropriate behaviors associated with driving an automobile? With supporting a topic sentence with two example sentences? Has he learned the route Roger Williams took when he left Boston for Rhode Island? To check this kind of memory, most people would say, "Give him the ignition key and put him behind the wheel," or "Have him write a paragraph," or "Give him a pencil and map to indicate the route."

Recall is not quite the same as *recognition*. Here, the student has only to demonstrate that he or she has met the same thing before. This kind of memory is also easily tested in school. To discover if Elizabeth has read her history assignment, the teacher may simply give her a list of possible answers to a question about the reading, only one of which is clearly correct, and have her check the correct one. Although recognition and recall are common, they are not necessarily understood to the satisfaction of all researchers in this field. For example, *free recall*, in which students tell everything they remember from their reading, is different enough from *aided recall*, in which they are given some retrieval clues, to have provoked countless studies by learning theorists (Andreas 1972).

A third kind of remembering relates to *relearning*. To discover if there is some residue from the past, the teacher can have students relearn material. Evidently, it is easier to learn material the second time around because portions of it were learned in the past, though seemingly forgotten. The seventh-grade student who "learns" her parts of speech more quickly than others in the group may not be more intelligent. She may be revealing indirectly that an older sister taught her the material years ago while "playing school." The kind of remembering, clearly, has implications for study skills teachers: negatively, it influences teachers' notions of intelligence, and, positively, it supports the belief that drill and direct teaching are never entirely wasted.

The kind of remembering that has playcd a lesser part in school programs through the years but which, in perspective, may be of greater importance, is sometimes called *redintegrative memory*. This occurs when an event and the circumstances surrounding it are recollected (or reintegrated) in the mind. Redintegrative memory is at work when an earlier experience is reestablished in the mind, usually on the basis of partial clues. A student remembers the entire plot, settings, and characters of a novel read several years before when the teacher mentions a single incident from the book; others reconstruct clearly in their minds laboratory experiments or events from history when one or two details come up in class discussions.

The concept of redintegrative memory has important implications, which are only recently being explored, for theories of thinking, learning, and intelligence. As new information and ideas come into the learner's mind, they are not stored as discrete pieces and bits but in packages or "big pictures"; that is, in larger contexts. As more and more material comes into the mind, is accumulated and organized, a richly interconnected data base develops and learning takes on a different character as new learnings are associated by analogy with what is already known. The preexisting memory structure, then, affects future learnings, retrieval systems, and the ways the learner understands the world. (For an analysis of this point of view, see Lindsay and Norman 1972.)

What does the notion of redintegrative memory mean to the study skills teacher? Clearly, the taking in of isolated bits and pieces of course content is not as valuable for understanding and remembering as the acquisition of organized blocks of material. Just as clearly, the *more* material the student takes in the better is that "richly interconnected data base"; organized blocks begin to relate and fit together to make fresh learning easier and remembering more effortless. This notion, too, has implications for the concept of intelligence. Evidently, the more information and ideas learners already have, the faster they will learn and the less they will forget. Those positive qualities associated with high IQ may have less to do with genetics and more to do with how much previous learning students have and how well they have organized it! New learning in content areas is never static or additive; it is always related, part and parcel, to the growing data base of the learner (Fincher 1976). It may be said, then, that the more previous learning a student brings into the classroom, the more he or she will acquire and retain.

STM and LTM

In addition to the four kinds of remembering listed above, psychologists recognize an even more basic distinction: that between short-term memory (STM) and long-term memory (LTM) (Baron, Byrne, and Kantowitz 1977). They note that visual and auditory information is retained in a *sensory storage system* for a very brief time, a half-second or less, and that this sensory storage system operates without conscious effort on the part of the learner. In order to be remembered for longer than a half-second, information must be transferred to the next memory system, the STM. It is retained here only by *rehearsal*. A classic example of the distinction between the pre-STM stage and STM may be found in the contrast between listening to a spoken sentence and using a telephone number just looked up in a directory. The sensory storage system retains the separate sounds and syllables only long enough so that the listener may piece them together into words and phrases. STM, on the other hand, allows the caller to retain a number long enough to dial it without having to recheck the directory. If the person wanted to keep the telephone number in his or her head, the caller would have to *rehearse* it by saying it over and over again until it "stuck." When rehearsal is prevented or interrupted, the information is dropped from STM. Obviously, STM has a limited capacity; more information is dropped than retained. It allows the mind to detect features, recognize patterns, and keeps stimuli around just long enough to ponder its significance. LTM, on the other hand, has an unlimited capacity. Once information gets into it, it stays. The problem is getting it out.

Retrieval Processes

Information and ideas, then, go from a short-term memory sensory storage stage to short-term memory and then to long-term memory. In the STM, it must be rehearsed to be remembered, but once in LTM, rehearsal is no longer necessary. Once there, it is there, seemingly forever and in magnificent abundance. The problem of getting it out is pivotal for all concerned with teaching and learning. Locating and retrieving material is so difficult that psychologists distinguish between what is *available* and what is *accessible*. All ideas and information are considered available in that they can be remembered if the conditions are right; material is accessible only if it can be retrieved. As Tulving states, "Accessible information is always available, but available information cannot always be accessible" (quoted in Baron, Byrne, and Kantowitz 1977, p. 160).

The Big Question for teachers and students is "How to retrieve?" There are several competing explanations of how human memory works, but one most representative of the kind of analysis currently in vogue suggests that long-term memory is *self-addressable* (Shiffrin and Atkinson 1969). This explanation says that the same plan used to store information is also used to retrieve it. If a student learns that *Roger Williams left the Massachusetts Bay Colony to set up a colony in Providence because he disagreed with the religious beliefs of the leaders of the Boston settlement* as part of a larger package of information organized by the teacher according to a structure or outline, which listed "Reasons for Establishing Early Colonies," then the student could retrieve the specific information by reviewing in his or her mind the larger organizational pattern of the structure or outline.

This cognitive view of memory divides it into three stages: encoding, storage, and retrieval. As Hilgard, Atkinson, and Atkinson (1975) explain it, *encoding* has to do with transforming sensory input into a form that can be processed by the memory system; if the information is to be remembered, then *storage* requires transferring the encoded information into memory; *retrieval* has to do with locating the memorized information when needed. They liken the three stages to an office filing system:

1. A phone message is received and encoded onto a typed sheet for the filing drawer.
2. This sheet is stored in the filing cabinet using the date, the caller's name, or the topic of the message.
3. When the information is later needed, it is retrieved by a search of the files.
4. Failure to find the information (that is, to remember) may be caused by (a) failure to encode, (b) neglect to store, or (c) inability to retrieve by using the caller's name, the date, or the topic.

Memory is not a grab bag of unrelated facts, ideas, incidents, images, or pieces of data. The material stored must be organized. If some rudimentary organizational patterns are lacking, the ability to reconstruct events and think in terms of remembered information and ideas would be hopelessly chaotic. It may be that the human memory is a vast, intricately interconnected network, not filled with isolated letters, syllables, words, or bits and pieces of information, but with patterns forming associative and semantic networks. Effective encoding, then, is the forming of new links in the network, of making new associations (Norman and Rumelhart, 1975). Retrieval is contingent upon the encoding and storage systems.

Forgetting

There are three traditional answers to the question, "Why do people forget things?" (A fourth explanation is derived from information-processing theory.) Each has implications for the classroom and the study skills teacher.

Decay through disuse. This explanation assumes that when learning occurs a *memory trace* (that is, some sort of physical change) is left in the brain. Ordinary metabolic processes somehow lead to a decay of the trace and, with the passage of time, the learning is lost. While it cannot be denied that organic changes in the nervous system may cause forgetting, most contemporary psychologists do not accept "decay through disuse" as a complete account of all forgetting. They cite common instances of learners reusing such motor skills as bicycling or driving with a clutch after decades of noncycling or driving with an automatic gearshift. They note, too, the ability of people approaching senility to speak a language unused since childhood or to vividly recall specific people and events of their youth—often when they cannot recall events of the present day.

Interference effects.   There is more evidence supporting the role of interference. Psychologists have long noted that new learning can interfere with material previously learned. *Retroactive inhibition* occurs, for example, when a student learns one list of nonsense syllables and then immediately learns a second list. Often the learning of the second list—as has been demonstrated in numerous experiments with experimental and control groups—interferes with the learning of the first. *Proactive inhibition* occurs when material previously learned interferes with the recall of newly learned information. Experiments have shown that the more lists of nonsense syllables a person has learned in the immediate past, the poorer will be his or her retention of new lists. However, two features of all experiments in this area are of importance to teachers: (1) both retroactive and proactive inhibition are less dramatic when the material to be learned is meaningful to the learner, and (2) a learner is less susceptible to interference effects when new material has been learned beyond the point of bare mastery (Hilgard, Atkinson, and Atkinson 1975, pp. 230–232).

Motivated forgetting.   Put simply, some forgetting takes place because learners want to forget. The material may have unpleasant associations, or perhaps it is too painful to recall. Because of the highly personal nature of motivated forgetting, teachers have little control over it. It is enough, perhaps, for them to recognize that some material will not be retained by students.

Processing break-downs.   The suggestion that long-term memory is "self-addressable" relates to the two-process theory of memory (Hilgard, Atkinson, and Atkinson 1975) and to various information-processing models. Such theories provide several explanations of forgetting, some of which account for the traditional explanations of forgetting described here.

1. Material may not have been "rehearsed" enough to get into STM.
2. Therefore, decay is possible before material is rehearsed and taken into STM and later into LTM.
3. Material may not have been transferred to LTM.
4. Not enough cues are available to locate it in LTM.
5. The coding system in LTM (the patterns of organization and network of associations) may be weak or ambiguous.
6. The coding system may be similar to or overlap with other coding systems causing cues to be ambiguous.

7. Both retroactive and proactive inhibition may be accounted for by the similar or overlapping coding systems.
8. If material is painful, the learner may instruct his or her "retrieval mechanism" to ignore it.

IMPROVING MEMORY

How can students be helped to remember more and better? Several answers to this important question have been implied:

☐ Encoding may be improved to provide sharper, richer, more striking, and better integrated representations of the material to be later remembered.

☐ Interference, particularly retroactive inhibition, may be controlled in the classroom at least to a limited extent.

☐ Overlearning may increase the chance that material is incorporated into LTM.

☐ Retrieval may be assisted if material is so organized that partial cues can lead to the recall of larger structures.

☐ Retrieval cues may be learned at the time of study to facilitate later retrieval.

Approaches to Memory Improvement

Six specific approaches to memory improvement are examined in this section. Teachers can help students remember through mnemonic devices, use of mental imagery, development of organizational and associative patterns and networks, self-recitation, overlearning, and relating.

Mnemonic Devices

These are any formal schemes designed deliberately to improve memory. They range from tying strings to fingers to simple rhymes such as "Thirty days hath September. . . ." One of the most effective is the *method of loci* (from the Latin word for *places*). The ancient orators would list the main points they wished to remember in their talk and associate each with a *place*, a building encountered in a walk through the town, or a room in a dwelling. As they spoke, they could move (mentally) from place to place, in sequential order, using the place to "trigger" in their minds the points they wished to make. The system clearly works (and has for more than 2,000 years). Today many people remember grocery lists by associating the rooms in their houses with wanted items from the supermarket shelves (a door which the cat scratches to get out with cat food, a kitchen sink with detergent, a closet with mothballs, etc.). In controlled laboratory experiments through the years, researchers have demonstrated that students using the method of loci do from two to seven times better than those who do not (Bower 1972).

Numeric pegword systems substitute words or objects for places. The learner memorizes a list of objects each associated with a digit (usually from 1 to 20) and then, instead of relating the new things to be remembered with places, he or she relates them to the objects on the list. Sometimes, a number-rhyme is used to select the object (1–gun, 2–shoe, 3–tree, etc.); sometimes, the shape of the number becomes the cue (1 looks like a pole, 2 like a swan, 10 like Laurel and Hardy, etc.). A student setting out to learn the names of American presidents in chronological order might associate Washington (#1) with pole (for pole to hang out wash), Adams (#2) with a swan (by the unlikely mental picture of the second president riding a swan), Jefferson (#3) with the picture of a tree outside Jefferson's home, and so on. Briefly described, pegword systems sound asinine and perhaps more trouble than they are worth. However, many are very powerful and have capacities that seem almost limitless (note the so-called "major" systems in which digits are based on consonants; Russell 1979, pp. 126–127) and provide the structure for many popular memory systems (see, for example, Lorayne, 1972).

Mnemonic devices should not be scorned by study skills teachers. Too many of them have proved effective for students through the centuries and are still being used by successful students (who distinguish a Bactrian camel from a dromedary camel by turning the initial letters on their sides to note the Bactrian has two humps and a dromedary one; or who remember the reciprocal of pi (0.318310) by simply remembering the phrase "Can I remember the reciprocal?" in which the number of letters in each word indicates the numbers!)

Why do these methods work? The answer lies in the way retrieval systems are used in free recall. The learner may not know where to look in LTM for the items to be remembered, but if he or she has used the method of loci or a pegword system in the learning stage, then he or she is provided with a set of library shelves or filing cabinets in which material can be systematically stored. Mnemonic devices are retrieval systems built into the encoding systems.

Mental Imagery

The mnemonic devices described contain an element of visual imagery (detergent is associated with a kitchen sink; Washington with a washing line pole, etc.). Psychologists have difficulty in defining mental imagery, but most agree that people can and do form pictures in their minds. Successful students frequently note that they remember details of laboratory experiments or incidents from novels by picturing in their minds the sequence of events, the physical backgrounds, the movements of characters or objects, even the atmospheric conditions.

Much of the experimental research in this area has centered upon the concept of memory as a dual encoding system, one part of which is verbal and the other pictorial, or "imaginal" (see, for example, Paivio 1971). The two parts are interconnected and often redundant, so that traces of the same item can be found in both "subsystems" at the same time. This research helps to explain why memory for concrete items, such as "bicycle" is better than that for abstract items, such as "truth"; both the *verbal symbolic process* and the *nonverbal imagery process* are at work on "bicycle," while only the verbal encodes an abstract word like "truth." The assumption of two separate processes, or subsystems, is in accord with recent research on split-brain (see Fincher 1976, pp. 49–74).

The use of mental imagery helps students remember. Enough evidence is in from teachers and successful students. The exact nature of the relationship between imagery and memory is still not completely understood, nor is it known if one is a necessary prerequisite for the other (Baron, Byrne, and Kantowitz 1977, p. 173), but it is reasonable to assume that any efforts teachers make to help students "see mental pictures" are steps toward better remembering.

Organization, Association, and Memory

From what has already been said about encoding, storage, and retrieval, it seems fairly clear that organization plays an important role in memory. If new material is encoded according to patterns, contexts, principles, associative networks, or other coding systems, it will be retrieved more easily. If "old" material, already stored in LTM, can have imposed on it some organizational system—no matter how artificial—it, too, will be retrieved more easily. One writer of a psychology book for the general public speaks of the human memory as "a vast, intricately interconnected network" (Russell 1979, p. 105). A standard college-level textbook says, "Memories are patterns of items, woven together by rules that impose varying degrees of *organization*; success in retrieval depends upon how much organization is present" (Hilgard, Atkinson, and Atkinson 1975, p. 243).

Considerable research evidence supports this view. In various studies through the years, people have been required to memorize lists of words, some with items randomized, some with items arranged according to some pattern. Inevitably, the people were able to remember lists arranged by patterns better than lists of random items. Whenever a pattern, a plan of organization, a principle, or a coding system is involved, learning and remembering improve (see Baron, Byrne, and Kantowitz 1977). Any of these organizational forms or patterns serve as a retrieval system for generating recall. In a sense, they are mnemonic devices!

What does all this mean for teachers? Clearly, new information and ideas presented in all content area classes should be organized in some fashion, whether by the teacher or by students themselves. The implications derived from research in organization and memory support many of the assumptions underlying discourse analysis (see Chapter 9) and traditional rhetoric (see Chapter 10).

Self-Recitation

The research on self-recitation goes back more than sixty years (Gates 1917). Recall during practice (reciting to oneself as material is studied) increases the retention of the material being studied. A student who reads through an assignment and then poses and answers questions on the reading will remember the contents better than the student who simply read the same assignment several times. As many teachers have noted, self-recitation forces the student to define and select what is to be remembered and gives him or her practice in retrieval. Self-recitation has been formalized by Robinson (1970) into a coherent "method": SQ3R (see Chapter 3). The generalization that self-recitation is an effective way of improving memory is supported by experiments in laboratory learning as well as by experiments with school learning.

Overlearning and Drill

What is the place in a study skills program of overlearning? Drill? Exercise sheets? Workbooks? Many modern teachers tend to look with disapproval upon such approaches to learning and study. "They carry too many connotations of the old-fashioned school at its worst!" remarks one teacher. This point of view is understandable; the concept of overlearning and drill is associated too easily with the kind of mindless, meaningless "busy work" which has characterized ineffective teaching in the past. However, misuse of drill sheets and workbooks in some classrooms does not alter the finding that *material to be long retained must be overlearned*. Enough research has been completed in this area to support the generalization.

For example, typical studies have required three groups to memorize lists of words by the serial-anticipation method, and then terminated one group at a criterion of one perfect recitation of the list, another group at 50 percent overlearning, and another at 100 percent overlearning. (For the 50 percent group, practice would be continued beyond the point of mastery for half as many trials as had been required of the first; for the 100 percent overlearning group, the number of trials would be doubled.) The same list would be relearned by all three groups at various periods of one to twenty-eight days later. Results of such studies consistently show that the greater the degree of overlearning, the greater the retention at all time intervals (Hilgard, Atkinson, and Atkinson 1975, p. 245).

Indeed, there is a place for overlearning and drill in most classrooms. Teachers need to maintain their reservations about the misuses of such approaches; they need to also make intelligent use of drills, exercise sheets, workbooks, and other devices. As long as the individual teaching-learning situation is meaningful to students, overlearning and drill have a place in the study skills program.

Relating

The five preceding approaches to memory improvement are generally included in the professional literature. One other is added here because it overlaps and highlights all others. Teachers in all school content areas need to develop strategies that encourage students to constantly relate one learning to another. As students take in new information and ideas, they need to relate them to previous learning. To effectively encode, store, and retrieve new material, it should be "contexted"; that is, packaged in such a manner that learners can relate it to other material. The relating may, in its grosser forms, be from the new piece of information to an irrelevant, disparate, even bizarre other piece of information (the reciprocal of pi to "Can I remember the reciprocal?" or Adams's place in the sequence of presidents to a picture of the second president riding a swan). Relating may be directly through mental imagery (remembering the climactic point in a short story by seeing the scene in the mind's eye). It may be through organizational patterns (recalling, for example, the sequence of events in a laboratory experiment by means of an outline on the chalkboard). In self-recitation and drill, it may be by relating what is already mastered to the next item to be learned.

Some questions for students that should permeate every study skills class are:

1. How does *this* relate to what I already know?
2. What does it remind me of?
3. What can I associate it with?
4. Can I picture it in my mind?
5. What can I link this picture to?
6. How does it relate to the topic as a whole?
7. What crazy things pop into my mind when I think of it?
8. How can I use the crazy associations to help remember?

9. How does this relate to what I learned before?
10. How does it relate to my life outside this class?

Interest and Memory

How does this material get from the STM into the LTM? Rehearsal plays a major role in transferring it from the sensory storage system to STM and a role in getting it from STM into LTM. But rehearsal is not the sole, nor the best, explanation for why a piece of information or an idea becomes part of long-term memory.

How can teachers help students move material from STM to LTM? This is surely one of the key questions in all teaching and, yet, ironically, it is one that is not always answered satisfactorily in books on experimental psychology! Serious studies in learning and memory present teachers with considerable data on learning and forgetting curves, the differences between verbal symbolic processes versus nonverbal imagery process, retroactive inhibitions, and models of two-way processing theories, but not much directly about what to many teachers is the most important question of all. "I can explain combustion for hours to that general science class," says one disgruntled colleague, "but I'm lucky if the material goes from that sensory storage system into *short-term* memory! The only way that group would put it into LTM would be if I set the building on fire!"

Perhaps more can be learned from Mr. Disgruntled Colleague (and from his friends, Mr. Less-Disgruntled and Ms. Not-Disgruntled-At-All) than from the experimental psychologists and learning theorists. What causes material to break into LTM? Most thoughtful teachers will say "interesting material and interesting activities." Most nonteachers would agree. But, now, the next question must be: What makes material interesting?

The answer here is suggested in a recent book on human motivation: "*The intensity of our interest in an activity as well as the amount of effort that we expend on it depends on our feeling of personal involvement in that activity*" (Kolesnik 1978, p. 195). Fortunately, strategies for increasing personal involvement have been practiced for years in many classes:

☐ Materials must be made interesting. If topics are not intrinsically interesting in their own right, someone (a teacher) must make them interesting by using examples, anecdotes, and other illustrative material that *relates* the "academic" content to the lives and concerns of the students. This means that teachers need not apologize for using analogies from professional sports, automotive mechanics, motorcycling, social life, or whatever catches the attention of students. Nor should teachers hesitate to go out of their way to relate the course content to the students in very direct personal ways by using personal references, stories, or examples that touch the lives of their clients (see Chapter 2).

☐ Role-playing and dramatics are not only fun but effective in physically involving students in the course content. McCaffery (1973) found that students not only enjoyed poetry study more when they *acted out* poems, but that they understood more and *remembered more* (see Chapter 10). Many studies have found role-playing effective in learning and remembering because, among other reasons, it directly involves participants (Stanford and Roark 1974).

☐ Small group discussions also promote maximum involvement. All students have opportunities to share, comment, and react; consequently, they feel more involved with the direction of the class than if they sat passively lecture-listening. Small group work may often lead to digressions but, when well-structured and carefully planned, it increases involvement and, hence, interest.

☐ Students are interested in activities they themselves plan. When personally involved in choosing the goals and activities of the unit or course, students generally feel more responsibility for learning outcomes. Many teachers have noted that student interest is higher when they plan, organize, and evaluate their own work.

☐ Individual projects, of course, increase interest. One generalization about human beings that psychologists from almost all schools of thought agree upon is that people are different. Each is shaped by unique biological inheritance, specific ways of responding to cultural influences, and particular personal experiences (Hilgard, Atkinson, and Atkinson 1975, p. 367). When teachers force all students into the exact same mold, day after day, they surely kill interest and involvement. Successful teachers have always known that, while common learning activities are justifiable, more learning occurs in the classroom when students are allowed to go off on their own and work through problems, conduct research, develop materials, and answer their own questions. Whenever teachers build into their course opportunities for personal projects, they do much to heighten interest in the course and, in the process, allow more course content to get from STM to LTM!

Improving Test-Taking Skills

Tests are administered for a number of reasons: teachers want to know how well their students have mastered certain skills and understood course content *and* how well their own teaching techniques are working; teachers, administrators, and parents want to know how their students compare to other, similar students throughout the country; school personnel want to diagnose the needs of particular students so that better or more appropriate instruction may be provided; and students want to know how well they are doing. The reasons vary from class to class and from test to test. One thing is sure—testing is part and parcel of schooling. Teachers and students, no matter what their individual persuasions and philosophies, have inherited, to a large extent, a tradition in America of test-taking and test-giving. They may agree with Ralph Nader that nationally-administered tests do not measure "important attributes" such as "judgment, determination, experience, idealism and creativity" (*New York Times* July 15, 1979), but they most probably concede that testing does have a place in the classroom. Successful teachers have always recognized that, if nothing else, testing helps give them at least minimal feedback on the effectiveness of their own teaching.

Guidelines

Because the reasons for testing and the types of tests vary so widely from class to class, it is difficult to articulate generalizations that hold for all grade levels, all content areas, all teachers, or all schools. The following six guidelines, however, direct attention to major issues and problems of concern to most study skills teachers.

Talk about tests and testing.   Many students survive and even profit from a dozen years of formal education without ever having opportunities to sit down with an informed and concerned adult to talk about the rationale for testing. They have been given standardized tests in reading and various school content areas, so-called "intelligence" tests (see Chapters 1 and 5) and countless teacher-made tests, yet no one has explained what "the curve" is, the penalties for guessing, the purpose of tests in general, or the inadequacies, weaknesses, and pitfalls inherent in the measurement of human attributes.

Many teachers have found that their students are less intimidated by standardized and teacher-made tests when they have had a chance to discuss such basic topics as course objectives, skills, affective and cognitive learnings, the bell-shaped curve, tally sheets, scoring, answer sheets, grading, and especially the purposes behind particular tests. High school and college students can discuss the history of the testing movement, the concept of IQ, the difficulties of measuring important human qualities such as creativity, taste, determination, or idealism, etc. Test-takers at all levels should have opportunities to discuss questions such as: What is the purpose of this test? Who developed it? Why? Who decided the answers? How? Why are we taking it? Will we be given the results? (Why not?) In what ways will this help me? My teacher? Am I being compared to others? Who are they?

Have students make their own tests. One of the most effective ways to teach about testing and give students insights into test-taking is to encourage them to frequently make their own tests. Some teachers make it a regular practice to have students *predict* test questions. As material is studied each day, the teacher reminds the class that a test must be given at the end of the week, unit, or course, and that they should be "on the watch" for good items. As the contributions are found, the teacher places them on the bulletin board or duplicates them a day or two before the test for class or home review. Other teachers stop before the end of the unit or course and note its specific objectives. Students then prepare together, as a class or in small groups, test items that measure a student's success in mastering the objectives. Teachers who take either of these approaches sometimes make the tests themselves and include student contributions, or use the best student ideas and add nothing themselves but editing.

Test-making is an excellent way of teaching about *kinds* of tests and test items. The difference between essay and objective tests becomes clear for many students for the first time, and the differences between objective test items (plus the advantages and disadvantages of each) become obvious: When is it best to use a true or false item? A sentence-completion type? A fill-in-the-blanks type? A multiple-choice? What is a "distractor"? Why use "distractors"? In what ways is an objective test better than an essay test? What can an essay-type do that a multiple choice cannot?

Cultivate test sophistication. After students have discussed the theory behind test-making and written a few tests themselves, they are on their way to "test sophistication." Now they can profit from some direct instructions in *how to take a test.* Although the research literature on measurement is vast, few studies have focused on the importance of teaching students the specific procedures needed to become test-wise; however, those studies have indicated that teaching test-wise techniques generally lead to improved performance by test-takers (see, for example, Erickson 1972). What can teachers do to cultivate test sophistication? Here are ten suggestions:

1. Bring in some actual test booklets and answer sheets. (If these are not available, make some "mock" copies that resemble the test to be taken.)
2. Go over the directions carefully and show students how to "test out" their understanding of the directions by checking the

sample exercises. Emphasize that time spent at this stage—before ever really "doing" an item—is time well spent.

3. Tell the students to keep the answer sheet beside their writing hand to avoid reaching over the booklet to mark (thus saving time and eliminating interruption of thought).

4. Tell the students to move systematically through the test, marking the answer sheet for answers they are fairly sure of, and then later go back to the "tricky" items.

5. Remind the students that they should not worry about doing every item but should move on at a slow, steady pace.

6. Explain the Right-minus-Wrong formula used in true-false tests. (Because guessing gives a 50-50 chance of getting each item right by chance, Wrongs are subtracted from Rights; therefore, students should omit really puzzling items.)

7. Remind the students to be super-cautious when they see words like *always, invariably* and *never.*

8. Tell the students to immediately eliminate the obvious incorrect answers in a multiple choice, and then come back later, if necessary, to think through the difficult choices.

9. Remind the students to watch for changes in the directions. Sometimes the test-makers shift from one format to another after several items.

10. For math problems, tell students to make quick "guesstimates." Often a common-sense guess will help narrow down the possibilities. If time permits, they can go back and apply the formula.

Show students how to take particular tests. The suggestions for developing test sophistication may be used to prepare students for most kinds of standardized, objective tests used in schools. There is nothing unprofessional or underhanded about preparing students to take a particular kind of test. The test-makers, as a matter of record, have worked to make their tests valid and reliable; they have usually done item-analyses to eliminate nondiscriminating items and have administered their tests to thousands of students throughout the country to establish norms. The one delimiting factor they have no control over is the test-taking sophistication of testees. It would be grossly unfair for Teacher A's class to be compared to Teacher B's class if A's had never taken, for example, any standardized reading test while B's had taken a different one each year for ten years! It may be said that Teacher A has a responsibility to expose her students to, at least, a mock version of a standardized reading test so that, when the class has to take one, they will not be unfairly intimidated. (See Erickson 1972.)

An example of teaching students how to take a particular kind of test is found in a three-year experiment at Springside School in Chestnut Hill,

Pennsylvania (Kintisch 1979). In order to improve test sophistication (and to improve verbal scores on the Scholastic Aptitude Test) teachers decided to help students (1) make more efficient use of time, especially in thirty-minute units; (2) respond more easily to multiple-choice test items; and (3) reduce their anticipation-anxiety. First, students were encouraged to use a stop watch for timed readings at home and in school to build efficiency and concentration. They kept records of their progress and moved from 400-word articles to 2,000-word articles. (They also created their own questions prior to reading, based on article titles, headings, and subheadings, as in the SQ3R method.) Second, they met in class to analyze their responses to each other's multiple-choice questions, evaluating their mistakes and developing ease in dealing with this type of question. Third, they had practice sessions in class handling ten-minute sustained silent readings of selected materials, learning to skim, scan, and adjust their rates to the level of difficulty of the material. In addition, students visited the building where the SAT would be given, and then discussed the test-taking experience with a teacher who had herself recently taken the examination.

The results showed a thirty-five-point gain (from the eleventh to twelfth grade) for students who had taken the "training sessions," in contrast to a twenty-one-point gain for students in a control group. "Many more students in the experimental group had increases of one hundred or more points than in the control group" (Kintisch 1979, p. 418). As the researchers noted, experiments such as this need to be carried out with larger samples and with different types of students. This modicum of evidence does lend support, however, to the suggestion: Show students how to take a particular test!

Show students how to take an essay test. Essay tests present special problems and require special preparation. Students at all levels need many practice sessions, much teacher guidance, and immediate feedback. Here are eight suggestions:

1. Give students many samples of the kinds of essay tests they will have to contend with. (Examples may be chosen from ones to be used later in the course, from other grade levels, or from other course instructors.)
2. Discuss the items, the specific instructions (word by word), the time limits, the ways students can block off their time to cover each item, etc.
3. If choice is allowed ("Answer three of the following five questions"), tell the students to save time by eliminating at once the ones they cannot handle.

4. Tell the students to sketch out an outline before writing. This allows time to think, and the process helps organize their thoughts. Remind students that the few minutes taken *before* writing to think through an outline is worth an extra hour at the end.
5. After the outline is done, tell students to check their answers to the following questions (these may be on the board for practice sessions):
   a. What am I supposed to do?
   b. What is the question?
   c. Are there several parts to the answer?
   d. Can I arrange these in any special order?
   e. Will my answer fit a pattern (such as cause and effect? Enumeration? Time order? Comparison and contrast?)
   f. What examples will illustrate my main point(s)?
   g. What vocabulary words are appropriate to this topic?
   h. Can I quote an authority? Refer to well-known books?
6. Tell the students to "show off" by including as much information as they can to prove they have studied the material.
7. Remind the students to proofread! Tell them to double-check for incomplete or run-on sentences, capitalization, punctuation, etc.
8. Emphasize appearance and legibility. Many students are their own worst enemies; they thoughtlessly pass in papers that look bad and influence the judgment of the evaluator. Some discussion of legibility and neatness ought to be incorporated into all practice sessions.

Set up systematic review systems.   One justification for test-giving (which even the severest critics of testing programs can usually accept) is that a test can be a learning device. The act of reviewing for a test may, in itself, serve as a learning approach to a topic. Students are forced to look for structures inherent in the material, for organizational patterns to help them remember, for useful mnemonic devices, for ways of picturing otherwise abstract ideas, and for relating what they are learning to what they already know. They are encouraged to exploit self-recitation, drill, and overlearning.

A systematic review of systems set up by the teacher or the group allows opportunities to discuss basic concepts associated with memory and forgetting, especially in high school and college classes. Teachers can discuss kinds of memory, free versus aided recall, retrieval, cues, redintegrative memory, STM and LTM, even information-processing theories of learning. These topics need not be considered the exclusive properties of the psychology class. If learning and memory lie at the basis of all study skills instruction, they should be a part of all content area classes. Students in upper elementary and middle-school classes can discuss the phenomenon of forgetting, and they may share experiences and discoveries about how people forget and how people remember. The method of loci, pegword strategies, SQ3R, drill, and remembering through pictures have roles to play at all educational levels.

Some teachers build a review system into the daily and weekly schedules of their classes, blocking off time within the period or unit to check on course objectives and review course material. Some schedule regular sessions each week for run-downs of the work done in preceding days. Some plan small group activities in which students focus on key topics and reread, review, and suggest test items. Most agree that a planned program of review is the best attack on cramming. Students begin to see that such approaches as self-recitation, drill, and overlearning need time, and that cramming is essentially nonproductive.

Idea Box
Memory and Test-Taking

Tell students that psychologists are not exactly sure how ideas and information get into the memory. Suggest that a team of interested students conduct a survey of students, teachers, parents, and other adults, asking, "What makes *you* remember something?" The team members may later organize the answers and report in a panel discussion or a brief duplicated copy of Survey Results.

Point out the value of *mental imagery* in improving memory. Encourage students to collect examples from their own lives relating how a mental picture helps them recall an event or experience in detail. A portion of class time may be devoted to sharing "personal pictures." Students may be led to realize that mental picturing is a legitimate and useful way for improving the memory.

To make students more aware of how memory works, have them suggest a topic (automobiles, Western movies, fast-food restaurants) and then check to see how much they can recall in sixty seconds about the topic (by making check marks on a sheet of paper). Next, give them a topic, perhaps from previous class discussion, and try the same timed count. This, or similar exercises, can lead into discussions on: What is memory? How does it work? Why do we remember more about some topics than others? Students may be led to see that the phenomenon of memory is still not completely understood, and that it is interesting, important, and improvable.

Explain what *mnemonic devices* are, and then have the class collect as many as possible. Students can collect these on 3 × 5 cards for a bulletin board display, or duplicate them so that all students have copies. Remind them that mnemonic devices may be silly, outrageous, even "naughty." The important thing is that they work!

One way to begin class discussions on the phenomenon of memory is to see how far back into the past individual students can remember. Students can often recall events from early grades, from preschool, and sometimes from infancy. A short session in which they share recollections can lead into more academic discussions on the nature of memory, forgetting, mental imagery, and the reasons why some events are remembered and some not.

Tell middle school and high school students about the four kinds of memory: recall, recognition, relearning, and redintegrative memory. Have them search their own minds for examples of each, and allow time for discussion. Discussion questions may include: Which kind of memory do we use most in school? Outside of school? Which are you, personally, best at? Why? How can you improve each kind of memory?

High school and college students may be introduced to the concepts of the sensory storage system, short-term memory, and long-term memory. They can research the characteristics of each by noting within a given time period (ten minutes before or after class) examples of information coming into the sensory storage system and examples retained in STM and/or LTM. A key discussion question might be: How can you remember items for this discussion if they did not go into LTM? Answers can lead to further discussion of concepts such as *attention, interest,* and *notetaking.*

What are *retrieval clues?* Most secondary school students are ready to deal with the idea of small cues being used to reconstruct larger, detailed memory pictures. While talking about memory in her course, one teacher regularly uses this assignment: "Before tomorrow's class—twenty-four hours from now—try to find an example of a retrieval cue at work in your own life. It may be that particular sight, sound, even smell, that helps you recall a vivid memory from years ago." She provides several examples, and then the next day devotes class time to sharing student examples.

How is your memory like a computer? High school and college students may be encouraged to do individual research (freshman college psychology textbooks in the library are a good source of information) and report to the group on their findings. Diagrams and illustrative comparisons can show the processes of encoding, storage, and retrieval. Questions for group discussion may start with: In what ways are your memory and computer memory alike? Different? Why cannot a man-made computer ever replace the human brain? What advantages have such machines over the brain?

Tie discussions on memory with lessons on notetaking. Remind students that human memory is a fragile thing and that notetaking generally enhances its power. Review basic notetaking skills (see Chapter 7) and encourage students to explore the value of notetaking to help get ideas and information from the sensory storage system to short-term memory to—hopefully—long-term memory.

A short unit on memory is a good place to review SQ3R (see Chapter 3): Why does SQ3R work to help memory? In what ways does it help with the encoding of new ideas and information? What part does self-recitation play in memory? High school students may explore some of the research supporting SQ3R as a learning-memorizing technique.

Give students this quotation from Kolesnik (1978, p. 105): "The intensity of our interest in an activity as well as the amount of effort that we expend on it depends on our feeling of personal involvement in that activity." Ask them to define interest. Ask them to explain the quotation in their terms: What does interest mean to you? What is personal involvement? What subjects are you most interested in? How are you more "involved" in them than in others? Is the statement true to your experience? Can you force yourself to become interested in a subject or topic? How? Such discussions may frequently establish a concern about learning, memory, and study that otherwise would not exist in a class.

Point out that some students approach tests with fear and trepidation. Note that fear often prevents success because it conditions the mind to failure. Allow class time to discuss fear of testing (and its consequences): Why do people fear tests? How can such fears be overcome? How can you best circumvent the "fear hurdle"? Informal class talk about widespread concerns may, in itself, do a good deal toward raising scores on school-wide tests.

Prior to regular class tests, take time to go over "Suggestions for Successful Review." These may be posted or duplicated for student notebooks:

1. *Select what is important.*   (Go through your notes and star the points that you believe are fundamental. Compare your starred items with those of friends. Are you in agreement? If not, why not? Check some of these with your teacher.)

2. *Review by predicting questions.*   (You can turn statements in your notes and in the book into questions. Try it. Now decide which are probably ones that *you* would put on a test. Find another student and test each other on your own questions.)

3. *Reorganize your material.*   (Use an entirely different system of organizing your class notes. This may involve extensive rewriting, but it is worth it. If your history notes, for example, are arranged chronologically, go back and arrange them by cause-and-effect, or by problems, or

biographically. Try rearranging math notes by terminology, by general principles, by definitions, or by kinds of examples given.)

4. *Change your point of view.*   (If you have approached the material from the memorizing angle, now try looking at it from the point of view of *application*. On a separate piece of paper, note all the ways a person could *use* the material. You'll find memorization improves.)

5. *Establish personal relationships.*   (Go through all your notes and jot down a *personal* association in the margin, no matter how offbeat or bizarre. Think of some way the piece of information relates to your life now, in the past, or in the future. Again, you'll find memory improves.)

6. *Overlearn.* (Don't stop while you are ahead! Keep going on and review, review, review. The research evidence indicates overlearning pays off in a big way!)

Remind students that one good way of learning a topic is to teach it to someone else: "After reviewing a topic thoroughly for a test in class, find a friend in this or another class and try to teach it to him or her." Note that this approach can be even more effective if the student-teacher makes up and uses a test: "As you review, make up a ten-item test which you can give to *your* student. That way, you'll discover how well you have taught—and learned."

Because vocabulary and special terminology is so important to all school subjects, encourage students to prepare special word lists before they take a test. Have them collect all possible words associated with the topic(s), list these, find definitions, and test one another out to make sure that, if nothing else, everyone knows the language.

Before the Big Test Day comes, take some class time to discuss the importance of the mind-body relationship! Remind students that no matter how much they have learned, their minds will not function efficiently if their bodies are tired and weakened. This is a good chance to discuss the importance of rest, sleep, proper eating, and exercise. It is a good opportunity, too, to discuss the perils of last-minute cramming. Remind students that overlearning is important but only if it is *concluded* several days before a test, and that late-night sessions before the BTD are nonproductive and, actually, self-defeating.

Before they take a standardized test, remind students to *survey:* "Don't plunge in until you have read through the directions carefully and skimmed the entire test!" Some teachers duplicate the following questions and discuss them in class:

1. How long is the whole test?
2. How much time will you have?
3. Do all questions count equally?
4. Which, if any, carry more weight?
5. Do the directions change "in midstream"?
6. Do you need a special pencil?
7. Is there a place for outlining or sketching in answers?
8. Can you use aids (such as tables)?
9. Are any questions related so that you have to do one before the other?
10. Have you written your name?

For important tests (such as the SATs), teachers may ease students into the testing situation by doing the following:

1. If possible, take them to the room or building where the test will be given so the physical surroundings will be familiar.
2. Bring a student into your class who has already taken the test to tell about his or her experiences.
3. Discuss the time schedule, the importance of prompt arrival, the possible breaks or recesses, and other features of the testing situation that may be unfamiliar to students.

If the test to be taken is machine-scored, teachers should remind students:

1. Make your marks full and solid.
2. Make any erasures clean.
3. Use the special pencil if it is required.
4. Don't make random or stray marks on the answer sheet.

For students who have never taken such a test, many teachers bring in a few answer sheets the day before and discuss each of these points, how the scoring machines work, and then allow students a chance to examine the sheets. Such seemingly basic steps actually help many students get higher grades!

Remind students again and again that "neatness counts"! Point out that studies have repeatedly shown graders favoring good-looking papers over sloppy ones, even though both contained essentially the same answers.

Some teachers emphasize these points by duplicating a list of "Warnings for Essay Test Takers":

1. Take time to form your letters and punctuations marks clearly.
2. Distinguish carefully between similar letters such as Q and G.
3. Write each letter the same way each time you use it.
4. Avoid "cute" flourishes, such as dots over "i" and artistic tricks at the ends of words and sentences.
5. Try to keep reasonable margins.
6. Don't crowd phrases or sentences together.
7. Bring and *use* a good quality pen.
8. Try to avoid abbreviations.
9. Double-check for run-ons, fragments, and misspellings.
10. Make sure you put your name on the paper.

Point out that testing has become widespread in our society. Suggest that individual students as a small group search out the uses to which testing is put today (such as for civil service positions, admission to special programs, and promotion in certain industries and businesses). Suggest, too, that the students try to discover (in their library) the names of some of the tests and, if possible, duplicate items found in sample copies so that all in the class can know the tests and what they are like.

Quote Ralph Nader's comments that tests cannot measure important human attributes such as "judgment, determination, experience, idealism, and creativity" (*New York Times* July 15, 1979). Ask students to respond orally (or in writing) to the question: "What can tests measure?" High school and college students may be encouraged to list famous, widely-used, and controversial tests, and then discuss in class the pros and cons of testing in general: Why test? Who profits? Who loses? Are there alternatives to testing?

Help students realize how testing works by encouraging them to construct a Humor Test. One class listed the reasons why people laugh (exaggeration, understatement, surprise, etc.) and then constructed a tape-recorded test which tried to discover the most powerful of their reasons. Later, the students and their teacher admitted that they did not discover much about humor in their ninth-grade class but did learn a great deal about the process of measuring a human characteristic.

Tell students that one high school guidance counselor says: "A test is a contest." Encourage them to conduct a panel discussion to explore the facets of this contention. Some may wish to argue against this point of view; others, for it. The discussion provides an opportunity to articulate many unexpressed feelings students have about testing in their lives.

References

Andreas, Burton G. *Experimental Psychology*, 2nd ed. New York: John Wiley and Sons, Inc., 1972.

Baron, Robert A.; Donn Byrne; and Barry H. Kantowitz. *Psychology: Understanding Behavior*. Philadelphia: W. B. Saunders Company, 1977.

Bower, G. H. "Mental Imagery and Associative Learning." In *Cognition in Learning and Memory*. Edited by L. Gregg. New York: John Wiley and Sons, Inc., 1972.

Erickson, Michael E. "Test Sophistication: An Important Consideration." *Journal of Reading* 16 (November 1972): 140–144.

Fincher, Jack. *Human Intelligence*. New York: G. P. Putnam's Sons, 1976.

Gates, Arthur I. "Recitation as a Factor in Memorizing." *Archives of Psychology* 40 (1917).

Hilgard, Ernest R.; Richard C. Atkinson; and Rita L. Atkinson. *Introduction to Psychology*, 6th ed. New York: Harcourt Brace Jovanovich, Inc., 1975.

Kintisch, Lenore S. "Classroom Techniques for Improving Scholastic Aptitude Test Scores." *Journal of Reading* 22 (February 1979): 416–419.

Kolesnik, Walter B. *Motivation: Understanding and Influencing Human Behavior*. Boston: Allyn and Bacon, Inc., 1978.

Lindsay, Peter H., and Donald A. Norman. *Human Information Processing*. New York: Academic Press, 1972.

Lorayne, Harry. *How to Develop a Super-Power Memory*. New York: New American Library, 1972.

McCaffery, Marilyn. *The Development and Evaluation of an Oral-Dramatic Approach for the Teaching of Poetry*. Ph.D. dissertation, Boston University, 1973.

New York Times. "Governor Signs Bill on College Testing." July 15, 1979, p. 23.

Norman, Donald A., and D. E. Rumelhart. *Explorations in Cognition*. San Francisco: Freeman, 1975.

Paivio A. *Imagery and Verbal Processes*. New York: Holt, Rinehart and Winston, 1971.

Robinson, Francis P. *Effective Study*, 4th ed. New York: Harper Row Publishers, 1970.

Russell, Peter. *The Brain Book*. New York: Hawthorn Books, Inc., 1979.

Shiffrin, R. M. and R. C. Atkinson. "Storage and Retrieval Processes in Long-term Memory." *Psychological Review* 76 (1969): 179–193.

Stanford, G., and A. E. Roark. *Human Interaction in Education*. Boston: Allyn and Bacon, Inc., 1974.

12

MOTIVATION, SELF-CONCEPT, AND THE STUDY SKILLS PROGRAM

Previous chapters have examined a variety of topics associated with the teaching of study skills. Specific topics (such as classroom listening, reading assignments, notetaking, library research, spelling, etc.) are the almost daily concerns of all teachers. Other topics (comprehension, thinking processes, memory, etc.) are important because decisions about daily teaching are based to a large extent upon a teacher's understanding of them. Underlying *all* discussions of these specific and more general topics are considerations of motivation and students' concepts of themselves as learners in the classroom.

Chapter 12 focuses on these two important areas. It examines four explanations of motivation, as derived from contemporary theory and research in psychology, and some of their classroom implications. The chapter then looks at what is currently known about self-concept and school achievement, and concludes with a set of guidelines for teachers to consider as they plan programs in study skills.

MOTIVATING STUDENTS IN A
STUDY SKILLS PROGRAM

Why does one young person spend hours each day in a dance studio or on a gym track in painful training for a ballet try-out or a regional field event? Why does another devote all spare time from a demanding job writing the first draft of a novel? Rebuilding old automobiles? Jogging? Cooking? Why does still another spend all time and energy trying to get ahead on the job? Another to working with alcoholics on Skid Row?

Bringing the questions into the classroom, why does Fred complete assignments on time, spend hours memorizing lists and formulas and preparing research reports, while David sits passively in the classroom with his eyes on the classroom clock? Why does Jill work thirty hours a week on a part-time job and another twenty on school tasks, while Bill refuses to learn or be taught?

Temperament, genetic inheritance, or physiological drives cannot account for the diversity and complexity of human behaviors—in the classroom or the world outside of it. Many theories have been advanced through the years to explain human motivation. None is accepted completely by all teachers, parents, or theorists. Four of the more influential explanations are examined here.

Psychoanalytic Theory

One of the most widely discussed explanations of human behavior comes from psychoanalytic theory. It rests, to a large extent, upon Freud's belief that all human behavior results from two opposing groups of instincts: the life instincts (or Eros) and the death instincts (or Thanatos). The first are life-affirming, positive, and conducive to growth; the second, generally, tend toward destruction. Eros, deriving energy from the *libido* (a kind of energy force for the life instinct) focuses on sex, birth, love, affection, caring, and similar activities; Thanatos focuses upon suicide, various forms of self-destruction, and aggression toward others. Put simply, the two basic human motives are sex and aggression, and these appear very early in a child's life (sex expressed in caressing, touching and stimulating body areas; aggression, by hitting, biting, damaging). At the core of the psychoanalytic theory is the notion that when parents delimit sex and aggression (as they must to insure some kind of tribal and community continuity), their expression becomes repressed and, instead of revealing themselves freely, they "go underground" and become unconscious motivations. It is these unconscious motivations that often determine many of a person's behaviors throughout life.

As psychoanalytic theory has evolved since the turn of the century, the concept of unconscious motivation has been one of its cornerstones. People tend to cover up—especially to themselves—their "real" motives for behaving in certain ways, and they sometimes do this by quite rational thinking. Two forces, comparable to the libido, operate in the "great cover-up": the *ego* (the rational dimension of personality) and the *superego* (or moral-judicial-ethical dimension). The ego sees *what is* and the superego sees *what should be*. When a person's thoughts, feelings, and actions become possibly dangerous to the person or others, the ego and superego step in and blunt the forces of Eros and Thanatos, either by valid intellectual judgments of what should be done or by a series of *defensive mechanisms*. These have been summarized in a number of popular and professional books (see, for example, Kolesnik 1978; Hall 1954), but because of their importance to teachers, they are briefly described here:

Repression. When possibly harmful urges, feelings, or memories arise and are opposed by the superego they are simply forced out of the conscious mind by the ego. (A student may have enormous feelings of hostility toward teachers but the student's ego forces him or her to submerge or conceal them. They are not destroyed; they continue to seek release, though often in some disguised form.)

Displacement. Sometimes feelings are channeled away from one object toward another; the urge remains but its expression is less obvious. (The same student may displace his or her hostility toward teachers by focusing upon school property, and destroying lighting fixtures, doors, windows, etc., in the building.)

Sublimation. This is a more wholesome form of displacement; the objects of feelings, usually associated with Eros rather than Thanatos, shift to the more socially-acceptable. (An adolescent with a strong sex drive, which his or her ego and superego cannot allow him or her to satisfy in a school setting, may develop a "crush" on the teacher, or even on the teacher's subject!)

Identification. Here the person incorporates into his or her own personality admired traits of a "loved" person. (A student frustrated by school work may identify with a rock star, or a teacher, so that some of that person's achievements are reflected back upon himself or herself; thus, adolescents often ape the mannerisms and dress styles of others.) As Kolesnik points out, this is often desirable: "Identification is used to alleviate anxieties about one's own shortcomings by attributing to oneself the strengths and virtues of others" (Kolesnik 1978, p. 35).

Projection. This seems to be the opposite of identification. The person alleviates feelings of guilt or anxiety by attributing to someone else his or her faults or problems. (The student who has trouble with mathematics argues that the teacher "doesn't know how to teach." The student with unsatisfied aggressions tends to believe the teacher is "out to get him.")

Regression. To avoid the difficulties of the present day, the individual moves back in time to a period when he or she was happier and more able to cope. (College students, faced with the problems of adjusting to adult expectations, sometimes act as if they were first-graders again! Others may have a temper tantrum or weep openly in an adult problem situation because such behaviors were acceptable at earlier periods of their lives.)

Can teachers profit from an understanding of psychoanalytic theory? So much of the behavior of successful and unsuccessful students may be explained by classical Freudian theory that it behooves teachers to at least examine and "think about" such theory in relation to their students. Adolescent "crushes," vandalism, refusal to cooperate in class, even open hostility have been explained by the application of psychoanalytic theory. Although other explanations of human motivation may be more in vogue in the 1980s, basic psychoanalytic concepts are still worth exploring as teacher try to motivate students in the classroom.

Psychoanalysis and teaching are examined in a number of books (see, for example, Hill 1971; Roberts, 1975); psychoanalysis, children, and adolescence are explored in others (see, for example, Erikson 1968; Bettleheim 1969).

Behaviorism

A theory more in vogue in the past decades has been behaviorism. Contrary to psychoanalytic theory, the heart of behavioristic theory is the belief that people behave in certain ways simply because they have learned to behave in these ways and not in others. Children, adolescents, and adults are not motivated by "life instincts," "death instincts," or other unconscious tendencies; they behave as they do because they have been so *conditioned*.

Behaviorists from John Watson through B. F. Skinner (1968, 1974) believe that all human behavior is learned (with the exception of biological drives, such as the need to eat, sleep, or procreate, and basic reflexes such as sneezing or blinking), and that behavior is learned (shaped or determined) by its consequences. Put simply, they say that behaviors which have pleasant results are repeated, and those which have unpleasant results are avoided. Behaviorist psychologists rarely discuss motivation because it is at the core of their theory: people (students, colleagues, friends, relatives, ourselves!) do things which will have pleasant consequences and avoid those that bring distress or pain. Teachers who emphasize prelearning activities in an effort to create "a desire to learn" are, to behaviorists, on the wrong track. "Desire" is out of teachers' hands, they say; the *consequences* of learning (which *are* in their hands!) are paramount. To motivate reading, for example, the teacher need not worry about building up a desire to read. Instead, he or she should directly teach the student to read and then make sure that the results of the experience are accompanied by positive (pleasureful) consequences.

This stimulus-response view of learning has great implications for schooling. Tom is told to learn ten new spelling words (his stimulus); he then studies the ten words (his response); he next receives an A on his spelling test (his reinforcing stimulus). Tom, therefore, *learns* the material. Motivation is built into the learning experience. The reinforcing stimuli—clearly, very important in teaching—include high grades, smiles, pats on the back, comments such as, "Super! You're doing a great job, Tom!," gold stars, honor roll mention, etc. Kolesnik (1978) lists types of *secondary* (or *conditioned*) *reinforcers* (as distinguished from primary reinforcers such as food or drink which, though used in animal training, are rarely found in school settings):

1. Social reinforcers (smiles, winks, remarks such as, "Nice going")
2. Symbolic reinforcers (gold stars, high grades, displayed papers, honors)
3. Tangible reinforcers (money, toys, records, tickets to rock concerts)
4. Activity reinforcers (being allowed to go on a field trip, to watch television, to attend a party)
5. Internal reinforcers (writing a story, completing a project, editing the school newspaper, participating in team sports; these require no external system of rewards and punishments)

One behaviorist (Bandura 1969, 1974) notes that behavior is also learned by imitation. Students (and people in general) set standards for their behavior and reward or punish themselves according to how well their behavior matches that of a selected model. His research indicates that students may pattern themselves on admired personalities and derive pleasures from dressing, speaking, or responding the way they do. "Imitation reinforcement" differs from the psychoanalytic idea of identification in that the model's traits, values, and behaviors arc not assimilated into the learner's personality, only imitated. No matter how viewed, imitation, as seen by the behaviorist psychologists, plays a role in school learning.

"What about negative reinforcement?" some teachers and parents ask. "If high grades and gold stars affect learning positively, won't Fs and Detention Room also influence behavior in school?" Clearly, just as people try to attain pleasure by their behavior, they try to avoid its possible unpleasant consequences. Negative reinforcers include punishments, deprivation, pain, and inconvenience. Behaviorists have studied the range of negative reinforcers (which are not necessarily punishments but usually unpleasant consequences of an act) and aversive motivations (which involve acts the learner wants to avert or escape from). They, too, conclude that these influence learning and serve, in their way, as powerful motivators. Students put themselves in learning situations to avoid verbal reprimands, loss of status, staying after school, being thrown off the team, poor grades, school suspension, and so forth. Most behaviorists, however, recommend punishment (the ultimate negative reinforcer or aversive motivation) only as a last resort because it (1) teaches students to avoid (that is, punishment) rather than seek out (rewards); (2)

promotes hostility and resentment; and (3) provides students with working models of an aggressive-type (since some students may identify with their punishers).

The educational implications of behaviorist theory have had considerable impact on schooling. Many teachers, for example, have accepted *programming* as a legitimate aspect of classroom learning. They have organized their courses and lessons to introduce students to new material in a sequential, step-by-step progression with much positive reinforcement built into the "program." Their students learn fresh material, are immediately rewarded, and move on to the next "bit" of new material and another reward. Such teachers have been supported frequently by published texts and course material of a "programmed" nature. Other teachers (and administrators and curriculum specialists) have tried to improve learning by spelling out their learning objectives in behavioral terms. Advocates of *performance objectives* (such as Kibler 1974, or Mager 1962) suggest that before programming can take place, the course objectives must be specified in behavioral terms; that is, in measurable, observable terms. The teacher, they say, should not teach the reading skill of recognizing main idea sentences but teach students, instead, so that they will be able to underline the main idea sentence in a specific paragraph on a specific page. Teachers who believe in performance objectives say that rewards, and other forms of positive reinforcement, are ineffective if the learning goals are fuzzy, overgeneralized, and vague.

Other teachers have accepted the basic tenets of behaviorist theory to develop classroom practices associated with *behavioral modification, contingency management,* and *behavior therapy* (see, for example, Krumboltz and Krumboltz 1972; MacMillan 1973; Craighead 1976). Undesired responses are eliminated by negative reinforcers or aversive motivation; desired behaviors are promoted by positive reinforcers. (For an excellent review of the theory and research in these areas, see Kolesnik 1978, pp. 74–107).

Cognitive Theories

Cognitive theories of motivation tend to reject the behaviorist's S-R (Stimulus-Response) or S-R-S (Stimulus-Response-Reinforcing Stimulus) models as simplistic. Instead, say cognitive theorists, behavior is changed not by stimuli alone but by how learners "think" and "feel" about the stimuli. If Tom's teacher is a "practicing behaviorist," she might set up a learning situation in spelling class by first providing a stimulus (the assignment, "Learn these ten words"), next allowing time for study (the response) and, then rewarding (or punishing) him immediately with his grade (the reinforcing stimulus). The motivation, as noted earlier, would be an intrinsic part of the total learning situation. If

Tom's teacher had been influenced by her reading in cognitive psychology, when setting up the lesson, she would try to provide for certain features behaviorists tend to ignore, such as Tom's previous knowledge of the stimulus and setting, his feelings about them, the values he places upon them, and especially the higher mental processes he uses in beginning, doing, and following up on the task. The main differences between the two approaches to motivation and learning is that S-R-S theorists pay little attention to the mental activity and emotional responses that precede, accompany, and follow learning, while cognitive theorists emphasize them.

Cognitive theories of motivation generally share this concern with how learners think and feel during learning. Individual theorists focus on different aspects of the learner's thoughts and feelings. Three of these are discussed here:

Causality. An important aspect of motivation (and of the learner's cognitive structure) is how he or she explains the events that happen to him. "Attribution theorists" (see, for example, Heider 1958; Weiner 1972) note that once children have reached the state in development where they can see cause-and-effect relationships, they begin to attribute causes to the things that happen to them. They may attribute them to internal causes, such as their own native ability or the effort they have expended in the task; they may attribute their success or failure to external causes, such as inherent difficulty of the task or simple "luck." A student's concept of causality, then, is a powerful influence upon his or her motivation and possible learning. Students who believe—rightly or wrongly—that *they* have some control over their lives (and school achievement) approach tasks differently from those who attribute success or failure to the nature of the job or "just plain luck."

Locus of control. Attribution theory has led to concern with the notion of locus of control. Some cognitive psychologists distinguish between individuals who tend to believe (whether rightly or wrongly is almost irrelevant) that their behavior is the result of their own personal decisions, initiated by them and controlled primarily by them, and those who tend to believe they are the victims of fate (Soloman and Oberlander 1974). Some research shows that students in the first group (the Internals) tend to accept the responsibility for their own learning and are motivated to complete learning tasks, while those in the second group (the Externals) perceive almost no relationship between what they do and what consequently happens to them (Rotter 1966; Phares 1957). (How many teachers have heard, "I got an A in the exam!" and "That rat gave me a flunking grade."?) Instruments to help teachers discriminate between Internals and Externals have been devised and used in several schools, and may help teachers, at least, identify students who believe they are "doomed to failure" (see, for example, Kolesnik 1978, p. 120).

Competence.   Some cognitive theorists now believe that most people have a desire to be Internals rather than Externals (White 1959). All human beings, they say, have a basic tendency toward competence or effectance. White, for example, sees people "not simply as the products of external influences but as reasoning organisms who can help to shape the course of their own development" (Kolesnik 1978, p. 122). Competence is the inherent willingness of people to take the initiative in shaping their lives instead of being the passive victims of fate. A student's motivation, then, is contingent upon his or her perceptions, knowledge base, values, and feelings. And most important for teachers, it is not something to be developed in school because *it is already present.*

Cognitive theorists have been interested in the higher mental processes that are involved in perception, in seeing cause-and-effect relationships, in inferring and predicting, and in thinking in general (see Chapter 5). They have also had much to say about problem solving, the discovery method, levels of aspiration, self-confidence, teacher expectations, and school underachievement. Because some of these discussions have had considerable influence on recent thinking about self-concept and schooling, they are treated later in this chapter.

Humanistic Psychologists

Closely related to the explanations of human motivations suggested by the cognitive theorists are those of the humanistic psychologists. Both groups tend to emphasize individuals' perceptions, thoughts, values, and feelings about themselves and the world around them. Both, too, tend to discount the psychoanalytic and behavioral views of the individual as a pawn, either the passive victim of unconscious desires, drives, and tendencies, or a highly-developed animal susceptible to training by S-R-S conditioning. Both are antimechanistic and antideterministic. Humanistic psychologists, however, particularly stress the importance of individual freedom, choice, decision making, and especially the striving toward self-fulfillment.

Much of modern humanistic psychology rests upon the work of Abraham Maslow, who suggested that motivation may be explained by an individual's striving toward growth (or "self-expression" or "self-enhancement"). Growth, the pivotal concept in Maslow's thinking, is defined as the satisfying, at successively higher levels, of a hierarchy of basic needs (Maslow 1970, 1977). At the base level come physiological needs (hunger, thirst); at the next level come physical needs for safety and security; at a third level come needs for love and belonging; at a fourth level come various esteem needs (such as to achieve, be competent, gain approval and recognition). At the top of the hierarchy come cognitive needs (to know, understand, explore), aesthetic needs (for beauty, order, symmetry), and, at the top, *self-actualization*, or the need to find self-fulfillment and realize one's potential.

Such a hierarchy provides a way of looking at motives and the relationships between and among them. The needs at the base level are biological, present at birth, and account for many childhood motivations; those at the higher levels have no basis in the physiological needs of the organism but are influenced by learning and the kind of society in which the individual is raised. These more complex psychological needs become important only after the biological needs have been satisfied. As Maslow and other humanistic psychologists point out, the needs at subsequent levels must be at least partially satisfied before those at higher levels become determiners of behavior.

It is only after the lower-level needs are satisfied that self-actualization becomes a prime source of motivation. Self-actualization itself is the highest level of human desire. The individual strives to become what only he or she can become: "himself" or "herself." After all basic needs (roughly, the first four levels of the hierarchy) are satisfied, the individual is free to explore, because he or she is no longer dependent upon others, the cognitive and aesthetic levels, and, finally, the self. Because each "self" is individual, every person has a different apex to his or her hierarchy. (All human beings are alike at the lower levels; individual distinctions become marked as one "grows" up in the levels.) Each person, then, has a different self to actualize because each has a unique set of abilities and potentialities to develop. The important feature to note in the humanist's description of human growth and motivation is that everyone wants to keep ascending the levels of the hierarchy of needs. Each person is constantly striving to attain, level by level, the person that he or she thinks and believes he or she can be.

Since Maslow first developed his "hierarchy of prepotency," many others have contributed to the development of humanistic psychology as a distinctive way of looking at human behavior (see, for example, Allport 1955; Combs and Snygg 1959; Rogers 1961). Three of their assumptions about human beings and their motivations are briefly discussed.

Most human behavior is purposeful.   Though humanistic psychologists may differ about specific elements in their theories, they generally agree that most behavior is directed toward a goal. Each individual is vaguely dissatisfied and strives to fulfill some need. Each perceives, however vaguely, some goal or goals, the attainment of which he or she believes will bring satisfaction. (Usually some obstacle presents itself; sometimes a confusion or multiplicity of goals becomes an obstacle.) Much human behavior and motivation may be explained simply in terms of the striving and the anxiety that attends it.

Sometimes human behavior does not seem purposeful. As people strive directly to attain a goal (and, indirectly, the next level of the hierarchy of prepotency), their behaviors are purposeful. At times, people exhibit behaviors which are *expressive*. Such behaviors are not aimed at a specific goal but are "acts in themselves," expressive of the individual's self at a given stage of development. For example, the student who plays the piano for an hour in the evening because she wants to is exhibiting *expressive* behavior; the one who plays because she is getting ready for a recital or lesson is showing *purposeful* behavior. The distinction is important for teachers because students, of course, exhibit both kinds of behavior in the classroom, thus confusing curriculum designers and lesson planners.

All people have a potential for growth. While all are limited to some extent by heredity or environment, these limitations are not as confining as sometimes believed (Kolesnik 1978, p. 154). Very few ever realize their full potential (that is, reach the apex of the hierarchy, real self-actualization), but the main source of everyone's motivation is to do so. Careless teacher talk about "unmotivated students" is, therefore, dangerous. Humanistic psychologists dismiss the labeling. To them, every student (because he or she is a human being) is motivated to satisfy needs, fulfill goals, and become self-actualized.

Teachers, parents, curriculum designers, administrators, and all those concerned with what happens to young people in schools and classrooms can derive important insights from the study of psychoanalytic theory, behaviorism, cognitive theory, and humanistic psychology. Each offers explanations of why people behave as they do. Each suggests strategies that adults may follow in motivating students. Before identifying some of these strategies, however, it is important to look at a topic which is receiving increasing attention in the professional literature: the effect of a student's self-concept on his or her school achievement.

SELF-CONCEPT AND SCHOOL ACHIEVEMENT

One of the most effective ways to introduce this topic is to retell Lowry's fable of "The Mouse and Henry Carson" (Lowry 1961; quoted in Purkey 1970):

> One summer evening a mouse scampered through the offices of the Educational Testing Service and triggered, quite accidentally, a delicate

mechanism just as the data for a student named Henry Carson was being scored.

Henry was an average high school student, unsure of himself and his abilities, whose scores on College Entrance Examination Board's tests would have been average or less. The mouse's accident caused the computer to "misfire" and the scores that emerged for Henry were striking: 800s in both verbal and quantitative areas!

When (as Lowry tells it) these scores reached lucky Henry's school, the word spread like wildfire. Teachers began to have second thoughts about Henry! Had they miscalculated? Had they so underestimated him? Counselors trembled at the thought of such talent wasted! College admissions officers made a bee-line for Henry!

Now a new world opened for him. He started to grow as a person and as a student. He began to be treated differently by his teachers, counselors, parents. A kind of self-fulfilling prophecy began. Henry excelled. He went to college. He graduated with honors. And (as Lowry ends the fable) he became "one of the best men of his generation."

The fable illustrates two of the basic points being repeated today by many psychologists and teachers:

1. The way students view themselves and their world are influenced powerfully by the ways others view them.
2. The ways they view the world and themselves affect their school achievement in ways previously not recognized.

Clearly, explanations of human motives found in psychoanalytic theory and in behaviorism cannot account completely for the change in Henry. Evidently, the attention cognitive psychologists have paid to how learners think and feel about themselves and the focus of humanistic psychologists on the growth toward self-actualization need to be reexamined in light of Henry's accomplishments and the accomplishments of students like Henry. What research evidence is available to teachers about the relationship between self-concept and school achievement? What evidence points to self-concept as a crucial factor in achievement as "inherited" ability? What can teachers do in the classroom to exploit this research, and to build strong, positive self-concepts in their students?

What evidence supports the belief that school achievement and self-concept are related? Many teachers have noted that students who feel good about themselves tend to do well in school, and those who do not feel good about themselves do not do well. Such teacher intuitions have been tested out in a number of school studies in recent years. One group of researchers, for example, used an "adjective checklist" with successful and unsuccessful high school juniors. They found that achievers scored themselves higher on such qualities as: optimistic, realistic, enthusiastic, reliable, clear-thinking, and intelligent. They concluded, after a study of their data, that school achievers (especially the males) generally felt more positively about themselves as people and as students (Shaw, Edson, and Bell 1960). In another study of 1,000 seventh-grade students, student self-reports were correlated with grades and found to be positively correlated (Brookover, Patterson, and Thomas 1964). In reviewing a number of studies from the 1940s through the 1970s, Kolesnik (1978) found that self-confident students tended to raise their own levels of aspiration, set higher and more realistic goals for themselves, accept failure, and find increased interest in tasks in which they have already succeeded. In short, success leads to success; the better students feel about themselves, the more apt they are to succeed further. It appears, too, that this generalization has no racial limitations. In a study of black students, Caplin (1966) found that those who indicated positive thoughts and feelings about themselves as achievers did, indeed, tend to have increasingly higher grades in school. After examining a wide range of studies in this area, Purkey (1970, p. 15) concluded, "Over-all, the research evidence clearly shows a persistent and significant relationship between the self-concept and academic achievement."

Success, then, leads to a positive self-concept and, in turn, more success. "How," a cynical teacher might ask, "do the initial successes come about that lead to subsequent successes?" An answer from experienced teachers might be, "By setting up classroom activities so that everyone can frequently succeed!" There is more to the problem, however, than this sensible answer indicates. Of course, if teachers plan classroom work so that each student experiences a degree of attainment, student attitudes toward the work and themselves will improve. Recent research indicates that students' self-concepts are also shaped by the ways other people look at them. Henry, in Lowry's fable, went on to do great things in college not because of his own specific achievement (remember, his test scores were a fluke!) but because people *expected* him to be good. The expectations of others—particularly teachers and parents—shape a student's self-concept just as much as his or her own previous achievements.

How students perceive teachers' (and others') views of them affect not only their levels of aspiration, their motivation, and school achievement, but their self-concepts. When teachers show they don't expect a high level of performance, they set up self-fulfilling prophecies which (too frequently) come true! This controversial notion has been explored and debated in a number of recent studies, the best known of which is Rosenthal and Jacobson's (1968) examination of the "Pygmalion effect." They identified students (who were actually randomly selected) as potential achievers and discovered that teachers treated these students differently. The teachers sent out subtle (and sometimes not so subtle) signals to the students showing that they were somehow "unusual." They indicated to the randomly selected students that "great things" were expected of them. The faith and confidence was evidently accepted, because the students (who were in no other ways different from those in the experimental population) began to perform better on school tasks and, at the end of the year, received higher grades. This particular study has been criticized by methodological groups (for example, see Thorndike 1968; Zanna 1975), but it still carries strong educational implications. As many successful teachers have realized through the years, "When students believe that *you* believe they can succeed, they often do; when they think that *you* think they are doomed to failure, they tend to fail." Solid research evidence to support—or disprove—this belief may never be attained because of the ethical problems involved in experimenting on human subjects. But the strong intuition of teachers remains: prejudging sets up self-fulfilling prophecies which may come true, to the student's advantage—or disadvantage.

It may be said with some confidence, then, that students' school achievement is indeed influenced by how they view themselves, and how they think others view them. However, underlying the fable of "The Mouse and Henry" lies another important research question: Does the self-concept determine achievement or does achievement determine the self-concept? Research does not have a firm answer, and (again, because of the ethical considerations involved in doing experiments on human subjects) may never have one. Inferences drawn from actual evidence obtained so far sometimes point one way; sometimes the other.

For example, in checking the self-perceptions of preschool children, investigators found in one study that those who thought well of themselves scored higher on later IQ and reading achievement tests. In fact, the scores on the self-perception test were excellent predictions of IQ and reading scores (Lamy 1965). In another study, measures of self-concepts were obtained as children drew pictures of themselves and responded to incomplete sentences. Again, scores were found to correlate highly with reading test scores when children entered school (Wattenberg and Clifford 1962). In reviewing research in this area, Purkey (1970, p. 25) noted, "The conclusion seems unavoidable: a student carries with him certain attitudes about himself and his abilities which play a primary role in how he performs in school."

Yet, as Purkey himself notes, the sword cuts both ways. Studies also indicate that performance affects self-concept. When students have a string of successes—or failures—their images of themselves change. In one study, students in one of two "bright and academically superior" seventh-grade classes were deliberately informed, just before taking a test, that they had failed an important previous test. The misinformed students did significantly less well on the second test and also dropped in scores on a measure of reported self-concept (Gibby and Gibby 1967). This tendency to score lower on self-concept measures after experiencing failure has been noted for both achievers and underachievers. After examining the available research evidence, teachers may conclude that they are dealing with a two-way street: "there is continuous interaction between the self and academic achievement," and "each directly influences the other" (Purkey 1970, p. 23).

Do some students have a strong, positive self-concept because they are innately "bright" or do they succeed in school because they have a good self-concept? This important question is unanswerable in terms of present research findings. However, the available evidence does support the belief that, given the options, teachers should do what they can to build in their students the belief that *they can succeed*. After working successfully for many years with so-called "adolescent slow learners," Canadian teacher Kenneth Weber entitled his "Practical Guide for Teaching the Adolescent Slow Learner," *Yes, They Can*! (Weber 1974). If teachers have a choice in how they view their clients—and they do!—it seems better for them to adopt Weber's positive stance than any less positive one.

DEVELOPING A STUDY SKILLS PROGRAM: GUIDELINES FOR TEACHERS

Guidelines for improving study skills are scattered throughout these chapters, some italicized to stand out on the page, others indirectly suggested or implied. Concluding this chapter and the book are six that underlie all attempts to improve the study skills of students—children and young adults. For many teachers, they sum up and capture in one brief verbal package the essence of the great human enterprise known as "teaching." They are presented here to stimulate (for individuals, groups of teachers, and others fascinated by "the great enterprise") further exploration, and possible discovery, in the issues and problems implicit in every encounter of Teacher with Students.

Know Your Goals

Workers in many fields are usually fortunate in facing defined tasks. The architect designing a three-bedroom ranch-type dwelling or the automotive mechanic replacing the brake linings on a car have their tasks sharply delineated, with clear lines of demarcation separating the immediate goal from all others. The surgeon treating a broken limb or the supermarket employee at the check-out counter have their goals specified and share with others well-defined standards for success or failure. Teachers too often spin out their working days in a world of conflicting, overlapping, and ill-defined tasks. Unfortunately, some respond by formulating simple survival goals ("Getting through the period" or "Keeping the kids quiet and in their seats") or trivializing their content commitments ("Today I'll teacher students to recognize a noun clause" or "the economic causes of the American Revolution"). Young teachers frequently start with commendable goals ("Teaching students to think," "to learn problem-solving techniques," "to read," or "to study") and too often adopt, to survive, trivial or management goals.

Successful teachers are most often successful because they learn (perhaps from the behaviorists) to break up their general goals into specific (teachable and testable) daily or weekly objectives. They come to realize that one does not "teach reading" but really sets up situations in which students learn specific reading skills, such as recognizing an author's organizational pattern, or sets of skills, such as SQ3R. They learn that one does not teach composition writing but rather creates activities and strategies that help students acquire specific thinking-writing skills, such as supporting a topic sentence with two examples or using a comparison-and-contrast pattern to develop a theme. They realize that one does not teach children and young adults How to Study but, rather, specific study skills.

A study skills program based on vague, but commendable, goals such as Improving Study Habits denies teachers the advantages of the architect, automobile mechanic, surgeon, or supermarket checker. The first, and perhaps most fundamental, guideline for teachers who want to establish an effective study skills program is to define and specify the exact goals of the program. Working on his own or with her colleagues, each teacher needs to spell out in a plan book (or in a public place) a Scope and Sequence of Study Skills. Critics of specificity and of lists of objectives in general are fond of noting that students never follow the lists, that they all grow and learn at different rates, and that, consequently, lists of objectives are idealizations. Teachers who choose to base their programs on a well-defined scope and sequence list of skills can recognize the objections of critics and derive some comfort from knowing that a task defined is more likely to be accomplished than one anfractuous and fuzzy.

(The Idea Box for this chapter includes, as its sole entry, a suggested Master List of Basic Study Skills with recommendations for grade placement, teaching, reteaching, and review.)

Know Why You Chose Your Goals

Teachers need to philosophize! It is not enough to specify teaching goals and then sequence them in orderly, logical patterns. Considerable cogitation needs to precede definition and placement. When teachers shy away from the responsibility of questioning and evaluating the validity of their teaching goals, they deny their own professionalism and become technicians. They need to think through their own lists of specific teaching objectives and decide how each contributes to the good of the student, the society, and the future of the race. Too often, teachers accept both general and specific teaching goals because "they are part of the curriculum," "they've always been included," or "we're expected to teach that." The development of "master lists" of objectives, in all content areas, should begin only after teachers—individually or in groups—have examined the pertinent research, assessed the pros and cons for the inclusion of each item, and measured the effect of the hoped-for learnings against reasonably valid epistemological axiological yardsticks. In short, philosophizing must precede curriculum-building, just as curriculum-building must precede teaching.

(Fortunately for teachers of study skills, it is relatively easy to justify the inclusion of most accepted specific objectives in an overall schema. If the general goal of the program is to teach study skills so that students can learn independently of a teacher, then one can defend using the periodical index, recognizing an author's/speaker's purpose, or using SQ3R. Such is not always the case in all content fields. How does a teacher of composition, for example, justify teaching ninth-grade students to *identify* a noun clause when the general goal of the program is to teach students to write clear, well-organized paragraphs? How can a teacher rationalize teaching how to distinguish between *simile* and *metaphor* when the general goal is to encourage the enjoyment of poetry? Informed philosophizing could reshape and restructure much content area teaching.)

Know Your Clients

Like Polonius's advice, educational admonitions become cliches to the ear and mind. The professional literature has so often counseled teachers to "Provide for Individual Differences!" that many teachers nod their heads ("yes, how true") and think about other matters. The inescapable classroom truth is, of course, that all students, despite their common humanity, *are* different in hundreds of subtle and not-so-subtle ways, and teachers do need to provide for some of these differences if lessons are to succeed. Children and young adults in even so-called "homogeneous" classes (there are none) are growing at different rates, bringing to the class varying experiential backgrounds, and viewing instruction from varying perspectives. They have different interests, goals, aspirations, values, attitudes, anxieties, and unconscious motives. They come into every class with special and unique handicaps, limitations, and possibilities.

And, as the humanistic psychologists point out, they each come with a unique, unified *self*, each trying to achieve self-actualization.

Mass instruction, therefore, is by definition nonproductive. Teachers cannot teach the same lesson or skill in the same way to twenty or thirty students in the same room at the same time. They try. They fail. "Success" can only be measured in relative terms like, "Forty percent of the class passed the Mastery Test!" Too many classrooms, in elementary schools, high schools, and colleges, become "screening" rooms, where the fortunate ones who do learn the lesson or skill are identified and set apart from the less fortunate. Gross discrimination (racial, sexual) is slowly being eliminated from American schools, but the more insidious form still prevails in classrooms where teachers treat "Provide for Individual Differences" as just another educational cliche.

How do teachers provide for differences? They first have to know their clients. At the "paper level," they can collect every bit of information that is written down: names, addresses, telephone numbers, standardized test scores, previous grades, and data and comments from cumulative records. At the "human level," they can talk to students, face-to-face, frequently, confidentially, socially, and publicly; they can encourage students to write as often as possible (reports, stories, poems, reaction papers) and read alertly and sympathetically in search of insights and communion; they can encourage students to respond to class work by creating collages, models, drawings, and slide-tapes, and study the products in search of clues to the creators' personalities.

At the "instructional level," teachers can give frequent check-tests, quizzes, exercises, and opportunities for oral response to assess the degree of learning for each segment of the Scope and Sequence; they can establish feedback systems that inform them immediately of who is learning and who is not.

How to provide for differences? Knowing students' successes and failures, strengths and weaknesses, backgrounds and personalities, is the first step. The second is using the vast array of successful techniques that have accumulated in classrooms and in the professional literature through the decades: differentiated assignments, individual projects, programmed workbooks and tests, small group instruction, library research projects, "solo reports," panel discussions, debates, drama, film-making; the list seems endless. Assigning all students the same task at the same time has proven to be an excellent way of screening those who can do the task from those who cannot. It has never shown itself to be the most effective approach to teaching.

When teachers truly know their students they tend to move away from mass instruction toward individualization. It is difficult to teach the entire class in the same way how to use the card catalog when one knows that Jack has yet to learn the alphabet, Susan's father is the town's

Head Librarian, Ted's parents told him that morning that they were separating, and Charlie does not know the librarian's meaning of the word *catalog!* It has been said that if every teacher really knew every one of his or her students, American education would be transformed overnight.

Know What Motivates Students

Books on educational psychology have traditionally distinguished between intrinsic and extrinsic motives. Although a clear line separating the two cannot always be drawn, considerable consensus exists about the items falling under each label. Extrinsic motivation, for example, includes approval-disapproval, rewards-punishments, praising-scolding, competition, testing, grading, and all forms of contingency management. Research through the years has indicated that all forms of extrinsic motivation work; students will indeed study to avoid disparagement and earn rewards of one sort or another. Some of the research indicates too, that, while positive feedback is generally more effective than negative feedback, feedback even of a negative nature is better than no feedback at all. (For a review of research in extrinsic motivation, see Kolesnik 1978, pp. 209–245). All forms of extrinsic motivation involve some reward, incentive, or goal extrinsic to the task itself, and have always been found in schools. Teachers who accept behaviorism as the best explanation of human motivation tend to favor these forms of motivation.

Intrinsic motivation, on the other hand, comes from within the student; consequently, teachers and learning theorists who favor forms of intrinsic motivation have tended through the years to look at students, at student interests, and at individuals in relation to the school curriculum. They talk about student-centered activities, interest inventories, problem-solving techniques in the classroom, curiosity, involvement, and the personal consequences of learning. They admit that students do complete school tasks to gain rewards (gold stars, high grades, teacher and parent approval)—and, in the process, learn. But they say "real" learning habits and a life-long predisposition to continue studying and learning best come about through intrinsic motivation.

Discussion of forms of intrinsic motivation constitute the bulk of many of the better books on teaching in the various content fields. Some of that vast discussion may be summarized here under the headings *topic*, *task*, and *student* because it is in the interrelationships of these three that much intrinsic motivation may be found.

Topic. When the topic is one to which students somehow relate, interest is increased. Although this seems axiomatic, some teachers still disregard the suggestion. As a result, one finds teachers "teaching" grammatical terminology, scientific abstractions, and elements of literary criticism to children and young adults who couldn't care less. This is not to say that a topic seemingly far removed from the immediate lives of students (noun clauses, matter, theme) cannot be related to learners. With imagination and careful planning, a teacher can find countless examples to bridge the gap between topic and learners (they *use* noun clauses; they are built up of matter; their very lives have themes). It is to say that many teachers either select topics thoughtlessly or fail to build necessary bridges. Most successful teachers have learned that seemingly unrelated, irrelevant topics can be related through good lesson planning (transformation grammar *can* be taught to fourth-graders). Many unsuccessful teachers have not selected topics wisely, have not specified and justified them, and have not related them to their students.

Task.   When the task itself is stimulating and challenging, interest is heightened. No one knows whether curiosity is a basic human need (at one of the biological levels of Maslow's "hierarchy of prepotency") or a psychological need developed by the environment, but it is apparent that all higher animals (students included) are powerfully motivated by an urge to explore their environments and satisfy their curiosity and need to know. Some successful teachers have always exploited student curiosity by creating learning tasks that challenge and stimulate. Thus, when a teacher assigning library research projects discovers that an eighteen-year-old student is called to jury duty and fears that the obligation will rob him of his summer's employment, she gives him the research question, "What are the exemptions from jury duty?" Other teachers have students find noun clauses in their own transcribed speech or the themes in their own favorite television dramas. Learning tasks may grow out of student uncertainty, doubt, perplexity, surprise, or wonder; they may take the form of experiments, library research, surveys, interviews, observations, the testing out of hunches and intuitions, and a hundred and one forms of problem solving. Inquiry and discovery lie at the heart of most school learning that is not directed exclusively toward a reward but toward the development of a life-long predilection toward studying and learning.

Student.   When the student is involved in the learning experience, interest and learning are increased. As long as classes of students are treated as classes and not as individual students, the effect of teaching is minimal. To insure the mastery of study skills (and content-area objectives), teachers must know their students, their needs, drives, interests, personal goals, aspirations, unconscious motives, attitudes, values, anxieties, and potentialities. Successful teachers have always made an effort to maintain and improve "feedback systems" with their classes.

They have encouraged much student writing, group and oral reporting, creative activities, and nonverbal reporting; they have also used a variety of observation techniques and interest inventories. On the basis of the information obtained about students, they have selected topics and developed learning tasks and strategies which involved the individual personalities of students. They have known that unless each student is personally involved in his or her own learning, much of the time and energy they expended in teaching are wasted. In short, they have known that listening to lectures on noun clauses or How to Use the Library are simply not as effective as, for example, locating a noun clause in one's own journal entry or finding in the library the probable causes of acne.

Build Student Self-Esteem and Levels of Aspiration

As noted earlier in this chapter, research findings to date tend to support the belief that student achievement in school is related to student self-concept. When students believe they can succeed, they tend to succeed; when they believe they are going to fail, they tend to fail. It was also noted that such generalizations may never be proven or disproven because of ethical constraints on researchers' ability to experiment further with human subjects. However, enough evidence from completed research and from the everyday observations of teachers exists to highlight this guideline.

What can teachers do to build student self-esteem and to raise levels of aspiration? Teachers who have worked successfully with "non-succeeders" try to help them break out of the failure cycle by sequencing into the school program many small successes. Such teachers, particularly those who work with so-called "slow learners," note that the expectation of failure is part of a cycle: because they see themselves as regular failures, such students do not try to learn even when topics and tasks are appropriate to them. Some become aggressive and rebellious, some retreat into silence and sullenness, and others work only for a passing grade. Successes and frequent, visible evidence of success help break the cycle.

Successes grow out of tasks—appropriate, meaningful, relevant tasks—which may be carried through to their conclusions rather briefly. For the students with a low "self-esteem quotient," the teacher needs to include with daily lessons a variety of activities that students will want to do and can do. Rather than present a class with a major unit on Using the Library or Understanding Subordinate Clauses, the teacher differentiates assignments and suggests that David locate one book on the shelves that tells him about Harley-Davidson motorcycles, and Tom find within a sentence he has just written in a review of a Rolling Stones record a sentence-within-a-sentence that "describes" the lead guitar player (pointing to the sentence). A backlog of small successes serves then as the foundation of the next success—and of a changing, more positive self-image. Learning to use context clues to discover the meaning of one unfamiliar word on a record jacket becomes the stepping stone to mastering the skill in general, and it's the beginning of a small break in the Failure Cycle.

But successes must be visible. Final quarter or semester grades are not enough. Students need frequent opportunities to see how they are developing. Teachers in remedial classes learned long ago that progress charts of different types provide a solid structure for continuing growth: as students successfully complete each task, they see before them evidence that the task is done and done correctly. Many teachers who use charts and graphs insist that (1) the charts not be established on a competitive basis, (2) failures are never coded in (only successes), and (3) charts be confined to a rather brief block of time (one or two weeks). Just as teachers need feedback to learn more about their students, students need constant feedback to discover how well they are learning. An A or B grade on a final exam is, for most students in most schools, a highly desirable achievement; a notch up on a personal graph or progress chart may be of greater significance for the learner convinced that he or she can't learn anyway!

For students who have already met with a modicum or more of success, progress charts may seem redundant, but the development of self-esteem remains a viable and important objective for their teachers. With more successful or more mature students, the notch on the graph may be replaced by a smile, a friendly wink of encouragement, or a few words after class. The gradual accumulation over a period of time of esteem-building encouragements may never be directly measurable on a paper-and-pencil-type achievement test, but decades of collective classroom experience indicates that such "signs and wonders" have more impact on school (and life) achievement than the results of the most impressive research findings. Teachers who make their students believe that "You can do it!" and/or "The sky's the limit!" still remain the foundation of a successful study skills program.

Believe that You, Too, Can Succeed

Teachers (as well as students, parents, and others) set up self-fulfilling prophecies for themselves. Some start with or develop through the years a conviction that they are "natural-born" teachers who are destined for success in the classroom, as other college classmates may have been bound for success in the law courts, the marketplace, or the stage. They send out signals: "I can teach that group," "*My* kids will know that material backwards and forwards," "I'll have them getting top grades in no time." Their students pick up the signals—as do parents, administrators, and other teachers. Powerful, productive self-fulfilling prophecies are set in motion; expectations are actualized.

Other teachers, unfortunately, begin their careers, or build up along the way, the belief that they cannot succeed: the system is against them; *their* students are incapable of learning; they, personally, are lacking some (undefined) "talent for teaching." They, too, send out signals: "The students are dull," "They aren't interested in schoolwork," "They are not motivated," "It's impossible to teach them a thing," "No one can teach under these conditions." (How many school visitors have been told, in a whisper loud enough to be heard in the back of the room, "This is my 'slow' class"?) Clearly, such teachers are setting up their own self-fulfilling prophecies.

Teaching success is contingent upon such an array of complex and interrelated variables that it may never be thoroughly understood. Students (all with individually different background, personalities, motivations, etc.) are brought together with teachers (with equally varied backgrounds, personalities, motivations, etc.) in the physical contexts of schools (which also are affected by differing forces and influences). It is difficult for objective researchers to identify and study specific variables, or even interrelationships of variables, and point to one or two and say, "Ah! *This* or *that* is what distinguishes successful from nonsuccessful teachers!" It is apparent, however, from the research that has been done and from decades of observation of teaching success and failure that the teacher's self-concept is a potent factor in the entire teaching-learning process. Just as students' achievement is affected by their self-concepts, so teachers are influenced by (1) how they feel about themselves, (2) how they think others feel about them, (3) how they feel about their students, and (4) how they think others feel about their students.

How can teachers improve *their* own self-concepts, develop *their* self-esteem and raise *their* levels of aspiration in the classroom? Many of the same strategies teachers use with their own students may be reversed and reapplied upon teachers themselves. The guidelines that conclude this chapter may be restated in somewhat different terms for teachers who want to restructure their self-concepts. (A productive exercise for individuals or groups of teachers would be to further develop this suggested list.)

Specify and sequence teaching objectives so that teaching can succeed. If "nothing succeeds like success," then teachers should not aim for unattainable goals that doom them to failure. Teachers may, over a period of time, produce dramatic improvements in class vocabularies, but, for today or this week, they are more likely to succeed by aiming at one or two specific (teachable and testable) objectives: (1) give, for example, a pretest on the ability to use context clues to get the meanings of unfamiliar words, (2) explain and show how people use this skill, (3) give dozens of examples from "real life" material, (4) provide practice with materials from the students' own lives, and (5) test again to measure success—for students and teacher.

Believe in objectives or "junk 'em." Much ineffective teaching results from the teachers' lack of belief in the value of the lesson objectives. It is difficult to work up teaching energy to teach a topic the teacher does not really care about. If a teacher does not believe that a content objective is important to the lives of students and the future of society, then he or she should search out objectives that are justifiable and hold a high priority in the teacher's scheme of things.

Stop labeling kids! One of the major obstacles to successful teaching is the unfortunate array of labels that linger on in classrooms. Intelligence, for example, is not thoroughly understood, yet words such as *dull, stupid, bright,* or *brilliant* remain in the classroom to blunt the perceptions of teachers and students. An examination of the research literature on motivation should curtail, once and for all, the indiscriminate use of the label *lazy,* yet it still interferes with the ways teachers see students, and, consequently, serves to stand in the way of many of the daily successes teachers need to build up their own self-confidence.

Know students. It is axiomatic that other workers and artists know their materials intimately, yet unsuccessful teachers regularly try to teach material (which, ironically, they may know well) to strangers. As the discussion has noted, children and young adults vary in respect to a hundred and one different qualities. Teachers who need to improve their own self-images as successful professionals need to better see the clients for whom such time and effort are expended.

Set up positive, productive self-fulfilling prophecies for teacher as well as students. If expectations lead to actualizations (and they seem to), then it behooves teachers to rephrase Weber's (1974) *Yes, They Can!* and say, "Yes, *they* can, and *I* can, too!"

Idea Box
Basic Study Skills

The Idea Box for Chapter 12 consists of this single entry: a suggested *Master List of Basic Study Skills, Grades 4 through 14.* The list is suggested and noninclusive. As individual teachers and groups of teachers develop their own study skills programs, they may add or delete specific items, reword others, edit, and assign grade level designations.

In Part 1 only, grade-level designations have been suggested: T for Teach, and R for Review or Reteach. The items in Parts 2 and 3 are not so coded. It is assumed that, as the Master List is reworked for specific students and teachers in specific schools, the grade-level placements suggested in Part 1 may be reassigned and placements for Parts 2 and 3 made in respect to the specific needs of students in individual schools.

PART 1:
INCOMING, OR RECEPTIVE, SKILLS

1. Determining one's purpose for listening or reading
   T: 4, R: 5–14
2. Determining the speaker's or author's purpose for talking or writing
   T: 4, R: 5–14
3. Predicting the speaker's or author's possible plan of organization
   a. Is it enumeration?   T: 4, R: 5–14
   b. Is it chronological?   T: 5, R: 6–14
   c. Is it cause and effect?   T: 9, R: 10–14
   d. Is it comparison and contrast?   T: 9, R: 10–14
   e. Is it generalization-plus-examples? T: 5, R: 6–14
   f. Is there a plan?   T: 4, R: 5–14
4. Noting the signal words or transitions in the talk or text
   T: 4, 5, 9 (with the
   plan), R: through 14
5. Recognizing a speaker's or author's main points
   T: 4, R: 5–14
6. Noting the supporting details or examples
   T: 5, R: 6–14
7. Following the sequence of ideas
   T: 4, R: 5–14
8. Keeping track (in writing or by mental review) of the main points
   T: 4, R: 5–14

9. Preparing a summary of the presentation
                                    T: 7, R: 8–14
10. Distinguishing between relevant and irrelevant material
                                    T: 6, R: 7–14
11. Drawing conclusions from the presentation
                                    T: 7, R: 7–14
12. Noting speaker or author bias
                                    T: 7, R: 8–14
13. Distinguishing fact from opinion statements
                                    T: 8, R: 9–14
14. Recognizing emotional appeals and emotive language
                                    T: 8, R: 9–14
15. Noting the speaker's or author's inferences
                                    T: 9, R: 10–14
16. Asking one's own personal questions (mentally or on paper) of the presentation
                                    T: 4, R: 5–14
17. Relating the speaker's or author's ideas and information to one's own life
                                    T: 4, R: 5–14
18. Predicting possible test questions
                                    T: 6, R: 17–14
19. Following spoken or written directions
                                    T: 14, R: 5–14
20. Using a study guide, outline, or study method (such as SQ3R)
                                    T: 6, R: 7–14
21. Noting unfamiliar concepts
                                    T: 6, R: 7–14
22. Using sound, structure, and context clues to get meanings of unfamiliar words
                                    T: 4, R: 5–14
23. Using the dictionary or glossary
                                    T: 4, R: 5–14
24. Using the table of contents and index in a book
                                    T: 4, R: 5–14
25. Using maps, charts, graphs, tables, and pictures (when provided)
                                    T: 4, R: 5–14
26. Using headings and other typographical aids in a book
                                    T: 4, R: 5–14
27. Using basic library research skills
    a. Periodical indexes   T: 6, R: 7–14
    b. Card catalogs   T: 6, R: 7–14
    c. Appropriate call number systems T: 6, R: 7–14

PART 2:
SYNTHESIZING, OR REFLECTIVE, SKILLS

1. Relating material to one's own experience and previous knowledge
2. Determining possible use of material for one's self
3. Building associations between the known and the unknown, new and old material
4. Guessing at the sender's message
5. Trying to reconstruct the sender's message in one's mind
6. Noting needed information
7. Guessing the sender's purpose
8. Recognizing the sender's patterns of organization
9. Organizing the information in one's own mind
10. Determining whether to retain and use new ideas and information.

PART 3:
REPORTING, OR EXPRESSIVE, SKILLS

1. Distinguishing reporting from other kinds of communication (poetry, narration, journal-keeping)
2. Recognizing and stating the purpose of a report
3. Identifying the intended readers or listeners
4. Deciding the main points
5. Selecting an appropriate organizational pattern (enumeration, cause-and-effect, comparison-and-contrast, time order, generalization-plus-examples)
6. Selecting and using appropriate transitional words and phrases
7. Dividing the report into sections or paragraphs
8. Selecting a topic (or main idea) sentence for each
9. Supporting topic (or main idea) sentences with appropriate details and examples
10. Choosing words appropriate to the task and readers/listeners
11. Selecting appropriate style or level of language
12. Proofreading written work
13. Noting and correcting spelling errors in written reports
14. Using appropriate punctuation in written reports
15. Using standard English grammar (and avoiding common errors)
16. Writing or typing legibly
17. Speaking distinctly
18. Seeking reader (or audience) response and criticism.

References

Allport, Gordon W. *Becoming: Basic Considerations for a Psychology of Personality.* New Haven: Yale University Press, 1955.

Bandura, A. A. *Principles of Behavior Modification.* New York: Holt, Rinehart and Winston, 1969.

Bandura, A. A., ed. *Psychological Modeling.* New York: Lieber-Atherton, 1974.

Bettelheim, Bruno. "Psychoanalysis and Education." *School Review* 77 (1969): 73–86.

Brookover, W. B.; A. Patterson; and S. Thomas. "Self-concept of Ability and School Achievement." *Sociology of Education* 37 (1964): 271–278.

Caplin, M. D. "The Relationship between Self Concept and Academic Achievement and between Level of Aspiration and Academic Achievement." *Dissertation Abstracts* 27 (1966): p. 979-A.

Combs, Arthur W., and D. Snygg. *Individual Behavior,* rev. ed. New York: Harper, 1959.

Craighead, W. E. et al. *Behavior Modification.* Boston: Houghton Mifflin, 1976.

Erikson, Eric H. *Identity: Youth and Crisis.* New York: W. W. Norton, 1968.

Gibby, R. G., Sr., and Gibby, R. G., Jr. "The Effects of Stress Resulting from Academic Failure." *Journal of Clinical Psychology* 23 (1967): 35–37.

Hall, C. S. *A Primer of Freudian Psychology.* New York: New American Library, 1954.

Heider, F. *The Psychology of Interpersonal Relations.* New York: John Wiley, 1958.

Hill, J. C. *Teaching and the Unconscious Mind.* New York: International Universities Press, 1971.

Kibler, R. J. et al. *Objectives for Instruction and Evaluation.* Boston: Allyn and Bacon, 1974.

Kolesnik, Walter B. *Motivation: Understanding and Influencing Human Behavior.* Boston: Allyn and Bacon, 1978.

Krumboltz, J. D., and H. B. Krumboltz. *Changing Children's Behavior.* Englewood Cliffs, N.J.: Prentice-Hall, Inc., 1972.

Lamy, M. W. "Relationship of Self-perceptions of Early Primary Children to Achievement in Reading." In *Human Development: Readings in Research.* Edited by I. J. Gordon. Chicago: Scott, Foresman and Co., 1965.

Lowry, H. F. "The Mouse and Henry Carson." Open address, Conference on Outstanding Students in Liberal Arts Colleges, Buck Hills Falls, Penn., March 29, 1961. (Quoted in William W. Purkey. *Self Concept and School Achievement.* Englewood Cliffs, N.J.: Prentice-Hall, Inc., 1970.)

MacMillan, D. L. *Behavior Modification in Education.* New York: Macmillan, 1973.

Mager, Robert F. *Preparing Instructional Objectives.* Palo Alto, Calif.: Fearon Publishers, 1962.

Maslow, Abraham H. *Motivation and Personality,* 2nd ed. New York: Harper and Row, 1970.

Maslow, Abraham H. "Theory of Motivation." In *Human Dynamics in Psychology and Education*, 3rd ed. Edited by D. E. Hamacheck. Boston: Allyn and Bacon, Inc., 1977.

Phares, E. J. "Expectancy Changes in Skill and Chance Situations." *Journal of Abnormal and Social Psychology* 54 (1957): 339–342.

Purkey, William W. *Self Concept and School Achievement*. Englewood Cliffs, N.J.: Prentice-Hall, Inc., 1970.

Roberts, T. B., ed. *Four Psychologies Applied to Education*. New York: John Wiley, 1975.

Rogers, Carl R. *On Becoming a Person*. Boston: Houghton Mifflin, 1961.

Rosenthal, R., and L. Jacobson. *Pygmalion in the Classroom: Teacher Expectation and Pupils' Intellectual Development*. New York: Holt, Rinehart and Winston, Inc., 1968.

Rotter, J. B. "Generalized Expectancies for Internal versus External Control of Reinforcement." *Psychological Monographs* 80 (1966): 1–28.

Shaw, M. C.; K. Edson; and H. Bell. "The Self-concept of Bright Underachieving High-School Students as Revealed by an Adjective Check List." *Personnel and Guidance Journal* 39 (1960): 193–196.

Skinner, B. F. *The Technology of Teaching*. New York: Appleton-Centry-Crofts, Inc., 1968.

Skinner, B. F. *About Behaviorism*. New York: Random House, 1974.

Solomon, D., and M. I. Oberlander. "Locus of Control in the Classroom." In *Psychological Concepts in the Classroom*. Edited by R. H. Cooper and K. White. New York: Harper and Row, 1974.

Thorndike, R. L. "Review of *Pygmalion in the Classroom*." *American Educational Research Journal* 5 (1968): 708–711.

Wattenberg, W. W., and C. Clifford. *Relationship of Self-concept to Beginning Achievement in Reading*. U.S. Office of Education, Cooperative Research Project No. 377. Detroit: Wayne State University, 1962.

Weber, Kenneth J. *Yes, They Can! A Practical Guide for Teaching the Adolescent Slower Learner*. Toronto: Methuen, 1974.

Weiner, B. "Attribution Theory, Achievement Motivation and the Educational Process." *Review of Educational Research* 42 (1972): 203–215.

White, R. W. "Motivation Reconsidered: The Concept of Competence." *Psychological Review* 66 (1959): 297–333.

Zanna, M. P. et al. "Pygmalian and Galatea: The Interactive Effect of Teacher and Expectations." *Journal of Experimental Social Psychology* 11 (1975): 279–287.

INDEX